THE ETHICS OF EVER

Why do we have children and what do we raise them for? Does the proliferation of depictions of suffering in the media enhance, or endanger, compassion? How do we live and die well in the extended periods of debility which old age now threatens? Why and how should we grieve for the dead? And how should we properly remember other grief and grievances?

In addressing such questions, the Christian imagination of human life has been powerfully shaped by the imagination of Christ's life—his conception, birth, suffering, death, and burial have been subjects of profound attention in Christian thought, just as they are moments of special interest and concern in each and every human life. However, they are also sites of contention and controversy, where what it is to be human is discovered, constructed, and contested. Conception, birth, suffering, burial, and death are occasions, in other words, for profound and continuing questioning regarding the meaning of human life, as controversies to do with IVF, abortion, euthanasia, and the use of bodies and body parts post mortem, indicate.

In *The Ethics of Everyday Life*, Michael Banner argues that moral theology must reconceive its nature and tasks if it is not only to articulate its own account of human being, but also to enter into constructive contention with other accounts—in particular, it must be willing to learn from and engage with social anthropology if it is to offer powerful and plausible portrayals of the moral life and answers to the questions which trouble modernity. Drawing in wide-ranging fashion from social anthropology and from Christian thought and practice from many periods, and influenced especially by his engagement in public policy matters including as a member of the UK's Human Tissue Authority, Banner develops the outlines of an everyday ethics, stretching from before the cradle to after the grave.

Michael Banner is a Dean and Fellow, Trinity College, University of Cambridge. He previously held chairs in the University of Edinburgh and at King's College, London. Alongside his academic career he has been a regular contributor to public policy discussions in diverse areas, chairing or serving on numerous UK government committees for more than twenty years.

The Ethics of Everyday Life

Moral Theology, Social Anthropology, and the Imagination of the Human

THE BAMPTON LECTURES
in the University of Oxford
2013

MICHAEL BANNER

OXFORD
UNIVERSITY PRESS

OXFORD

UNIVERSITY PRESS

Great Clarendon Street, Oxford, OX2 6DP,
United Kingdom

Oxford University Press is a department of the University of Oxford.
It furthers the University's objective of excellence in research, scholarship,
and education by publishing worldwide. Oxford is a registered trade mark of
Oxford University Press in the UK and in certain other countries

First published 2014
First published in paperback 2016

Published in the United States of America by Oxford University Press
198 Madison Avenue, New York, NY 10016, United States of America

British Library Cataloguing in Publication Data
Data available

Library of Congress Cataloging in Publication Data
Data available

ISBN 978–0–19–872206–9 (Hbk.)
ISBN 978–0–19–876646–9 (Pbk.)

To Sally-Ann Gannon
for each everyday

Acknowledgements

Though works of this kind appear under the name of a single author, only if they were written on a desert island without any books are they likely to be the work of an individual (and even that individual will have incurred debts to others in his or her pre-wrecked life). Far from working on a desert island, I have benefited from close collaboration and engagement with and support from countless colleagues, and am conscious of my immense good fortune in working alongside those who have generously shared expertise, understanding, and insights which exceed my own.

My very first and warmest thanks must go the electors to the Bampton Lectureship at the University of Oxford for electing me for 2013, thereby providing the encouragement and opportunity to turn an early idea set out in a short proposal into a series of lectures, and now into a book.

The first outing for my initial ideas about the shape and nature of the topic was provided by David Ford's 'Home Seminar' in Cambridge back in the autumn of 2011. (By happy coincidence, David Ford is to be the next Bampton Lecturer in 2015.) It is difficult to conceive of a more fruitful, constructive, and collaborative atmosphere than the one which David Ford fosters, so it was an excellent place to take first steps. Particular themes were developed and tested by lectures and seminars in the Department of Divinity and Religious Studies in Aberdeen (where I benefitted especially from discussion with Brian Brock, Bernd Wannenwetsch, and John Swinton) and in the School of Divinity at the University of St Andrew's (where Alan Torrance, Stephen Holmes, and Ann Loades, amongst others, offered helpful criticism). Other material in the book was greeted with considerable (but good-natured and constructive) scepticism at the Sandra Day O'Connor College of Law at Arizona State University in Phoenix (where Geoffrey Murphy and Jim Weinstein were generous hosts and inquisitive critics). James Faubion's graduate seminar in the Department of Anthropology at Rice University, Houston (where I had the pleasure of being a visiting fellow), provided encouraging and enriching discussion—and James Faubion himself was a patient and learned guide on matters to do with the anthropology of morality. A version of Chapter 1 was given to a meeting of the D Society in Cambridge, chaired by Sarah Coakley, and, so I believe, was clarified as a result of comments and suggestions (including from the chair), and especially by the chastening remarks of the respondent, Chuck Mathewes.

I was greatly assisted by taking part in James Laidlaw and Hallevard Lillehammer's reading group at the University of Cambridge CRAASH (Centre for Reasearch in Arts, Social Sciences, and Humanities) in Philosophy and Social

Anthropology, and also by taking part in a similar group on modern reproductive biology orchestrated by Sarah Franklin. James Laidlaw has generously shared his work prior to publication, and as one of the leaders in the development of the anthropology of morality, has been an invaluable tutor. I also owe thanks to Carrie Humphrey, another such leader in the field, for guiding my reading and being ready to discuss diverse topics in social anthropology even with a novice.

My most extensive tution in social anthropology has been provided by Lesley Sharp of Barnard College, Columbia University, New York. She responded warmly to email enquiries from an unknown source in Cambridge, and has now become a highly valued colleague and friend. Her work has been of the very first importance for me in thinking about the topics in this book.

Trinity College is generously supportive of scholarly endeavour in many different ways, and I express wholehearted thanks to the College for enabling me to make various research trips, attend conferences, and bring Lesley Sharp and James Faubion to Cambridge to lead seminars. Trinity sponsors a summer scheme for Harvard students, and I was fortunate to be able to work with Isabel Herbert over one summer when she helped me greatly to survey and think about changes in representations of Christ's life and death in Western art. The College also granted me a period of sabbatical leave in the Lent Term of 2013, thus allowing me to prepare my lectures for Oxford. (I am grateful to Chris Stoltz for efficiently and effectively taking on certain of my duties while I was on leave.) Above all, of course, the College provides a community of fellow enquirers from whom one can gain enlightenment, counsel, and encouragement. Two Trinity anthropologists have answered a variety of enquiries and questions (Hoenik Kwon and Nick Thomas), but perhaps the brunt of questioning has been patiently borne by Tessa Webber (a distinguished palaeographer), to whom I have turned on numerous matters medieval for unfailing and generous assistance. Adrian Poole and Angela Leighton, both in English Literature, and John Marenbon and Simon Blackburn in philosophy, have also ably and helpfully fielded many, what must have seemed rather random questions. I am particularly fortunate that one of the foremost anthropologists of morality and of Christianity, Joel Robbins, has recently come to the Sigrid Rausing chair in Social Anthropology in Cambridge and to a fellowship at Trinity. His encouragement of my work, especially in the latter stages of the completion of this manuscript, has been outstanding and is deeply appreciated.

In preparing the lectures to be given in Oxford, I was fortunate that Chuck Mathewes, on leave in Cambridge from the University of Virginia, took the initiative along with Patrick McKearney in organizing a small group to meet and respond (gently and constructively, but not uncritically) to draft chapters. Kevin Grove and Giulia Conto also took part in sessions that were enormously valuable in concentrating my mind, directing me to further reading, and in shaping ideas. I acknowledge a very real debt to this group for their wholehearted and generous engagement with the lectures and the ideas they seek to explore. Patrick McKearney kindly read a later draft of the book and offered substantial comments, and was especially tireless in pointing me to useful material along the way.

When I gave the lectures in Oxford, Rob Waller (Principal of Harris Manchester College) and Brian Mountford (of the University Church), were graceful hosts. Eric Southworth loyally attended the entire series, and went above and beyond loyalty in reading and commenting in detail on a first draft of the book based on the lectures he had already endured. His friendship and acumen are both of the highest kind. Nigel Biggar's graduate seminar in Christian ethics provided an occasion to respond to various questions and to attempt clarifications. Both Nigel Biggar and Josh Hordern mildly (but persistently) pressed various important points to which I hope I have at least begun to provide adequate answers in what follows.

Jane Heal (of St John's College, Cambridge) read a penultimate draft and suggested clarifications and improvements. Anthony Kenny read much earlier material and, as so often in the past, was generously encouraging and constructively critical.

Anthea Smith at Trinity College worked hard to produce the very fine illustrated handouts which accompanied the lectures, and subsequently in preparing the manuscript for Oxford University Press. David Torrance was impressively efficient in helping me tidy up the final version, creating the bibliography and checking quotations and footnotes, as well as in offering perceptive observations along the way. And I am grateful to the Bampton Electors for a contribution to funding his very great assistance.

It is a pleasure to work with Tom Perridge at OUP in bringing a manuscript to press. I am grateful to him and the two anonymous readers who provided careful and insightful comments on my draft. I was glad, of course, that these reports were broadly supportive of my approach and argument, but equally glad of requests for clarifications at various points which I have now provided, and which, so I hope, will prevent misunderstanding of what I have taken myself to be doing (and not doing).

The first instalment of Oliver O'Donovan's new work, *Self, World and Time*, came into my hands too late for me to do anything other than simply acknowledge that there is yet another major contribution to the field from which I have yet to learn, but at least it reminds me to acknowledge all I have learnt from Oliver in the past (though it is doubtless by no means all that he could teach me were I a better student).

A debt of a different kind is owed to Agi Lloyd, a fount of wisdom, support, and encouragement. Over many years, George and Jane Cassidy have provided practical and generous friendship for which I am profoundly thankful.

Were I on a desert island, my chosen companion would be Sally Gannon, whose contribution to my ongoing interest in everyday life is incomparable.

Trinity College, Cambridge
December 2013

Contents

List of Illustrations

Introduction: Last Words and First Words: On Creeds, Christ, and the Human Condition

Bampton Lectures have sometimes been last words—in one or other, or sometimes in both senses of that phrase. The lectures of my distinguished predecessor but two as Dean at Trinity College, Cambridge, Bishop John Robinson, were his final work (published as *The Priority of John*[1])—indeed, he did not live to give the lectures drawn from the book, which were delivered on his behalf by his Cambridge colleague Professor Charlie Moule, himself a sometime Bampton Lecturer. Whether those lectures were a last word in the other sense—the last and authoritative word on John Robinson's subject, namely the relationship of John to the other gospels—is a question for others who are competent to judge, as I am not.

I am not expecting my lectures, or even the book based on them, to be a last word in either sense. Indeed I feel bound to confess to the Electors who did me the honour of inviting me to contribute to this distinguished series that if my lectures or book turn out to be a last word, it will be only in the gloomy not the sunny sense of the phrase. In his preface to *The Priority of John*, John Robinson reports that the Bampton Lecturer is 'expected by tradition to produce something of a *magnum opus*'. He cites no authority for this tradition—and even were it undoubted and established, it must be said that Anglicans, of whom I am one, have what might be termed, in Facebook parlance, a 'complicated' relationship with tradition. In fact, I might mention (and I trust that it will not count as speaking ill of the dead), that John Robinson was not a man who felt wholly constrained by customary expectations. And I will have to claim a similar liberty in relation to the tradition he alleges to exist, since the lectures and the book which they have now become, are neither *magnum opus* nor last word, but very much, for reasons I must explain at the outset, a first word.

---

[1] J. A. T. Robinson, *The Priority of John* (London, 1985).

Before I do that, however, let me mention the terms of the will of John Bampton, sometime Canon of Salisbury, who died in 1751 and established by that will a set of eight 'lecture sermons' to be given in the University of Oxford from a list of subjects including 'upon the Articles of the Christian Faith, as comprehended in the Apostles' and Nicene Creeds'. The title I gave to the lecture series (though I have chosen a different title for the book), was *Imagining Life: Christ and the Human Condition*, and was intended to point to an aspect of certain articles of those creeds which is really quite obvious but seems not to have been much remarked upon— that in the creeds, the moments of Christ's life which are noticed prior to his resurrection and ascension are paradigmatically human.[2] Christ, it is recounted, was conceived, born, suffered, died, and buried, thereby passing through regular stages along life's way—so regular indeed, that these stages would likely feature in any outline syllabus for a course in social anthropology.

The life of Christ has, of course, been a subject of extended and profound meditation within the Christian tradition. Around those credal moments, Christ's human life has been imagined, represented, enacted, expounded, and interrogated, not only through the drama of the liturgy and the liturgical year, but also through sermons, prayers, through biblical commentary, exegesis, and contemplation, in doctrinal, moral, and philosophical theology, in art of all kinds (in paintings, mosaics, statues, and tapestries), in devotional writings, mystery plays, poems, and other forms of literature, in hymns, oratorios, cantatas, spirituals, and every other type of musical work—and so on. Through these highly diverse and virtually countless engagements with the life of Christ, that life has been brought to an imaginative realization and in that realization a particular architecture of the human and of human subjectivity (with certain emotions, attitudes, and perceptions), has been explored, staged, elaborated, and commended. Thus the general imagination of the human has been shaped, inflected, modulated, and arguably enriched in so many ways by this particular imagining as to defy the production of a simple catalogue.

These credal moments of conception, birth, suffering, death, and burial are not only paradigmatically human, however, in the sense of being moments of interest and concern in every human life, but are furthermore, for our contemporaries (and not only for our contemporaries), sites of contention and controversy in which what it is to be human is at stake. Conception, birth, suffering, death, and burial are at once universal and at the same time almost universally troubling aspects of the human condition—they both structure, but also often perplex, the narratives of every human life, such that these moments of existence are not only ones in which what it is to be human is lived out, but also occasions in which the human is discovered,

---

[2] The constraints of the lectures and a certain logic militated against any engagement with the anthropological significance of the imagination of Christ's post-mortem existence, but here I simply note a boundary placed on the project.

disputed, contested, and constructed. These contestations come to our attention especially (but not only) in controversies to do with contraception, IVF, abortion, euthanasia, and the use of tissue and body parts, to take some current examples to which I shall return later in the book; but it is of the first importance, I believe, to notice that the enshrining, shaping, framing, and exploration of what it is to be human goes on not just on these boundaries where conundrums and dilemmas are to the fore, but in the regular practice of everyday life.

Some questions thus emerge. If Christian reflection, beginning from these events in Christ's life, authorized by the creeds, and continued in multiple and quite different modes of engagement, amounts to an intense imagining of the human, how does the Christian representation of human being relate to other representations of the human? In particular, how does it relate especially to present-day cultural norms and expectations and to newly emerging modes of being and relationship, as these are currently shaping and framing human life? How can the Christian imagination of human life (dwelling on and drawing from the life of Christ), come into conversation with or engage these other moral imaginaries of the human?

But here we meet a problem—the problem which explains why this book cannot hope to be a last word, but only a first word. The conversation I am envisaging can only begin and proceed if we not only conceive a moral theology somewhat different from the standard, textbook kind, but also review and reconfigure its relationship with moral philosophy and social anthropology. This is just because the complex set of relations, misrelations, and non-relations between these disciplines serve, so I suggest, to discourage—even to disable—the sort of conversation about the human which those credal moments themselves invite and ethical seriousness itself demands. There is, it seems to me, no well-established practice of everyday ethics (as I dub the subject of this conversation), to which this book could simply content itself with making a contribution; and there is, for example, no settled engagement between moral theology and social anthropology of the kind which would facilitate that practice.[3] The purpose of the book is to encourage the development of moral theology's very own everyday ethics—that is, as I shall attempt to characterize it in

---

[3] The key words there are 'no well-established practice' and 'no settled engagement'. I am very happy to notice two important studies published when I was in the middle of the work for my lectures and book, which signal an emerging sense that moral theology and Christian ethics need to reconsider their intellectual relationships, especially through an engagement with the social sciences in general and through a turn to ethnography in particular. See C. Scharen and A. M. Vigen, eds., *Ethnography and Christian Theology and Ethics* (London, 2011) and P. Ward, ed., *Perspectives on Ecclesiology and Ethnography* (Grand Rapids, MI, 2012). My concerns, interests, and approach lie at something of a tangent to these two volumes, but the methodological issues which principally concern them are plainly deserving, on another occasion, of more explicit treatment than I can give them here.

Chapter 1, an ethics not of hard cases, but of the life course. But this book can aspire to do no more than to take initial steps towards that goal. These will be first words, not last words.

As Jeffrey Stout famously and wisely said, discussing methodology is a bit like clearing your throat; you can only do it for so long before people begin to lose interest. True enough—and I am tempted to take that moral very much to heart by proceeding straight to the main subject of the book which is an attempt to practise everyday ethics, rather than beginning with a chapter which is about why and how one might attempt such a thing. (And any reader who wishes to do so, can perfectly well begin at Chapter 2.) But since the approach I am taking may seem somewhat unusual to those already familiar with the study of ethics, a bit of throat-clearing may be of some help, even if not absolutely essential, in orienting the reader to the strategy of what follows.

The first chapter, then, amounts to a 'preliminary expectoration' (to borrow Kierkegaard's term from *Fear and Trembling*). Its main theses are simply stated. First, moral theology does not embrace and practise everyday ethics as it should (and I hazard some reasons why this might be so, and I use the word 'hazard' advisedly, since my diagnosis of this deficiency is offered tentatively and is not essential to the argument of the book). Second, I suggest that moral philosophy is an unhelpful and unpromising partner for a moral theology which would fulfil its obligation to contribute to a conversation concerning everyday ethics, since moral philosophy has turned its back on morality as a social phenomenon, whereas the practice of everyday ethics requires familiarity with morality in its social context. Third, I suggest that moral theology will be more likely and better able to provide an everyday ethics, just insofar as it gains some distance from moral philosophy and engages more fully than it has to date with social anthropology. It is for sub-sequent chapters (the substance of the book) to vindicate (or not) the promise which an engagement with social anthropology holds for moral theology.

It will be apparent already perhaps, and if not will certainly become appar-ent very quickly, that this book is very wide ranging in its scope and subject matter—human life, after all, is a not inconsiderable topic. The spectre of A. E. Housman immediately comes to mind, also a sometime fellow of my college in Cambridge (though not a Bampton Lecturer), who had a rather harsh line in criticism. Of Jowett's translations of Plato he said that they were probably the finest translations we have of works of Greek philosophy from someone who knew neither Greek nor philosophy. More to the point, however, are words in his review of an edition of a particular classical work by a former colleague: 'The width and variety of his ignorance are wonderful; it embraces mythology, palaeography, prosody, and astronomy, and he cannot keep it to himself.'[4]

---

[4] Cited by D. Feeny, *Caesar's Calendar: Ancient Time and the Beginnings of History* (Berkeley, 2007), xii.

A latter-day Housman reviewing my lectures and the resulting book might likewise compliment me on my willingness to share my ignorance unparsimoniously. One must, however, be prepared to sin boldly, as Luther put it—that is to say, to proceed incautiously but cheerfully into the territory, doing the best one can, just because the territory really does deserve to be surveyed. Each of the topics I introduce—conception, birth, suffering, death, burial, and mourning, and the practice of memory—warrants at least a hefty book in its own right, and I am only too aware of merely opening up some lines of discussion from the point of view of moral theology, without treating them exhaustively. Better and more accurate maps will be made in due course, but this initial map will serve towards that goal even if it is itself possessed of what might generously be described as a certain simplicity.

In converting lectures into a book, I have decided to leave the lectures much as they were for the sake of trying to maintain the clarity of argument which the lecture format encourages. I have, however, added to the text here and there, though chiefly with footnotes that sometimes elaborate or support the argument, sometimes nuance it, or sometimes indicate substantial questions and problems which a fuller treatment would have to take up and address. The material drawn upon is very diverse and the juxtapositions between different elements of the evidence sometimes very sharp (some might say harsh). The reader may be advised then, to read the text through for the first time without reference to the notes, relying on the summaries which appear in the introductory sections of each chapter as guides to the thread of argument, and only returning to the notes if any points in the main text seem deserving of further study (or so wholly incredible that the reader wants to know whether they can possibly have any support above and beyond mere assertion).

So, since the first chapter wonders what has inhibited the practice of an everyday Christian ethics, the uninhibited may safely pass over to the chapters that follow and which start to answer the main and central question: how does the Christian imagination of conception, birth, suffering, death, and burial bear on the human life course, and envisage and sustain a Christian form of human being?

1

Moral Theology, Moral Philosophy, Social Anthropology, and the State We Are In: On (the Lack of) Everyday Ethics

I INTRODUCTION: THE STATE WE ARE IN

The moments of Christ's human life which are mentioned in the creeds, namely his conception, birth, suffering, death, and burial, have been the subject of sustained attention within the Christian tradition. This prolonged meditation on the life of Christ has been conducted not just, nor even most importantly, in dogmatic theology, but also in liturgy, prayer, art, poetry, music, and so on, and amounts to an intense imagining of the form of human life. But since these moments are the regular elements of any human life, the imagining of the human from this starting place adds up to a critique (implicit or explicit), of other forms of life which construe conception, birth, suffering, death, and burial and so on, possibly in quite different ways.

If, however, we ask the question which rather naturally occurs at this point (that is, how does this representation of the human engage with and contest other contemporary representations?), we immediately confront a difficulty: the state we are in. The state we are in is a matter of the practice of and relations between three disciplines which might be expected to contribute to the discussion we envisage: moral theology, moral philosophy, and social anthropology. The body of this book will attempt to present what I am terming an everyday Christian ethics in its critical engagement with other imaginations of human being. But the challenge of doing so is the greater just because of the current relations—or misrelations—between moral theology, moral philosophy, and social anthropology, which presently inhibit or discourage the task I have in mind. Moral theology itself, I suggest, is disinclined to take up the construction of an everyday ethics, and may perhaps only overcome this disinclination as it clarifies its own self-understanding and its understanding of its relationship with these other two disciplines. As it does so, and in particular as it learns to engage more closely with social anthropology, it will also equip itself to conduct an enquiry into everyday life in the way it needs to be conducted—so the remaining chapters of the book seek to show.

Since the space of one chapter does not allow for a conspectus of the field, I make no more than preliminary and quite limited remarks about each of the disciplines which concern me at this point. I shall suggest (in section II) that in various ways moral theology is misconceived (at least, in so far as the subject is expressed in textbook and popular conceptions of it), as comprising an ethics of hard cases. So practised, moral theology is insufficiently interested in the social; specifically it lacks a concern for the plausible narration of moral lives, and this lack of concern has doleful consequences for its apologetic, or as I would prefer to say, its therapeutic or evangelical responsibilities and potential. I will briefly explain (in section III) why moral philosophy fails to help moral theology to a better self-understanding and practice, and is indeed part of the problem not the solution, since moral philosophy's relationship with the social (and naturally enough therefore, with social anthropology), is itself disordered. I will then (in section IV), turn even more briefly to social anthropology itself, with which I propose to engage throughout the rest of this book. The purpose at this point will be merely to notice the nature of social anthropology's intellectual ambition to depict the human—an ambition which, for the reasons given in the discussion of moral theology, should be of great interest to that subject. (In addition, I note two further reasons why this is an especially auspicious time for moral theology to open up relations with social anthropology.)

What these preliminary remarks intend, then, is to set out a *prima facie* case for reconceiving the practice of moral theology in the light of the concerns and reservations about it and moral philosophy which are here discussed, and further to indicate how anthropology may assist moral theology (methodologically and materially), in a practice which better displays and explicates the character of Christian life. Through its encounter with social anthropology, moral theology may be deepened, challenged, corrected, and advanced.

Behind the different considerations of these three sections, there is a unifying theme, which I can sum up in the contention that as the three disciplines are currently practised, only social anthropology is genuinely and thoroughly interested in what I mean to refer to by 'morality'—and conversely, that what I consider the misdirection of moral theology and of moral philosophy, has to do with their lack of interest in this morality.

I use the word 'morality' here to refer to an everyday practice which exists on the ground—the practice of appraising ourselves and others against notions of the good, or the right, or the fitting. But suppose we ask whether and how morality, in this sense, is an object of attention or analysis for theology or for philosophy. Alternatively, suppose we ask about the relationship between morality as an everyday practice and morality as it is treated, conceived, understood, and described in theology, philosophy, and social anthropology. We will find ourselves concluding that moral theology's misdirection (which may stem in part from its roots in the subject's original and continuing fascination with what we might call difficult questions) involves its own self-willed alienation from morality (in the sense I am now using it to refer to an extant social practice), and further that this alienation entails its own therapeutic incapacity—a notion I shall explain presently. Furthermore, we will conclude that moral philosophy achieved its own perhaps more self-conscious rejection of morality through its self-definition in the modern period, involving as it did the repudiation of anthropology. So, since the parting of the ways between moral philosophy and social anthropology left social anthropology holding the cards when it comes to the comprehension of morality as a practice of everyday life, it follows that a better moral theology will crucially need to find a way to engage with social anthropology if it is to equip itself for its proper tasks, including as they do the fashioning of an everyday ethics.

II THE ODDITY OF MORAL THEOLOGY

Moral theology and Christian ethics, in their textbook forms, are really very odd; that is, as they are conceived and conveyed by a typical course or syllabus, and as they are received by students of the discipline, as well as more widely.[1] So conceived we have a moral theology which is curiously uninterested in everyday ethics, in the social context of our ethical actions, and in social anthropology.

Suppose we were to broach the subject which newspapers like to refer to as 'the crisis of old age' with a student who has taken a course in Christian ethics. This crisis consists in the fact that since we (at least in the affluent world) are living far beyond the 64 years which was the life expectancy of a male in the UK in 1945, we have a high chance of experiencing a period of debility and dependency before death, and that the burden of delivering adequate care for those so dependent poses a considerable social challenge. My guess is that

---

[1] It is important to stress that the point I am making here is about a dominant conception of the subject which continues to exert its sway in a variety of ways. I am definitely not saying that there is no good moral theology and my debt to colleagues in the field will be obvious at many places in what follows. My point is thus analogous to Fassin's and Laidlaw's contention that anthropology lacks an anthropology of morality (see 'The Promise of Social Anthropology' in this chapter); it is not, as they see it, that there has been no good work relevant to this topic, but rather that the topic has not been recognized and understood as belonging centrally to the discipline's practice—and that this failure skews the subject and its development, and prevents social anthropology from having the shape it properly should.

thus prompted the student will talk about euthanasia (good or bad), and possibly mention too, advance directives, living wills, and assisted suicide—in other words, the student will likely reproduce the topics which the typical handbook on bioethics has in a section entitled 'the end of life'. But about the quotidian challenges of growing old, and about what it would be to live well, ethically, and Christianly, in this particular stage of life, I would be surprised if the student has much to say immediately and without further reflection. What he or she has learnt as belonging to the subject matter of ethics is a set of question about the acceptability or otherwise of managing one's exit from this stage of life, but nothing much about what it might be to live it well.

Or let us take the reflective Christian layperson and suppose we touch on the subject of reproduction. Such a person would almost certainly have a view on the rights or wrongs of abortion, have things to say about contraception, and perhaps about IVF—but on the subject of whether and why one should want 'a child of one's own', to use the current language, and what children are or are for, I doubt that he or she would be so articulate. Again, what has been learnt is the importance of addressing the licitness (that is, the acceptability or otherwise) of certain ways of becoming, avoiding, or ceasing to be pregnant—but about why and whether one should want to be pregnant at all, and what it means to have a child, ethically speaking, I suspect that our informant might be (surely quite remarkably) uninformative.

What both student and layperson have absorbed, it seems, is the notion that Christian ethics is an ethics of hard cases—for this is how the subject is predominantly presented and received. If it is thought to have anything to say about conception, birth, suffering, death, and burial, it will be as those life moments throw up dilemmas, many of which are extraordinary, unusual, and tragic. But about the everyday experience and understanding of those events, about the normal passage of the life course, and its more general shaping and structuring by a conception of what it is to be human, Christian ethics can seem to have little or nothing to say.[2] I do not suggest, of course, that the asking and answering of difficult questions is, to use the language of the tradition, illicit—but rather that the dominant conception which sees the asking and answering of difficult questions as at the very core of moral theology diminishes the subject, and specifically stands in the way of it taking up the task of shaping an everyday ethics, as I am calling it. Hard cases are not unimportant; but they represent siren voices for moral theology when moral theology becomes so besotted with them as to take the view, in effect, that they comprise the scope of its tasks and responsibilities.

---

[2] Which is why the treatment of ethics by historians, whether of the early church or of later periods, such as, for example, Peter Brown, Wayne Meeks, and John Bossy, can be so refreshing and potentially liberating for the moralist, reminding him or her of the possibility of conceiving of ethics within the context of a richly described social world.

How did this come about? How did it happen that Christian ethics is generally regarded as essentially concerned with addressing and resolving hard cases? Well, genealogy in cases such as this is not easy and an adequate genealogy would identify multiple and complex causes of the way things are. But according to Jack Mahoney in *The Making of Moral Theology*, 'The single most influential factor in the development of the practice and discipline of moral theology is to be found in the growth and spread of confession.'[3]

As Mahoney tells the story, the subject's beginnings in the so-called Penitentials was indeed in response to the practice of auricular confession. These handbooks (possibly Welsh and sixth century in origin, but certainly reaching England and mainland Europe via Irish missionaries), were written to guide confessors by fixing 'a tariff of penances to be enjoined for various sins',[4] thereby avoiding a confessional post-code lottery. Mahoney regards these 'practical...ready reckoners'[5] of sins and penance as a 'fascinating and repelling literature'[6]—and though he doesn't specify in what way they are so, it may be granted that Columbanus's decree 'that for a particular transgression the penitent should "abstain for three years from the more tasty food and from his wife"'[7], is likely to be judged one or other, and possibly both.

These early attempts to articulate sins and assess liability for them would be given further encouragement by the Fourth Lateran Council of 1215, which in Canon 21 required auricular confession at least once a year. It was the routinization of the practice of confession which led to the further strengthening of moral theology in its characteristic form as a juridical calculus of sins and penance, both in the later medieval summas, and also in the development of the tradition after the Council of Trent, epitomized in the work of St Alphonsus Liguori. Of course, confession in daily practice dealt not necessarily with difficult conundrums, but with the prosaic and the routine. But the means of advance in this science, as in the common law tradition, is through the weighing of hard cases and the making of nice distinctions—and it was this tendency that gave us the probably mythic but properly celebrated maxim which can be regarded as the apogee of this tradition, namely that the sin of watching animals copulate is in proportion to the size of the animals and in inverse proportion to your distance from them.

However the fostering and cementing of moral theology's interest in difficult questions is to be explained, what is beyond dispute is that by the time of the Second Vatican Council the weaknesses of this tradition of moral theology and its particular emphases were commonly rehearsed within Roman Catholic

---

[3] J. Mahoney, *The Making of Moral Theology* (Oxford, 1987), 1.
[4] Mahoney, *The Making of Moral Theology*, 6.
[5] Mahoney, *The Making of Moral Theology*, 15.
[6] Mahoney, *The Making of Moral Theology*, 6.
[7] Mahoney, *The Making of Moral Theology*, 10.

circles. Moral theology, it was said in the 1960s, needed to regain its theological bearings.[8] It had become unbiblical, legalistic, individualistic, and preoccupied, rather negatively, with sin and its avoidance.

Protestantism had made similar complaints four hundred years earlier, though with a good deal more attitude.[9] But it could be said that it generally failed to move constructively beyond mere moaning and thus remained in a wholly dialectical relationship with the difficult questions tradition, such that ethics (understood to mean casuistry), became for many Protestants an 'inherently doubtful enterprise'[10] (to use Hauerwas's phrase)—which it definitely should not be. For there is nothing in these complaints about the tradition, whether put bluntly or more circumspectly, which alleges that there is no place for the consideration of difficult questions—simply that it is not the *only* thing that moral theology should do.[11] For moral theology to be wholesome, so to say, it needs to locate mere casuistry, however sophisticated, in a wider and richer context. Thus if the Protestant tradition was ahead of Vatican II in seeming to make some of the same complaints which were to resurface four hundred years later, it was in error in rejecting, in effect, the very practice of moral theology rather than doing what Vatican II sought to do, which was to conceive the subject more fruitfully and to encourage it to develop along new lines. (It was only with Barth and Bonhoeffer, it might be said, that Protestantism brought some sustained theological attention to the question of how moral theology, or ethics in the preferred Protestant parlance, could properly be conceived and practised rather than simply repudiated.)

---

[8] Of course, official pronouncements both before and after the Council made their complaints in a very particular style of diplomatic and allusive indirection. Thus Pius XII's assertion of the importance of scripture to moral theology (in *Divino Affiante Spiritu* of 1943), and Vatican II's injunction (in its decree on priestly training, *Optatam Totius*), that not only dogmatic theology, but 'the other theological disciplines' should be 'renewed through a more living contact with the mystery of Christ and the history of salvation', and furthermore that 'Special care must be given to the perfecting of moral theology', are meant, as Mahoney puts is, as a 'rebuke' to moral theology; see Mahoney, *The Making of Moral Theology*, 303. That moral theology's 'scientific expositions, nourished more on the teaching of the Bible, should', as the decree has it, 'shed light on the loftiness of the calling of the faithful in Christ and the obligation that is theirs of bearing fruit in charity for the life of the world', is one of those 'shoulds' which implies a 'doesn't'.

[9] Luther's *Ninety-Five Theses* begin as follows: '1. When our Lord and Master Jesus Christ said, "Repent", he willed the entire life of believers to be one of repentance. 2. This word cannot be understood as referring to the sacrament of penance, that is, confession and satisfaction, as administered by the clergy.' (M. Luther's *Works*, trans. H. J. Grimm, vol. 31 [Philadelphia, 1957], 25.) Luther's point, of course, is not to reject the practice of confession, but a particular understanding of it, and specifically any understanding which fails to reckon with the fact that penance cannot properly be a matter of a single and discrete outward act, but only of a permanent transformation of inner attitude, through the agency of God's grace. For further discussion, see J. T. McNeill, *A History of the Cure of Souls* (Chicago, 1951), ch. 8.

[10] S. Hauerwas, *The Peaceable Kingdom* (London, 1984), 52.

[11] This point must be underlined and stressed. I make no suggestion that casuistry is improper. Of course, attending to tensions or even what appear to be contradictions in moral thought and practice can be a vital element in the refinement and application of a moral vision or scheme.

But let us go back and consider what the nub of any complaint against the difficult questions tradition should be. And I take a cue here—but only a cue—from Mahoney's, to my mind, perceptive suggestion that 'for all its preoccupation with sin and its busy cataloguing and subdividing of sins, from the family trees of Cassian and Gregory onwards, moral theology has not always appeared to take sin itself seriously enough.'[12] Mahoney's own development of this thought need not concern us, but we may treat the remark as suggestive—and add to it the thought that the same moral theology, in not taking sin seriously, has just as well failed to take seriously the character of the good, for perhaps almost inevitably in treating the one lightly it treats the other so too.

The hard cases tradition, so we might say, is always in danger of effectively satisfying itself with telling us that the good is good and the bad is bad. Of course, it might arrive at a determination of good or bad with arguments of great sophistication. But it nonetheless succumbs to an inherently Pelagian temptation just as it fails to locate either the good or the bad in what I will later refer to (borrowing a phrase from the work of an important contemporary social anthropologist), as 'psychologically and socioculturally realistic' narratives. (Were Luther's neat anti-Pelagian mantra that 'man by nature has neither correct precept nor good will'[13] accepted, moral theology would not act as if the good is natural in such a way that it needs no well-developed or considered narrative context to explain its character and existence—nor as if the bad, although perhaps necessarily in some way more mysterious than the good, does not itself require or deserve such a contextual understanding.) No matter how we explain it, however, we need to note moral theology's historic and continuing unwillingness to undertake the sort of cultural engagement which the Vatican Council seems to have envisaged and wished for. Without that engagement, what results, I think, is a moral theology that treats the good and the bad as lightly as each other (even if it prefers one to the other), and shows no sustained interest in the deep character and logic of different forms of life. It follows that such a moral theology has the capacity neither to support the imagination and practice of the good, nor to engage critically and therapeutically with the imagination and practice of the bad. The hard cases tradition, in other words, is content essentially to determine or judge hard cases; but the task of moral theology, properly conceived, so I maintain, must be not only to judge, but to understand and characterize the lives out of which our actions, good or bad, plausibly, persuasively, or even compellingly arise. With such an agenda, moral theology becomes a very challenging enterprise indeed; but without such a hermeneutic agenda, moral theology will remain

---

[12] Mahoney, *The Making of Moral Theology*, 32.

[13] From Luther's *Disputation Against Scholastic Theology*, trans. H. J. Grimm, in *Luther's Works*, vol. 31 (Philadelphia, 1957), proposition 17.

fundamentally incapable of a therapeutic or evangelical engagement with contemporary life.

Let me try to explain further what may appear to be a rather dense point by referring to Freud's complaints about the inadequacies of the treatment, other than his own analytic treatment, of what were termed 'neurotics' in his day. '[T]he estimate in which neuroses are still held by the majority of doctors' is revealed by the fact that '[t]he doctor says to the neurotic patient: "There's nothing wrong with you, it's only a question of nerves; so I can blow away your trouble in two or three minutes with just a few words." '[14] With the mere diagnosis, then, the doctors' work is done. Of course Freud had come to his own position via the practice of hypnosis, and the practitioners of hypnosis manifestly took the treatment of neuroses more seriously than did the majority of doctors. But hypnosis, while right in reckoning that these complaints were more intractable than supposed by those who would address them with a sweep of the hands and a few words, failed nonetheless, according to Freud, to offer a genuine therapy:

> In the light of the knowledge we have gained from psychoanalysis we can describe the difference between hypnotic and psychoanalytic suggestion as follows. Hypnotic treatment seeks to cover up and gloss over something in mental life; analytic treatment seeks to expose and get rid of something. The former acts like a cosmetic, the latter like surgery.[15]

My suggestion is, of course, that moral theology in the limited mode which it takes in the difficult questions tradition, is analogous to the hypnotists', or even to the 'it's only nerves' approach, in failing to reckon with the necessity for 'the accomplishment of serious work'[16] if one is to address aberrant behaviours—or, for that matter, if one is to locate the good as well as the bad in the social contexts in which they arise and have their appeal, force, and meaning. Moral theology which simply classifies an action as right or wrong, even if it backs up this identification with the firm directions of a stringent confessional or other pastoral practice, has thereby offered nothing by way of treatment, and at its best is simply cosmetic. Such a practice may (or more likely, may not) prevent (or rather suppress) what it aims to prevent, but a more serious treatment would demand some more 'serious work'. Such serious work would go behind the symptoms, and would seek to understand and address the deeper individual, social, and cultural drives of which any symptoms are an expression and which may still exist even if the symptoms are in some way dealt with. Only with such cultural engagement could moral theology be a properly therapeutic practice.

---

[14] Sigmund Freud, *Introductory Lectures on Psychoanalysis*, trans. J. Strachey (London, 1973), 503.
[15] Freud, *Introductory Lectures*, 504.   [16] Freud, *Introductory Lectures*, 505.

Why has moral theology in some of its dominant forms avoided this serious work? After all, even if the practice of moral theology has been shaped by confession and thus pushed into being an ethics concerned with the determination of hard cases, it might still have resisted its confinement by this concern, and branched out beyond a simple 'it's only nerves' approach and have resolved to understand the sources and grounds of human action, good or bad.

I suggest that we can identify a further and typical element in the picture in an unresolved tension in the work of John Paul II, evident in his encyclical letter *Evangelium Vitae*.[17] The tension is between, on the one hand, John Paul II's powerful pastoral sense of the need for careful engagement with modern culture, and on the other, his lingering faith in what might be called peeping Thomism[18]—that is, a nostalgic confidence in the epistemological and persuasive force of the natural law. This latter element, like confession, has been an extremely influential factor in shaping moral theology and has in turn itself discouraged the 'serious work' of comprehending contemporary social life, thought, and action. As it is, unable to resolve the tension, the Encyclical ends up highly conflicted as to which of two different projects it should pursue: either providing a genealogical understanding of characteristic contemporary patterns of moral conduct, or, alternatively, simply identifying them as wrong.[19]

The tension is plain to see. On the one hand the Encyclical draws attention to the development of 'a new cultural climate... which gives crimes against life a new and—if possible—even more sinister character'. The sinister character, as the Encyclical will explain, is just that 'choices once unanimously considered criminal and rejected by the common moral sense are gradually becoming socially acceptable'.[20] So, for the Encyclical, the conversion of what was the crime of abortion into a right is the most striking element in what it sees as 'a conspiracy against life' and 'a veritable "culture of death"'.[21] According to *Evangelium Vitae* then, 'powerful cultural, economic and political currents' explain the choice of courses of action which were once unthinkable; and insofar as it holds to this line, the Encyclical is implicitly committed to a genealogical analysis which would, in principle, attempt to come to terms with contemporary life and thought in the sense of providing a careful and full understanding of it.

On the other hand, however, the Encyclical is held back by the thought that what is at stake here are 'essential and innate human and moral values which

---

[17] John Paul II, *Evangelium Vitae*, English trans. (London, 1995).

[18] To borrow what is said to be Ralph McInerny's coinage.

[19] I have discussed the Encyclical and these issues at greater length in 'Catholics and Anglicans and Contemporary Bioethics: Divided or United?', in *Issues for a Catholic Bioethics*, ed. L. Gormally (London, 1999), 34–57, and draw on some of the discussion in this chapter.

[20] John Paul II, *Evangelium Vitae*, para. 4.

[21] John Paul II, *Evangelium Vitae*, para. 12.

flow from the very truth of the human being and express and safeguard the dignity of the person'[22]—so that what is 'urgently called for is a general mobilization of consciences'[23], for it is the conscience which bears witness to the value of life, a 'value…which every human being can grasp by the light of reason'.[24] With this counter thought, expressive of one reading of the natural law tradition, the Encyclical seems to recoil from the project of understanding that it otherwise entertained. For with a return to the possibility that a simple apologetic appeal to the moral law and conscience will overcome the 'culture of death', the Encyclical fails to take at all seriously the depth, character, and compelling logic, so to say, of this culture of death which it has itself conjured up as seemingly socially compelling and powerful.

It is telling of the conflict here, of course, that the Encyclical hesitates before the 'linguistic phenomenon' of the 'widespread use of ambiguous terminology, such as 'interruption of pregnancy', wondering whether this phenomenon 'is itself a symptom of an uneasiness of conscience'.[25] This is a perfectly appropriate question—but what the Encyclical here declines to allow and recognize, is that even if such terminology was perhaps originally and is even now sometimes used euphemistically and for the sake of a delicate conscience, in much contemporary usage it is just as often employed as a morally neutral description of what is deemed a morally neutral act. The termination of a pregnancy really is, for this way of thought, a termination of a pregnancy and not the killing of a child; the latter description is not implicitly regarded as the accurate, though too explicit account of what is going on. So what we have in this usage is not, then, a case of people calling things they know to be bad by names which consciously serve to conceal that fact, but of people using what they take to be morally neutral terms to refer to what is genuinely thought to be so. The 'culture of death', as John Paul II dubs it, is not a culture with a bad conscience which must be carefully guarded from reminders of what it secretly knows, but a culture which has come, quite genuinely, to regard as beyond moral critique what is, for the Encyclical, beyond the moral law.

The Encyclical hesitates here then, and fails to understand and come to terms with our contemporary circumstances, just because of that nostalgic peeping Thomism, the wistful epistemological Pelagianism, which holds on to the lingering hope that an appeal to conscience and the natural law, like the insistence that 'it's only nerves', will be enough to overcome our modern neuroses. This is but one strain in the thought of John Paul II, and his contribution to moral theology is richer and more subtle just because it is only that. But amongst his admirers there are those who are appreciative chiefly

---

[22] John Paul II, *Evangelium Vitae*, para. 71.
[23] John Paul II, *Evangelium Vitae*, para. 95.
[24] John Paul II, *Evangelium Vitae*, para. 101.
[25] John Paul II, *Evangelium Vitae*, para. 58.

of the natural law strand in his work, and who illustrate only too clearly what happens when it gains the upper hand. Thus when one such admirer ends a chapter of a book setting out the context and resources of (to use the book's title) a *Catholic Bioethics for a New Millennium*, with the following question, we should sense a problem:

> Do Christians believe and are they willing to live the creative and hopeful teach-ings of their tradition about life, sexuality, marriage, and family—reformulated and developed appropriately with the aid of the best of contemporary moral think-ing? Or do we prefer to acquiesce in the wholesale commodification and destruc-tion of early human life, the disintegration of marriage and the marriage-based family, the consumerization of sex, the blanket sterilization of individuals and societies and the abandonment of the disabled and the elderly?[26]

Such a question suggests that any serious interest in the comprehension of our contemporary cultural context has vanished, and we are left with a clarion call of the sort sounded by a trumpet played in deep space. However well the trumpet is played, no one will hear it.

We need a different moral theology. Not a moral theology of hard cases, nor one which simply names the good and denounces the bad. Somehow, if the seeming paradox can be excused, we need a moral theology which can fathom what we may casually refer to as the 'unfathomable' choices and wishes of contemporary life. But there is no real paradox, of course, in fathoming these unfathomable cases, just because the forms of life lived out amongst us are not really unfathomable in practice, but only unfathomable from where we may currently stand, with our particular limitations of experience and knowledge and failures of imagination and insight. What choices do I have in mind? Well, it might be the choice of people who wish to amputate healthy limbs because they feel incomplete *with* them;[27] or it might be the choice expressed in the demand for gender reassignment; or it might be in the choice to persevere, against the odds and at huge cost (in all senses), with immensely burdensome IVF treatment; or it might be the wish of parents to have returned to them for burial or cremation slides of tissue created in the course of post-mortem exam-ination of their children; and so on. These wishes and actions are, to many of us, more or less opaque or puzzling—even bewildering. But a moral theology which cannot fully comprehend these desires and the life stances from which

---

[26] A. Fisher, *Catholic Bioethics for a New Millennium* (Cambridge, 2012), 37.

[27] To take an example from C. Elliott's book, *Better than Well: American Medicine Meets the American Dream* (New York, 2003); Elliott, while frankly admitting that 'nobody really under-stands apotemnophilia' (235), properly attempts to understand the desire for amputation of healthy limbs by locating this desire, at least as a place to begin, in a cultural context which com-bines radical individualism, consumerism, and competitiveness with a search for self-fulfilment. What is clear is that the desire will only be understood if we start to identify and reckon with these and other cultural drivers.

they come, no matter whether it judges them good or bad, no matter whether it sees them as expressions of or threats to Christian life and action, fails in its intellectual responsibilities. The difficult questions tradition, in failing to naturalize both the good and the bad—in failing to render these courses of action 'psychologically and socioculturally realistic'—leaves us merely with that silent trumpet call.

It is plain how such a moral theology must fail, in addition, to be therapeutic or evangelical, in what I take to be O'Donovan's sense of the term,[28] and as implied by Karl Barth in an aside in his discussion of abortion. Having contended that 'a definite No must be the presupposition of all further discussion' on this subject (and that point does not concern me here and now), Barth comments that 'the question arises, however, how this No is to be established and stated if it is to be a truly effective No'.[29] His answer is that the Church 'could and can tell and show humanity which is tormented by life because it thinks it must live it, that it may do so'. Thus he says that the Protestant Church:

> neither could nor can range itself with the Roman Catholic Church and its hard preaching of the Law. It must proclaim its own message in this matter, namely the Gospel. In so doing, however, it must not underbid the severity of the Roman Catholic No. It must overbid its abstract and negative: "Thou shalt not", by the force of its positive: "Thou mayest", in which, of course, the corresponding: "Thou mayest not", is included. . .[30]

Karl Barth's contention that the 'no' of the law must be outdone, so to say, by the explication of the law as evangelical permission and promise, is an important desideratum for moral theology. But moral theology will only find its therapeutic and evangelical voice and vocation insofar as it understands and locates the bad in its own compelling form, and as it narrates the good as a form of life with its own logic and sense. Both the 'no' and the 'thou mayest' must be provided with real and rich contexts if the passage from one to the other is to be navigated.

My purpose here has not been to provide a survey of moral theology. On the contrary, my purpose has been very limited. My interest and the interest of the substance of this book is in making a contribution to what I am terming an everyday ethics. Moral theology however, so I suggested, will need to reconceive its practice if it is to develop such an ethics, since in its dominant self-presentation, reception, and form, it is an ethics of hard cases. In the previous pages I have hazarded a diagnosis of this state of affairs. I have suggested

---

[28] O. M. T. O'Donovan, *Resurrection and Moral Order: An Outline for Evangelical Ethics*, 2nd ed. (Leceister, 1994).

[29] K. Barth, *Church Dogmatics*, III/4, trans. A. T. Mackay et al. (Edinburgh, 1961), 417.

[30] Barth, *Church Dogmatics*, III/4, 418.

that moral theology's origins as a guide for confessors, combined with certain epistemologically Pelagian tendencies, may explain its being disinclined or ill-equipped to take up the task of narrating the form of human being which an everyday ethics requires. (I suggest later that in taking up the tasks of an everyday ethics, moral theology will need to reconceive its relationships with moral philosophy and social anthropology, turning away from the first and engaging more closely with the second.) But nothing rests on this particular and tentative diagnosis; exactly why moral theology is as it is, is not my chief concern. My concern is that it should be what it currently is not—an everyday ethics, which is at once both therapeutic and evangelical. It will be such, however, only as it engages more fully than it has with the wider cultural context. And it will do this just as it takes social anthropology, and not moral philosophy and bioethics, as a useful dialogue partner—for philosophy, as I will argue, only serves to confirm moral theology in a certain intellectual isolation and abstraction, by itself resolutely turning its back on the social in general, and social anthropology in particular.

III THE EVEN GREATER ODDITY OF MORAL PHILOSOPHY: THE PHILOSOPHY OF WHAT?

Moral theology is odd. Moral philosophy is odder—and itself a further part of 'the state we are in'. Moral theology sometimes shows scant interest in the social context of moral action; moral philosophy, however, in its leading forms, dissociates itself from the social altogether, resolutely failing to reckon with the fact that morality must be understood as a social practice.

Let me come at this from something of an angle, by asking how moral philosophy relates to social anthropology. To anyone standing on the academic touchline, involved in neither subject, it would be a reasonable thought that since both subjects can be expected to have an interest in morality, the practitioners in the one discipline should surely take account of work in the other. What we find, however, is that moral philosophy has, for the most part, no interest whatsoever in social anthropology.

It would be telling, though tedious, to catalogue the general indifference of moral philosophy to social anthropology. So let it suffice to note just how unrewarding it would be for the interested enquirer to consult standard works in philosophy in an attempt to discover what philosophy has been willing to learn from social anthropology's treatment of morality (such as, to name three significant and authoritative tomes, the ten-volume *Encyclopedia of Philosophy* edited by Craig,[31] the three-volume *Encyclopedia of Ethics*

---

[31] *The Encyclopedia of Philosophy*, ed. E. Craig (London, 1998).

edited by Becker and Becker,[32] and the five-volume *Encyclopedia of Bioethics* edited by Reich).[33] The general message of the first two of these works is that anthropologists face certain moral problems in the conduct of their research with which philosophers can help, and that while they are at it, these helpful philosophers can also sort out the dreadful muddle which anthropologists have got themselves into over relativism. There is no indication, however, of any interest in the substance of the work of social anthropology; no interest, in other words, in the human and moral worlds which anthropologists discover and describe.[34] The *Encyclopedia of Bioethics* seems, in principle, to be more open to attending to perspectives from social anthropology, but not in practice.[35]

How has it come about that moral philosophers have no interest in the moral practice which is the concern of social anthropology? On what understanding of morality on the part of moral philosophy does this disinterest make sense?[36] The two key protagonists in giving modern moral philosophy its character and (lack of) interests are Kant and Mill. And for all that those two are usually opposed one to the other, on this matter they effectively stand shoulder to shoulder.

---

[32] *Encyclopedia of Ethics*, 2nd. ed., eds. L. C. and C. B. Becker (London, 2001).

[33] *Encyclopedia of Bioethics*, ed. W. T. Reich, rev. ed. (New York, 1995).

[34] See K. A. Appiah, 'Anthropology', in *Encyclopedia of Ethics*, eds. Becker and Becker, and 'Anthropology, Philosophy of', M. H. Salmon, in *The Encyclopedia of Philosophy*, ed. Craig.

[35] The editor, William Reich, in recounting the history of the development of bioethics, tells of the widening of the subject's intellectual engagements. Developments in kidney dialysis, heart transplantation, and in the ability to prolong life 'stimulated a renaissance of traditional medical ethics and, simultaneously, fostered unprecedented, new interdisciplinary conversation. Theology, philosophy, law, and sociology had previously engaged issues arising from medicine, health care, end of life science, but rarely in dialogue. By 1970 the disciplines now contributing to bioethics were finding one another.' The *Encyclopedia of Bioethics* does not, however, fully bear out this sense of a new meeting of minds or disciplines. Social anthropology, when it appears, seems to stand next to bioethics at best, rather than to engage with it or modify it. On many occasions it doesn't appear at all. Thus the long article, in eight separate contributions, under the heading 'Reproductive Technologies', concludes with sections on 'Ethical Issues' and 'Legal and Regulatory Issues', which plainly do not allow for a treatment of the considerable body of work that social anthropology has contributed in this area. In the same way, the article in many parts, on 'Genetic Testing and Screening' has sections on 'Legal Issues' and 'Ethical Issues', but no anthropological perspectives. There are, it is true, discrete contributions, often of great merit, from particular anthropologists: thus Arthur Kleinman's article 'Medicine, Anthropology of', is an elegant account not only of what medical anthropology brings to an understanding of medical practice and the experiences of illness, but also a critique of the limitations of bioethics in its standard forms, in which, so Kleinman argues, what is at stake for patients and families in their particular contexts and circumstances is occluded by a search for and imposition of supposedly universal categories and framings. But Kleinman's article, along with other contributions such as Sarah Franklin's essay on 'Life', are, we might say, *in* the *Encyclopedia of Bioethics* but not *of* it. For notwithstanding the editor's assurance that the disciplines which might contribute to bioethics started to 'find one another' in the 1970s, the evidence of genuine engagement is not readily found here.

[36] For a more extended development of these points, see Banner, 'Moral Philosophy: The Philosophy of What?', *Studies in Christian Ethics* 24 (2011), 232–41.

In his most fundamental contribution to moral philosophy, in *Groundwork of the Metaphysic of Morals*, Kant announces that it is:

> a matter of the utmost necessity to work out a pure moral philosophy cleansed of everything that can only be empirical and appropriate to anthropology...When applied to man [philosophy] does not borrow in the slightest from acquaintance with him (in anthropology), but gives him laws *a priori* as a rational being.[37]

This magisterial stipulation, which he barely deigns to defend, has been immensely influential for moral philosophy's self-understanding in the last two hundred and thirty years—and can be regarded as a highly creative piece of boundary work, since with it Kant invented social anthropology as a discipline distinct from philosophy, just by banishing its subject matter from philosophy. Philosophy thus turned its back on any real interest in the descriptive and empirical, and was content to be prescriptive, whereas social anthropology took up the task of attending to the particulars of social practice. And since 'pure reason is itself practical' to borrow Kant's programmatic slogan (i.e. since reason alone can determine the moral law), a philosophic morality need have no truck with actual practice—and thus anthropology is assigned to a very specific place.

Mill, with whom Kant is usually contrasted, follows a parallel path in beginning his ethics with an entirely prescriptive move, stating that:

> there ought either to be some one fundamental principle or law, at the root of all morality, or if there be several, there should be a determinate order of precedence among them; and the one principle, or the rule for deciding between the various principles when they conflict, ought to be self-evident.[38]

For this role, and on the basis of his notorious proof of it, Mill offers the principle of utility ('or as Bentham latterly called it, the greatest happiness principle'). With a further piece of breath-taking cheek Mill asserts that 'It would be...easy to show that whatever steadiness or consistency [the] moral beliefs [of mankind] have attained, has been mainly due to the tacit influence of a standard not recognised',[39] namely that very principle of utility. Discerning the tacit influence of an unrecognized standard is surely likely to be difficult rather than easy; but with only a feeble feint towards an argument to establish his ethical principles, as expressive of ethical practice, Mill moves on.

Both Kant and Mill claim to vindicate popular moral thought and the core of common morality, Kant with arguments of some subtlety,[40] Mill with very little argument at all. The claims of both on this point have, however, little more to be said for them than that they manifest the air of breezy confidence

---

[37] I. Kant, *Groundwork of the Metaphysic of Morals*, 389, in H. J. Paton's translation, published as *The Moral Law* (London, 1948).

[38] J. S. Mill, *Utilitarianism*, ed. R. Crisp (Oxford, 1998), 51.

[39] Mill, *Utilitarianism*, 51.

[40] See the references and discussion in Banner, 'Moral Philosophy: The Philosophy of What?'

with which a developer assures a planning enquiry that the proposed redevelopment of a district is true to and will retain that district's quintessential character and community spirit—even while a road is driven through the middle of it. The fact is, both approach morality with a more lively commitment to judging it than to comprehending it—and this ought to surprise or trouble us. It should surely seem at least mildly perplexing for moral philosophy to begin and proceed in such a resolutely stipulative and prescriptive manner.

We can get at the problematic character of such beginnings for moral philosophy by asking ourselves the following seemingly simple (perhaps even simple-minded question): what is moral philosophy the philosophy of?

It sounds a rather easy question. The philosophy of science is, plainly enough, the philosophy of (or about) science. The philosophy of art is, again, plainly enough, the philosophy of (or about) art. So, once you get going, the answer here seems equally obvious: moral philosophy must be the philosophy of or about morality. Certainly. But this seemingly simple-minded line of questioning alerts us to the always potentially problematic nature of the relationship between any philosophy of such and such, and its subject matter. It can't just be taken for granted that this relationship is unproblematic and straightforward, since a question about the adequacy of whatever species of philosophy to its subject can always be asked.

Take the philosophy of science for example. The philosophy of science as it was rendered in many courses and authoritative texts in the 1960s, 1970s and even later, was arguably very much the philosophy of physics (with dashes of chemistry) and in this regard it reflected the influence of logical positivism and the work of Hempel, Feigl, and Carnap, for example. A student might have been forgiven for wondering what had happened in all this to, say, biology. Furthermore, even without asking about the scope of the philosophy of science, its relationship to the disciplines to which it did undoubtedly refer was not itself straightforward. True enough, the philosophy of science of the day said more about physics than it seemed to say about biology; but whether what it said about physics was truly said was quite another matter. The burden of Thomas Kuhn's celebrated challenge (in *The Structure of Scientific Revolutions*), for all the rhetorical flourishes which accompanied it and to which his critics could only too easily take exception, was that the philosophy of science bore little relationship to the practice of science. And yet if a philosophy of science—or of art, or religion, or morality—is to be a philosophy *of* that something, it has to be a philosophy with some relationship to and concern for the phenomena. Any map from above must somehow mesh with a map from below (or explain the lack of fit).

So, what is moral philosophy the philosophy of, if it manifestly prescribes to practice, rather than taking any trouble to describe it? As the philosophy of science was in danger of becoming the philosophy of science as imagined by philosophers (until it regained some contact with the realities of scientific practice), so in the case of moral philosophy in its dominant form—it certainly talks about morality (or 'morality'), but the precise referent of the term remains in doubt.

Such a philosophy has the bioethics it deserves—a bioethics that misunderstands and misconstrues the ethical, rather than explicates it. I will return to this point later, but let me note that it is characteristic of bioethics grounded in a bluntly prescriptive moral philosophy, that it will often (and unsurprisingly) be uncomprehending of moral practice and only too ready to dismiss it. Take the wish of the Alder Hey parents to have returned to them the tissue of their children which had been retained without their knowledge or consent after post-mortem examination. At the time of the associated controversy, John Harris, a very talkative bioethicist, commented as follows: 'preoccupation with reverence and respect for bodily tissue' which 'has come to dominate discussions of retained tissues and organs in the wake of the Alder Hey revelations' is 'quite absurd, if understandable.'[41] Harris's confidence that what he fails to make sense of is absurd (albeit, *understandably* absurd), has a certain charming innocence and naïveté about it—like the innocence of someone who comes across a book in Arabic script and solemnly pronounces that it is merely scribbles. This is the bioethics, of course, which moral philosophy has willed and deserved—a bioethics so removed from social intelligence, that moral practice, even the everyday practice of grieving parents, remains wholly opaque to it.

Schopenhauer put this all rather well: of philosophical ethics, in the Kantian tradition, he notes that though it 'may carry on its disputations and make a show in the lecture halls... real life will make it an object of ridicule. I must, therefore, give the teachers of ethics the paradoxical advice of first looking around a little at the lives of men.'[42] Or, to put it another way: the moral terrain as it appears to those who navigate that terrain on the ground, may or may not be the terrain as it is represented on certain neat and tidy maps as they are devised from the sky. But it is certainly far from self-evident that the maps from above can serve simply to correct the map from below. Which brings us to social anthropology, that subject which Kant invented when he decreed that moral philosophy should be done entirely indoors, so to speak—or at least within ten miles of Konigsberg.[43]

---

[41] Cited by A. V. Campbell and M. Willis, 'They Stole My Baby's Soul: Narratives of Embodiment and Loss', *Medical Humanities*, 31 (2005), 102.

[42] A. Schopenhauer, *On the Basis of Morality*, trans. E. F. J. Payne (Indianapolis, 1995), 121. Alternatively, in a letter (of 1910) Charles Péguy makes the following apposite observation: 'Je compte. . . que vous ne réglerez point ces débats par les méthodes kantiennes, par la philosopie kantienne, par la morale kantienne. Le kantianisme a les mains pures, MAIS IL N'A PAS DE MAINS.' (That is—'I reckon. . . you will not settle these debates by Kantian methods, philosophy and morality. Kantianism has pure hands, BUT IT HAS NO HANDS.') C. Péguy, *Œuvres complètes en prose* (Paris, 1992), III, 331. I am grateful to Eric Southworth for referring me to this remark.

[43] There are, of course, other traditions in moral philosophy than those represented by Kant and Mill. I have limited the discussion to these two, however, because these have been most

IV THE PROMISE OF SOCIAL ANTHROPOLOGY

Moral theology must, like moral philosophy, 'learn to look around a little at the lives of men'. Both moral theology and moral philosophy, for their own reasons, have shown little interest in the social and in the findings of social anthropology.[44] But if moral theology is to set out an everyday ethics which would sustain and support the Christian imagination of the human, and yet address pastorally and therapeutically other ethical imaginaries and forms of life, it must attend to the psychological and sociocultural depth of the different forms of life which we encounter. And to do this, it should be willing to learn from social anthropology, which can assist moral theology, so I hope to show in subsequent chapters, both methodologically and materially. In engagement with social anthropology, moral theology can learn the better to display and explicate the character and form of the Christian life—and to engage constructively and therapeutically with other forms of human being, fathoming the unfathomable choices against which that silent trumpet sounds so ineffectively.

My interest in subsequent chapters is principally in the particular findings of social anthropology as they bear on the moments in the life course which concern us. For example, in a later chapter I will take up Lesley Sharp's telling discovery and depiction of the subtle work that goes on between the recipients

---

influential for contemporary moral philosophy, especially for bioethics. An alternative line of thinkers manifestly interested in moral practice would include such important figures as Aristotle, Hume, and Wittgenstein (and amongst contemporary writers, Raimond Gaita, David Wiggins, and Cora Diamond, to take just a few examples). As conceived by this tradition, moral philosophy would stand in a thoroughly un-Kantian and un-Mill-like relationship to the practice (and the anthropology) of ethics; it would not blithely propound theories against which practice is found wanting, but would struggle to understand the grounding of and connections between our feelings, thoughts, and judgments, and other phenomena of moral life. It would take seriously social anthropology's discovery and description of our moral worlds. This is not, however, the moral philosophy of the mainstream, and especially as that moral philosophy has informed the practice of bioethics.

The omission of Alasdair MacIntyre in the list of alternatives to the dominant tradition may seem odd—and certainly, as has often been noted, his work has appealed to many social anthropologists as providing a more promising partner for anthropological thinking than either Kantian or utilitarian traditions. There are, however, distinct limitations in MacIntyre's work, especially in its later development: for an excellent critique see J. Laidlaw, *The Subject of Virtue: An Anthropology of Ethics and Freedom* (Cambridge, 2014), ch. 2. But of course, without any later developments, the very starting point of MacIntyre's *After Virtue* (London, 1981), has a strongly and troublingly prescriptive flavour: 'we have', he says, '—very largely, if not entirely—lost our comprehension, both theoretical and practical, of morality' (2). To say the least, a sweeping charge that modernity is morally amnesiac is not one which suggests a great openness to the need to attend to, and the possibility of learning from, moral practice. In fact, given what we will refer to below as the ubiquity of the ethical, it surely has all the implausibility of a declaration that the speakers of such and such a language have failed to grasp its grammar.

[44] I am aware that the term 'social anthropology', rather than such alternatives as 'cultural anthropology' or 'sociocultural anthropology', could be taken to mark certain theoretical presuppositions and commitments. I use the term in current British usage for the disciplinary area which concerns me, without meaning here to take any position on the deeper questions.

of organs and the close kin of deceased donors, in negotiating and construct-ing a morally nuanced relationship in the emotionally fraught and unfamiliar territory where the life of one person is sustained by tissue from one who has died in, most likely, tragic circumstances.[45] Such material findings from social anthropology, in relation to conception, birth, suffering, death, and burial, will provide Christian moral theology with insights to assist with the explication of its own account of the human, as well as allowing it to come into critical conversation with significant and realized alternatives.

The ability of social anthropology to contribute to moral theology in this way arises from its very nature. The key point is one I have already alluded to on a number of occasions, by relying on Joel Robbins' characterization of the central ambition of anthropological work. As Robbins puts it, the best social anthropology is concerned to give an account of how people live which is 'at once psychologically and socioculturally realistic'.[46] 'It is relatively easy', he says, to satisfy 'one or other of these requirements', that is, 'to provide a cred-ible account of how individuals live their lives and make decisions', or alter-natively, 'to offer detailed discussion of how cultural meanings, norms and values shape social life in profound ways'. But those who do one or other well 'stumble' in doing both: then psychologically realistic accounts 'tend to thin out the cultural and social, while socially and culturally realistic accounts often leave individuals looking more or less like puppets'.[47]

I have already suggested that it should be the ambition of moral theology to narrate the good and the bad in a fuller sense; to locate each in a context which renders them fathomable. But if it is to do this, then moral theology must itself learn to explicate moral lives as psychologically and socioculturally real-istic, whether it means to commend those lives, or to engage with them criti-cally and therapeutically. What social anthropology intends, in other words, is the comprehension of the social against which moral philosophy (in certain dominant traditions) has turned, and in which moral theology has, misguid-edly, been uninterested. Moral theology will not, of course, engage uncritically with social anthropology, as we shall see in what follows. But on this central point it should be willing to learn what is to be learnt from social anthropol-ogy's methods and findings, and should especially be willing to take account of and reckon with the social comprehension of the good and the bad to which anthropology aspires.

---

[45] L. Sharp, *Strange Harvest: Organ Transplants, Denatured Bodies, and the Transformed Self* (Berkeley, 2006).

[46] J. Robbins, 'Where in the World are Values? Exemplarity, Morality and Social Process' (forthcoming). He is commending C. Humphrey's work, especially her 'Exemplars and Rules: Aspects of the Discourse of Moralities in Mongolia', in *The Ethnography of Moralities*, ed. S. Howell (London, 1997), and also 'Reassembling Individual Subjects: Events and Decisions in Troubled Times', *Anthropological Theory*, 8 (2008), 357–380.

[47] J. Robbins, 'Where in the World are Values? Exemplarity, Morality and Social Process'.

That key point stands on its own. But two relatively recent developments in social anthropology encourage the further thought that this is an especially auspicious moment to begin a conversation between moral theology and social anthropology. The developments lie in the contemporary identification of the anthropology of morality and, separately, of the anthropology of Christianity, as two distinct fields deserving of particular and focused anthropological attention.

Only five years ago, Didier Fassin wrote that were the project of 'moral anthropology' recognized as it should be,[48] then 'moral anthropology would be an entry in social science dictionaries and encyclopedias, it would be presented in student textbooks and taught in humanities courses—which it is not'.[49] (In other words, had we undertaken five years ago, let us say, an exercise analogous to the one we imagined undertaking for moral philosophy, but asking here what we might learn of anthropology's interest in morality from a survey of recent and major reference works of the kind which students might employ, we would have to say that we would have learnt very little.)[50] So, for Fassin the question becomes, 'why is there not a moral anthropology?'[51]

Five years later that question has joined a class of questions which includes the following: 'why are there no white swans?', 'why does it never rain in Cambridge?' or 'why are politicians universally admired?' For the anthropology of morality is now not merely a budding but a burgeoning field. Fassin has himself recently edited that great marker of the establishment of a new field, the Companion—in this case *A Companion to Moral Anthropology*[52] which follows on the heels of and has contributions from the major figures in what

---

[48] That is, to use his words, 'an anthropology which has morals for its object—in other words, which explores how societies ideologically and emotionally found their cultural distinction between good and evil, and how social agents concretely work out this separation in their everyday life'; D. Fassin, 'Beyond Good and Evil? Questioning the Anthropological Discomfort with Morals', *Anthropological Theory*, 8.4 (2008), 333.

[49] Fassin, 'Beyond Good and Evil?', 336.

[50] Thus, to cite a few examples: *The Encyclopedia of Social and Cultural Anthropology*, eds. A. Barnard and J. Spencer (London, 2002), has no entry for 'Ethics' or 'Morality'; *The Companion Encyclopedia of Anthropology*, ed. T. Ingold (London, 1994), has no essay on morality or ethics, and only one (erroneous) reference to ethics in the index. The very much larger four-volume *Encyclopedia of Cultural Anthropology*, eds. D. Levinson and M. Ember (New York, 1996), has some quite extensive discussions of professional ethics (i.e. questions raised by the practice of ethnography), but little to counter the impression that morality as such is not an object of key anthropological concern. Of course, this seeming lack of interest in morality within social anthropology may itself go some way towards explaining philosophy's lack of interest in social anthropology's treatment of morality, to which I alluded in the last section—just because there can seem to be no such treatment. Certainly, however, philosophy's disdain for the empirical treatment of morality, and social anthropology's less-than-obvious engagement with morality, conspired to ensure a less-than-busy intellectual traffic between the disciplines on this theme.

[51] Fassin, 'Beyond Good and Evil?', 336.

[52] D. Fassin, ed., *A Companion to Moral Anthropology* (Oxford, 2012).

has been dubbed the 'ethical turn'[53] in recent anthropology.[54] The ethical turn represents a conscious and sustained attempt to correct the occlusion of ethics from anthropological attention, and to advance beyond earlier and tentative ventures towards the rehabilitation of the ethical through the development of the conceptual and analytic tools for a careful study of the nature, form, and character of ethical life.[55]

Crucial to the value of this anthropological reappropriation of the ethical for moral theology, given some of moral theology's failings already noted, is very specifically anthropology's attempt to overcome the narrowing of the moral to codes and laws by insisting on what has been termed the 'ubiquity of the ethical'; or, to borrow a slogan of Lambek's, by maintaining that 'the ordinary is intrinsically ethical and ethics intrinsically ordinary'.[56] The stress on the ordinariness of ethics is part and parcel of the characteristic interest of social anthropology in the reproduction of the social (that is, in its persistence and continuity), and thus a healthy corrective to the concerns of moral theology (and more so of bioethics), where the interest in difficult questions is an interest especially in what is novel, contentious, and changing. Anthropology's

---

[53] M. Lambek, ed., *Ordinary Ethics: Anthropology, Language, and Action* (New York, 2010), 'Introduction', 5.

[54] Those major figures include Lambek, Faubion, Robbins, Laidlaw, and Humphrey. An early contribution is M. and A. Edel, eds., *Anthropology and Ethics: The Quest for Moral Understanding* (Cleveland, 1959), but a concerted interest in the subject is generally reckoned to begin with S. Howell, ed., *The Ethnography of Moralities* (London, 1997). For our purposes the work of M. Lambek, J. D. Faubion, J. Laidlaw, and J. Robbins is most important. For Laidlaw, see his review of Jarrett Zigon, *Morality: An Anthropological Perspective*, in *Ethnos*, 74, (2009), 436. And see further J. Laidlaw, 'Social Anthropology' in *The Routledge Companion to Ethics*, ed. J. Skorupski (London, 2010) and J. Laidlaw, 'For an Anthropology of Ethics and Freedom', *Journal of the Royal Anthropological Institute*, 8 (2002), 311–32, and already cited, *The Subject of Virtue*. For Faubion, *An Anthropology of Ethics* (Cambridge, 2011) is the most significant statement, but see also, 'Toward an Anthropology of Ethics: Foucault and the Pedagogics of Autopoiesis', *Representations*, 74 (2001), 83–104. For Lambek, in addition to the book already cited, see 'The Anthropology of Religion and the Quarrel Between Poetry and Philosophy', *Current Anthropology*, 41 (2000), 309–20, and 'Value and Virtue', *Anthropological Theory*, 8 (2008), 133–57. For Robbins, see works already cited and also *An Anthropology of the Good* (forthcoming). See also M. Heintz, ed., *The Anthropology of Moralities* (New York, 2009) and J. Zigon, *Morality: An Anthropological Perspective* (Oxford, 2008).

[55] It should be noticed, of course, that anthropology's lack of interest in morality as a topic was more than a chance occurrence—as Laidlaw argues, the presuppositions of Durkheimian social theory in effect prevented social anthropology coming to terms with the ethical. As Laidlaw puts it, 'an anthropology of ethics will only be possible—will only be prevented from constantly collapsing into general questions of social regularity and social control—if we take seriously, as something requiring ethnographic description, the possibilities of human freedom', and this the Durkheimian approach did not allow. (Laidlaw, 'For an Anthropology of Ethics and Freedom', 315, and now see ch. 1 of Laidlaw's *The Subject of Virtue*.) Laidlaw's critique of social theory on this point removes, I would suggest, one of the central grounds of theological suspicion of the social sciences; in other words, the 'ethical turn' reconfigures the landscape in such a way as to disarm some elements in J. Milbank's important critique of the social sciences in *Theology and Social Theory: Beyond Secular Reason* (Oxford, 1990).

[56] Lambek, 'Introduction' to *Ordinary Ethics*, 3.

concern with the reproduction of the social is a concern with the everyday, the routine, and the normal—and thus may serve to remind moral theology of where its work might, at the very least, begin.

Just as social anthropology is newly interested in morality, so is it also newly interested in Christianity. There is a complex story to tell here (just as there is about the new-found interest in morals), and specifically as to why Christianity has been excluded, to a certain extent, from anthropological attention. It is not necessary to delve into this story here, however, so I shall simply cite a recent and suggestive survey of the anthropology of Christianity which explains the gap with reference to a number of thoughts. Christianity has seemed either too similar (lacking 'the degree of cultural alterity that has until quite recently been definitional of an apt disciplinary object'[57]); or too different (the 'conservatism or political quietism of so many of the Christian communities anthropologists encounter in the Global South' rendering them 'disappointing subalterns' to use one striking phrase, or 'culturally repugnant others whom it is best to avoid', to borrow another[58]); or too superficial a phenomenon to be worthy of attention ('the Christianity of converts is often treated as epiphenomenal, merely a thin veneer laid over an enduring prior culture and as such not worthy of research'[59]). However that may be, according to these same commentators, 'The combined force of political prominence, demographic growth, and visible piety has made Christianity unavoidable in many ethnographic settings, as well as newly important at home, and has therefore made the development of the anthropology of Christianity not only possible, but also something many anthropologists have come to see as necessary.'[60] Thus, along with the anthropology of morality, the anthropology of Christianity is now emerging as a vital element in the understanding of contemporary patterns of social change and existence.

The emergence of these two new subfields within anthropology provides further reason for moral theology to attend to social anthropology, above and beyond the interest moral theology should have in the central ambitions of social anthropology to describe the forms of human moral action. They promise fresh perspectives on moral life and practice, and Christian life and practice, from a discipline which is highly sensitive to the construction of identities and the dynamics of social action. Such perspectives, whatever issues may need to be addressed regarding the assumptions which inform them, may serve to deepen, challenge, or correct the theologian's own constructions of Christian

---

[57] J. Bialecki, N. Haynes, and J. Robbins, 'The Anthropology of Christianity', *Religion Compass* (2008), 1139–58. And for one leading example of the new genre, see J. Robbins, *Becoming Sinners: Christianity and Moral Torment in a Papua New Guinea Society* (Berkeley, 2004).

[58] Bialecki, Haynes, and Robbins, 'The Anthropology of Christianity', 1140, quoting D. Maxwell on 'disappointing subalterns' and S. Harding on the 'culturally repugnant other'.

[59] Bialecki, Haynes, and Robbins, 'The Anthropology of Christianity', 1141.

[60] Bialecki, Haynes, and Robbins, 'The Anthropology of Christianity', 1141.

ethical life and practice, as well as to place this life and practice in relationship to other forms of human being.

These particular developments suggest that the engagement between moral theology and social anthropology which is demanded by the need for the practice of a critical everyday ethics, takes place at an especially promising moment in the development of social anthropology. But the main point is that the ethnographic endeavour promises insight and understanding of the kind moral theology itself needs to develop.

Juliet du Boulay's *Cosmos, Life, and Liturgy in a Greek Orthodox Village*[61] serves as an indication of what moral theology might gain from the work of an anthropologically informed and theologically sensitive observer. In this fine study, an 'ethnographic theology', as one reviewer has referred to it,[62] du Boulay narrates the life of the village Christianly, that is to say, as that life is construed and constructed by the cosmology and liturgy of Orthodoxy. This life is not built on and cannot be imagined by reference to the handling of a few difficult cases or the application of some general principles. Instead, du Boulay's perspicuous presentation of the warp and weft of everyday life refers us to the richness of a religious imagination, which by means of rituals and routines, serves to shape the forms and patterns of daily existence, with their particular and characteristic modes of knowing, feeling, thinking, and acting.

It must be the ambition of a Christian moral theology which seeks to explicate an everyday ethics, to describe the moral life as it is shaped by a religious imagination, holding up to view the framework of perceptions, meanings, emotions, concepts, and attitudes that are formed by that imagination in its various realizations. This imagination proposes a self-fashioning and the generation of a distinctive sensibility and subjectivity, to be expressed in a particular form of life. What we currently lack and what we need is a coherent and perspicuous account of the practice of the Christian life, which would, in a space of cultural contestation, describe and sustain this form of life as a particular way of being human in the world (especially as the human is discovered in the moments of conception, birth, suffering, death, and burial from which we began), in conscious and therapeutic dialogue with other accounts.

It is for the remaining chapters to demonstrate that an engagement with social anthropology, which seems promising in theory, really is so in practice, and will assist moral theology in undertaking its proper work. But let me reiterate that social anthropology promises to challenge and correct moral theology, as well as deepen and advance it—it is not a matter here then, of anthropology simply providing tools ready to hand for a moral theology which already knows very well what it is doing. I suggest that the encounter is more dynamic

---

[61] J. du Boulay, *Cosmos, Life, and Liturgy in a Greek Orthodox Village* (Limni, 2009).
[62] M.E. Kenna, in *Journal of the Royal Anthropological Institute*, N.S., 17 (2011), 205.

than that, and can be expected to tax and test moral theology, and in so doing, shape its own self-understanding.

V SEEING THE WORLD IN CHRIST: THE *MÉRODE ALTARPIECE*

The *Mérode Altarpiece*, now in the Cloisters Collection in New York, constitutes an invitation, somewhat like the invitation made in this first chapter. But perhaps to see the invitation for what it is, the picture has to be seen with fresh eyes. It is an annunciation, and we have seen hundreds of pictures of annunciations, so even if we are seeing this particular picture for the first time, we are viewing it in relation to countless other images in our heads. We should endeavour, however, to see it as it might have been seen for the first time in 1425 when the picture was newly painted. For newly innocent eyes will be shocked by this picture (see Plate 1).

Along with the donors in the left-hand panel (probably a young married and as yet childless couple), we see the non-negotiable components of an annunciation: an angelic messenger and a young woman. But the artist—sometimes referred to as the Master of Flémalle, sometimes said to be Robert Campin, but no one knows for sure—has boldly struck out on his own against the traditional representations of the scene, so that in 1425 the viewer would certainly have been surprised by this depiction.

First of all, the picture is revolutionary in terms of its artistic technique. We can see this at once simply by putting it side by side with, say, a fresco of the annunciation painted by Fra Angelico, in San Marco, Florence. That fresco dates from probably ten or fifteen years after the altarpiece, and is representative of the sort of imagery found in frescos, panels, and in manuscript illuminations from the early fifteenth century. Next to the *Mérode Altarpiece*, the fresco seems to come from another, earlier age.

The Master of Flémalle, or Robert Campin, or whoever, is one of a group referred to as the Flemish or Netherlandish Primitivists—though their technique is anything but primitive. These Flemish painters made astonishing discoveries regarding the depiction of light, volume, and weight—discoveries that achieve their greatest effects in the work of Jan van Eyck (in his *Arnolfini Portrait* of 1434, for example).[63] Suffice to say that the picture in front of us already shows the possibility of a new and really quite breathtaking realism in comparison with the somewhat flat work which precedes it. Seeing a painting

---

[63] First, the artists understand and depict light as the ground of colour; second from sculpture, these painters discover and learn to depict the volume of figures; and third, they have learnt how to root their people to the ground.

by one of these painters for the first time in the 1420s would surely have been rather like seeing colour television back in the early 1960s.

Standing in front of the picture in 1425, however, it would be not only its technique you would notice; not just 'how' the picture is painted, but also 'what' is painted will strike you. The painting is as revolutionary with regard to the 'what' as with regard to the 'how'—for as well as a realism in how the scene is represented, our artist is reaching after another sort of realism regarding the annunciation itself.

To notice this, we need to take note of something we can very easily miss, but would not have been missed by a contemporary viewer. What we have here is an interior; so much is obvious. What we won't know without some further information is that this is what one distinguished critic describes as the 'first true modern interior'[64] in the history of art. Interiors in this sense are unknown prior to the 1420s when this picture is painted—previously when someone is shown inside a building, it is by means of a cut away, cross-section technique whereby we can see the exterior along with the interior. It is the sort of view of an interior that we get if we take the front off a doll's house. Annunciations had been located in various spaces, in grand classical loggias, in gardens, courtyards, ruined temples, or oratories, even sometimes, in knowing anachronisms, in churches—but always from outside. The painter here, however, gives us a room in a way it has never been seen before—as if from the inside. And all at once, for the first time, we are brought dramatically up close, in to the very midst of this intimate moment. Previously the viewer had looked on at the annunciation; now the viewer is present.

But there is another way in which the previous role of the viewer as mere spectator is subverted by the painter; as well as placing us in the midst of this newly private and thus newly intimate moment, he has particularized and specified the interior so that the space the viewer enters is very definitely of the painter's times. The interior is a perfectly regular domestic room, the fittings and fixtures of which amount to 'an inventory of the furnishings in a late-gothic home':[65] an adjustable bench, a folding oval table, a fire screen, brass candle sticks, a kettle or cauldron hanging in an alcove over a basin, a rack with towels, a jug on the table, a book (probably a Book of Hours) resting on a velvet or silk bag on the table, a prayer roll under that book, and yet another book in Mary's hand with the sheet-like covering to wrap and protect it. (So perhaps not just any 'late-gothic home', but a rather bookish one.) The point is, however, that the bookish Mary is sitting in a regular room as it would have looked in 1425, when the picture was fresh off the easel. The approach is 'prosaic, almost anecdotal',[66] and the same effect could be achieved in our day

---

[64] O. Pächt, *Van Eyck and the Founders of Early Netherlandish Painting*, trans. D. Britt (London, 1994), 50.

[65] D. de Vos, *The Flemish Primitives* (Princeton, 2002), 33.

[66] de Vos, *The Flemish Primitives*, 33.

by picturing Mary in a regular and firmly contemporary living room: there would be, very probably, a sofa (not the bench), a couple of armchairs, a coffee table, a wide-screen TV instead of a fire place, some lamps or spotlights, pictures on the wall, framed photographs on a mantelpiece, curtains at the windows, a laptop or an iPad or perhaps both where the Book of Hours sits open, and a Kindle in Mary's hands.

The Master of Flémalle and the other Flemish realists 'took [biblical] scenes remote in place and time' and, as one critic puts it, 'almost literally brought them home to the viewer, into his own life, his own age and his own milieu. Legendary events were depicted as if they had just happened, or were still happening, at the moment when the painter recorded them, and in the places best known to him and his public'. 'Christ in Flanders' is how that critic denotes the trend—what it amounts to here is Gabriel and Mary in 'the living room of a Flemish bourgeois house'.[67] Five hundred years later Stanley Spencer will attempt a similar thing—not Christ in Flanders, of course, but Christ in Cookham. The effect is the same, however—the biblical events are taking place in a street, in a home, near you.

But this is not all. There is another choice which the artist has made in depicting the annunciation which further serves the purpose of making the scene more regular, more everyday, and more mundane. We shall need to look quite closely—somewhat more closely than the scholar, writing about this work, who tells us that 'the Virgin Mary looks up from an open book...interrupted in her reading by the Angel Gabriel'.[68] She is very definitely not interrupted and she does not look up. Gabriel has entered the room very quietly—with only the faintest of breezes (perhaps from the flapping of his wings), only just enough to extinguish the candle and cause the pages of the book on the table to flutter. He has entered so very quietly indeed, that he is unnoticed, and Mary remains quietly engrossed in her book.

Very unusually then, the painter has chosen not to depict the moments which are normally depicted, the two moments of drama in the story. In the first moment Mary is perturbed: 'she was troubled and wondered what sort of greeting this might be'. In the second, she assents to her newly revealed vocation: 'behold the handmaid of the Lord'. And depictions of Mary choose one or other moment: so she is either disturbed, perplexed, quizzical, concerned, at a loss, mystified, thrown, baffled, or confounded by Gabriel's salutation; or, at the conclusion to the conversation, she is accepting, resolved, humble, compliant, modestly giving her consent to the divine calling, sometimes a touch fearful. The artist has chosen neither of those two obvious moments—and instead has Mary quietly unaware. She doesn't even notice at all, and we only just see

---

[67] Pächt, *Van Eyck and the Founders of Early Netherlandish Painting*, 66.
[68] M.W. Driver, 'Mirrors of a Collective Past: Re-considering Images of Medieval Women', 75, in *Women and the Book*, eds. J. Taylor and L. Smith (British Library, 1997).

the baby Christ who enters through the unopened window as he will enter the unopened womb. The conception of Christ is going on with barely more than a mild breeze to flap the pages, and the angel is, at least for the moment, invisible. Mary sticks to her book. (Or as Pächt puts it more solemnly, there has been a 'drastic neutralization of the protagonist's response'.[69])

Why has the artist placed us firmly in an interior, a contemporary interior, and on top of that, has chosen a moment in the story which almost no artist before or since has picked? Standing before this picture with the eyes of the painter's contemporaries, we would surely wonder what this realistic, private, modernized, interior annunciation is all about—an annunciation which overlooks those dramatic moments when Mary is either deeply perplexed or humbly assenting, and chooses instead to bring us up close to Mary lost in her reading, before she is aware of the choice she will confront.

It has to be said that the general domesticating tendency in the Flemish painters of this period (the 'Christ in Flanders' motif), has rather troubled or perplexed commentators who have been inclined to offer diametrically opposed accounts of what is going on, though I'm inclined to think that the whole truth is found in neither of the alternatives we are given.

On the one hand, some see this domestication as a symptom of a secularizing trend which uses religious themes as a mere pretext for 'depicting everyday objects that had yet to establish themselves as suitable subjects in their own right';[70] it is as if, on this account, what these painters really wanted to do was to paint a still life, or a Vermeer, but having arrived on the scene two hundred years too early, have to content themselves with painting religious scenes grudgingly, making them as secular as they can.

Others, on the opposite side of the controversy (such as Panofsky), see the everyday realism in these painters as a façade behind which lies a profound and secret religious iconography, even when the subject is not in any way obviously a religious one. The high-water mark of this approach is Panofsky's elaborate, not to say rococo, interpretation of van Eyck's *Arnolfini Portrait*, which sees the everyday objects and articles in these pictures as carrying various religious messages which it is our task to decipher or decode. Thus, for example, a candle is never just a candle but a sign of the light of the world; a cauldron or basin is never for washing but signifies the washing away of sins; shoes are never thrown aside because, well, that is what we do with shoes, but because we are meant to think of the command to Moses: 'take off the shoes from thy feet, for the ground on which you stand is holy ground'.

As a way of approaching the pictures of this period and indeed of any other period, these alternatives look limited, even if neither is simply and straightforwardly wrong. It is perhaps best to say that theologically speaking, the

---

[69] Pächt, *Van Eyck and the Founders of Early Netherlandish Painting*, 63.
[70] Pächt, *Van Eyck and the Founders of Early Netherlandish Painting*, 56.

alternatives look very meagre indeed if they are taken to exhaust the options for depicting the religious—as if to be present to the world, the religious, or the divine, must either be blatantly mythological, so to say (with as many angels and flashes of light and heavenly choirs as you can gather on the canvas, for without them we have only the secular), or if it is not present in that fashion, must lie behind the everyday secular world in some sort of cryptic, da Vinci code fashion. It is as if, on these alternatives, the religious is either a very heavy layer on top of the world we know, or is somehow mysteriously concealed behind it, like the most difficult clue to a deeply challenging puzzle. It is either above the surface or below the surface but never on the surface.

I think the painter intends something else, and that in his 'humanization of sacred history', as Pächt terms it, he is choosing neither in favour of anti-religious secularizing, nor meaning to maintain the religious through some system of signs and signals: what we might think of as a game of metaphysical nudges and winks. For even though it seems that almost no one previously chose to treat the annunciation as he does by isolating this particular moment, and almost no one followed him afterwards, I don't think that we should say he is making a mistake, as one critic has it. The painter is not making a mistake, but a point and a rather important one. Or perhaps it is better to say that he is issuing an invitation.

By this domesticating realism, by locating the annunciation in a real bourgeois home of 1425 and taking us into the interior of this home, and by taking one step further still, picking the moment in the story when the religious is most unobtrusively and quietly present, our painter has turned *The* Annunciation into *An* Annunciation—not for the sake of trivializing the scene, but for sake of universalizing it. He has presented the event of annunciation as a real and regular moment, not as an exceptional one. A young woman, bible or prayer book in hand, is lost in her thoughts, and on the verge of being addressed by a divine word. She will conceive this divine word and in conceiving it the divine will become flesh. But as the painter gives us this scene, it is no longer merely a particular, however important, event in Palestine 2000 years ago. This is no longer an unprecedented and unrepeatable and exceptional moment of divine action, but a form of God's general engagement with the world in sitting rooms in Flanders just as well as in a room in Palestine.

By representing the religious as quietly and unobtrusively present, the picture invites not only the young donors to the left, but other viewers to conceive their conceivings in the light of the conception of Christ. What does it mean, this picture invites us to consider, for the conception of Christ to be not an historical fact alone, not an occurrence in one human life, but an event which may be repeated as it governs, inflects, or modulates later conceptions, whether in Flanders in 1425, or here and now?

It is an invitation, then, to begin the work of everyday Christian ethics. Our lives—all lives—pass through those credal moments, of birth, conception, suffering, death, and burial. In the coming chapters, I will ask and answer with some first words, the general question analogous to the particular one implied by the painter: how can the Christian imagination not only of conception, but of birth, suffering, death, and burial too, be brought to bear on our conceivings, births, sufferings, deaths, and burials, for the sake of fashioning an everyday ethics which would support and sustain a Christian form of human being?

2

Conceiving Conception: On IVF, Virgin Births, and the Troubling of Kinship

I INTRODUCTION: ON CONCEIVING CHRIST (NORMATIVELY SPEAKING)

In staccato fashion, the Apostles' Creed notices paradigmatically human moments in Christ's life: he was conceived, born, suffered, died, and buried. But these moments would very likely appear in any syllabus for a course in social anthropology—a point which brings to notice the fact that these events are not only paradigmatically human, in the sense of being of special interest and concern in any human life, but also sites of contention and controversy, where what it is to be human is discovered, constructed, and contested. Conception, birth, suffering, burial, and death are the occasions, in other words, for profound and continuing questioning which comes to particular attention in, but is not limited to, the controversies to do with IVF, abortion, euthanasia, the use of bodies and body parts post-mortem, and so on. Thus many questions arise. How do the moments of Christ's life (as they are evoked in the Creeds and as subjects of extended reflection in theology and sermons, in prayers and liturgy, in art and literature) represent human life? And how do these representations relate to present-day cultural norms and expectations and newly emerging modes of relationship, themselves shaping and framing human life? And, furthermore, how does the Christian imagination of human life, which dwells on and draws from the life of Christ, not only articulate its own, but also come into conversation with and engage other, moral imaginaries of the human? I suggested earlier that asking and answering this question will require of moral theology something of a reconceiving of its nature and tasks—and that, in particular, a newly conceived moral theology must learn to engage especially with social anthropology. Subsequent chapters, beginning with this one, will seek to explore the possibility and value of such an

engagement with the aim of developing the everyday ethics which moral theology has neglected to provide in its obsession with hard cases.

'They say, don't they, "A man can have two sons, but he can't have two
fathers"?', remarks Augustine in a sermon preached soon after Christmas,
probably in Hippo, and generally dated to 418.[1] 'They say, don't they'. But
of course, *we* do not. We have become accustomed to the array of possibilities opened up by the new reproductive technologies and to their creative
potential in relation to relationships. We, unlike 'they', are familiar with the
thought that, courtesy of what are collectively termed Assisted Reproductive
Technologies (and hereafter referred to as ARTs), a child may indeed have two
fathers and more than one mother for that matter. In principle (with donor
egg and donor sperm), a child may have a biological father and a social father,
and a biological mother and a social mother. And if the embryo was carried
to term by a surrogate who did not contribute the egg, then the child may
have a fifth potential parent in the gestational mother. (And with the possibility of 'mitochondrial mothers',[2] further permutations emerge.) Or, to put the
point pithily by borrowing the title of an article by Charis Thompson: '"Quit
snivelling cryo-baby, we'll work out which one's your mama"—kinship in an
infertility clinic'.[3]

Conception and kinship have much to do with each other—or at least, it is
often assumed to be so. And for anthropologists, kinship has been historically a
fundamental category of analysis and concern, going back to the subject's early
origins in the late century in, for example, Morgan's *Systems of Consanguinity
and Affinity in the Human Family*, and equally prominent in the work of such
a key figure as Malinowski. Just recently, 'kinship has returned to the pages
of anthropology journals with a vengeance',[4] the interest being renewed and
reinvigorated especially by ARTs (and by anthropology's discovery of its own
early practitioners' uncritical reliance on the so-called 'folk theory', as will be
explained presently).

---

[1] But perhaps somewhat earlier according to a recent translator; Augustine, Sermon 51, in *The
Works of Saint Augustine: A Translation for the 21st Century*, pt. 3, *Sermons* (Brooklyn, NY, 1991),
trans. E Hill; on this point see note 1 to Sermon 51. Hereafter all quotations from Augustine's sermons will be from this series of Augustine's works, in which eleven volumes cover the sermons.
Citations will give the sermon and section number.

[2] See M. Richards, G. Pennings, and J. B. Appleby, eds., *Reproductive Donation: Practice, Policy
and Bioethics* (Cambridge, 2012), 1.

[3] C. Thompson, '"Quit Snivelling Cryo-baby, We'll Work Out Which One's Your Mama"—
Kinship in an Infertility Clinic', in *Cyborg Babies: From Techno-Sex to Techno-Tots*, eds. R.
Davis-Floyd and J. Dumit (London, 1998), 4–66.

[4] S. Franklin, 'From Blood to Genes? Rethinking Consanguinity in the Context of
Geneticization', in *Blood and Kinship: Matter and Metaphor from Ancient Rome to the Present
Day*, eds. C. H. Johnson, B. Jassen, D.W. Sabean, and S. Teuscher (New York, 2013), 285. That this
field remains an important stimulus to anthropological work is evidenced by Sarah Franklin's
new study, published too late for me to take into account: *Biological Relatives: IVF, Stem Cells and
the Future of Kinship* (Durham, NC, 2013).

The contrast with moral theology is quite striking—modern moral theology has seemed to have very little to say about kinship, and what it has said has seemed not always to be shaped by theological insights or concerns and unaware of the discussions within social anthropology. Anthropology's service to moral theology here then, is twofold, so I shall suggest. First of all, acquaintance with the discussions within social anthropology should, at the least, encourage moral theology to attend to a category of huge moral significance, which moral theology seems to have neglected. We will always need an understanding and ethics of kinship since kinship is such a general and important aspect of our social lives even when it is not contested. But, in the second place, as it takes up the task of thinking about kinship with the help of anthropological reflection, moral theology will discover even from its own resources the capacity to respond radically, therapeutically, and evangelically to the current social framing and use of ARTS as illuminated by social anthropology. Crucial to that framing are two related notions: first, that of 'the desperation of childlessness', and second, the idea that that desperation can be best addressed by obtaining 'a child of one's own'. In other words what this chapter will suggest is that, as moral theology attends and responds to recent work in anthropology which has sought to trouble certain dominant conceptions of kinship, and furthermore attends to the sustained reflection on the conception and kinship of Christ which has occurred within the Christian tradition, it will find that it has more to contribute to the understanding of the new reproductive technologies than is commonly supposed. (It will have more to contribute, that is to say, than the narrowly construed and extremely constrained discussion of the licitness of the use of the technologies which has been the central concern of moral theology in this area to date.) In particular, it may contribute to a therapeutic deconstruction of the framing I have mentioned, for moral theology will not only deny the existence of (and repudiate the desire) for the child of one's own of supposed contemporary longing, but will also deny the tragedy of childlessness which that child is intended to relieve.

The path I shall take in bringing an order to the wide-ranging materials and issues we need to consider is as follows:

First (in section II), to grasp something of the normative significance of the imagining of Christ's conception, to ask what influence the conceiving of Christ's conception has had on the conceiving of other conceptions, I return to Augustine's sermon and consider how Augustine, compelled by the story of Christ, himself troubles regular notions of kinship, challenging certain common understandings of it.

Secondly (in section III), I try to place this sermon in the wider context of its before and after. The 'before' consists in the complex reconsideration of relatedness that occurs in the early Christian world. Thus the writings of the New Testament privilege spiritual kinship over what we might term for now 'natural' or 'biological' kinship. (Thus, the church is the Israel of promise not of blood, and the brothers, mothers, and sisters of Christ are those who do the will of God.) This privileging was taken up in the early church in the institutions of avowed celibacy and baptism, whereby alternative patterns of kinship were promulgated well beyond the monastery. Especially in the rite of baptism, and in particular in the role taken by godparents, Christianity scripted a practice which preferred kinship that is made over kinship that is given. (Further on we shall return to the sense in which the rite gives children their meaning within Christianity, effectively effacing natural kinship in various ways, and so bearing especially on the pretension of natural kinship to deliver a child of one's own.)

We return to the troubling of kinship by IVF and ARTs in section IV. Here we note something of a paradox. On the one hand, the practices of the infertility clinic have served to underline the anthropological critique of anthropology's own previous assumption that kinship is given, not cultural. That is, the new procreative technologies are taken to expose what anthropologists should have known and didn't, namely that there is no natural kinship. On the other hand, however, the ethnographic study of the use of IVF reveals that very many of the consumers of these new technologies typically use them, in diverse ways, to 'chase the blood tie' (to borrow a resonant phrase). That is to say then, that the notion of kinship which the technologies themselves are said to challenge, is the notion which remains one of the driving forces shaping the consumption or use of those technologies. The modern troubling, in other words, can seem not to have troubled kinship much at all—just in so far as it is the desire for a child of one's own that drives the technologies' consumption.

In conclusion, then, we ask about the Christian appraisal and critique of this technology, which can seem too concerned with the licitness or otherwise of the use of these technologies, and insufficiently concerned with taking account of the difference which the reality of spiritual kinship should make to our being in the world. My point is not that the regular discussions of these topics are straightforwardly poor; they are not. It is rather that they typically fail to take seriously the Christian reconstruction of kinship, which believes neither in the tragedy of childlessness, nor in the possibility of answering that tragedy by obtaining a child of one's own.

In broad terms then, my purpose in what follows is to allow reflection on the conception of Christ from within the Christian tradition to engage with the contemporary use and framing of the new technologies, and with the questions about genealogy and kinship that they are thought to pose.

II AUGUSTINE AND FATHERS WHO COUNT

'They say, don't they, "A man can have two sons, but he can't have two fathers"?'
Well, we don't say that anymore. Once upon a time (a phrase which sometimes

indicates the beginning of a fairy tale and so should put us on our guard), conception made kin—it was both necessary and sufficient. But now? As the anthropologists like to say, kinship has been troubled by these new technologies—and even if contributing biological material to conception is judged sufficient to create kinship (and perhaps it is not), it is certainly not necessary (although the common use of the word 'real' in relation to fathers and mothers seems to indicate a certain determined homage to or hankering after a world in which conception really does count). We—so one title from a social anthropologist has it, summing up in the most seemingly radical terms the results of the recent troubling of a supposedly simple traditional notion—live 'after kinship'.[5]

So, 'They say, don't they, "A man can have two sons, but he can't have two fathers"?', but we do not. But then, of course, neither did Augustine. He quoted the adage only to challenge it. For in his sermon preached in the Christmas season, Augustine was himself troubling kinship on account of a conception as irregular as any that have occurred in the wake of modernity's very own miracle birth following in vitro fertilization, that of Louise Brown in 1978. Indeed, in the light of the conception that interested him, Augustine was compelled to reconceive links between conception and kinship, and thus to disturb some accepted assumptions.

Augustine begins the sermon to which I have referred in the conversational fashion that the recording of his sermons by scribes has preserved. He reminds his congregation that he had put off solving a problem which he had raised on Christmas morning 'because there were many people celebrating that day's feast with us, who usually find explanations of the word of God rather a bore'. (This is the first instance known to me of a clergyman expressing ambivalence about the presence of a large congregation on Christmas day, but certainly not the last.) 'But now', he continues, 'it is only people who want to listen that have come together here'. Indeed since 'the games on today have blown many people away from here',[6] Augustine is certain that those who are left are truly in earnest; thus he can give careful and detailed attention (the sermon is some twenty-five pages long in the recent English translation) to the problem whose solution he had postponed on Christmas day, to do with certain supposed difficulties in or inconsistencies between the genealogies of Christ. One particular awkwardness is in Joseph having different fathers in the two lists (Jacob according to Matthew and Heli according to Luke).

Augustine's argument is long and its various twists and turns need not detain us. For our concerns, the main issue is that posed by an imagined objector who claims that 'He [Joseph] oughtn't to be called a father, because he didn't

---

[5] J. Carsten, *After Kinship* (Cambridge, 2004); though, as we shall see, the title doesn't mean quite what it might be taken to mean.

[6] Augustine, Sermon 51, 1.

beget his son'.[7] Augustine's answer is that a father can be a father even without being, biologically, the progenitor of that son. So though Jesus was 'not born of Joseph's seed',[8] Joseph is nonetheless, says Augustine, truly the father of Christ.

Augustine argues his point as follows. There can be marriage even if the partners do not 'come together in the flesh, but are tied together in their hearts'.[9] In such a marriage, as was the marriage of Joseph and Mary, 'she was chastely a wife' and he 'was chastely a husband'. But just as she was chastely a wife, so also was she 'chastely a mother', and he, by analogy, 'was chastely a father'. That is, just as sexual intercourse is not necessary to their being wife and husband, so it is unnecessary to their being mother and father. Indeed this possibility of 'begetting a child chastely' without sexual intercourse is realized in adoption, for 'people who adopt children beget them chastely in the heart, though they cannot do so in the flesh'.[10] Thus, 'from this you must go on to observe that it can happen that one man not only has two sons, but also two fathers... [O]ne who begot him from his seed, the other who adopted him out of love'.[11]

Nor should it be supposed, continues Augustine in rounding off his argument, that 'the custom of adoption is foreign to our scriptures'[12]— that it is merely a matter, as it was, of Roman law and custom. Far from it: 'adoption is something that has a long history, and is familiar to the documents of the Church'. In the Old Testament it features in the stories of those (such as Sarah, Rachel, and Leah) who 'adopt children born of maidservants from their husbands' seed',[13] and in the New Testament the notion of adoption occurs repeatedly 'and very significantly'[14] in the writings of St Paul.

In holding that Joseph was a father 'not by the flesh but by love',[15] Augustine has reimagined the nature of kinship, against a model with which he and his hearers and imagined objectors were plainly familiar. This model regarded sexual intercourse as necessary for making fathers fathers (and mothers mothers).[16] But defending the fatherhood of Joseph was not his major objective—'I

---

[7] Augustine, Sermon 51, 26.   [8] Augustine, Sermon 51, 16.

[9] Augustine, Sermon 5, 21. This claim and others that follow (for example, that the patriarchs were so chaste they only married and had sexual intercourse for the sake of procreation and would have been 'tremendously happy' had they been 'shown a way of having children without sexual intercourse': Sermon 5, 23), would come to represent severe burdens on the development of a Christian sexual ethics, though that is another story. As the editor notes, Augustine, in effect and to put it in modern terms, would seem to prefer IVF to natural intercourse.

[10] Augustine, Sermon 51, 26. And adoption is so real that when 'a man becomes the son of someone whose seed he was not born from. . . the one who adopts him has by this act of will more rights over him than the one who begot him has by nature'.

[11] Augustine, Sermon 51, 27.   [12] Augustine, Sermon 51, 28.

[13] Augustine, Sermon 51, 28. And 'if women were allowed to claim as their own children ones they had not given birth to themselves, why should men not be allowed to claim as their own ones they had not begotten with their physical seed, but with adoptive love?'

[14] Augustine, Sermon 51, 28.   [15] Augustine, Sermon 51, 30.

[16] Augustine, Sermon 51, 23. He would hardly have felt the need to argue the point were the claim for Joseph's fatherhood not controversial, even if in making his case he relies on certain obviously current notions about adoption.

have said all this in case anyone should insist that you cannot rightly list two fathers of one and the same person, and then go on to bring a sacrilegious charge of lying against one or other of the evangelists who relate the genealogy of the Lord'.[17] That is, in other words, he sets out to prove that Joseph really is the father of Christ in the context of establishing his major claim, namely that Joseph himself could have two fathers, one by adoption. But lest the insistence on the reality of the fatherhood of Joseph should be thought mere improvization determined principally by the need to save the scriptures from a tight spot relating to the fatherhood of Joseph himself, it is important to place this sermon in the wider context first of the pre-history (to which Augustine refers) of the Christian disturbing of kinship, and second, of the post-Augustinian practical elaboration of this refashioned kinship. Placed in this context, his argument can be seen to emerge out of matters of general and wider importance in Christian thought and thus not to be determined merely by the necessity of explaining the awkwardness of Christ having two grandfathers on his father's side.[18]

III TROUBLING KINSHIP BEFORE AND AFTER AUGUSTINE

According to Luke's account of John the Baptist's preaching, John's call to repentance opened with a hyperbolic denunciation of any simple reliance on the claims of kinship: 'Do not begin to say to yourselves, "We have Abraham as our ancestor"; for I tell you, God is able from these stones to raise up children to Abraham'.[19] This warning against complacent reliance on the salvific sufficiency of mere ancestry need not be taken to presage a total discounting of the claims and privileges of ancestry and kinship—it may warn only against complacency. Ancestry may remain necessary, even if not by itself sufficient. But, as it turns out, this proclamation that the fulfilment of God's promises need not be constrained by lineage and inheritance opens a story the outworking of which will lead to the claim that the fulfilment of these promises not only need not be, but in actual fact is not so constrained: 'I tell you this brethren, that flesh and blood will not inherit the kingdom of God',[20]

---

[17] Augustine, Sermon 51, 29. '[E]nough has been said to show why it shouldn't bother us that the ancestry of Christ is reckoned through Joseph and not through Mary; it's because, just as she was a mother without carnal desire, so he was a father without carnal intercourse. So the generations come down through him and they go back up through him' (Sermon 51, 30).

[18] In addition, Augustine's sermon on this theme might be placed in the context of other reflections on kinship, such as, for example, Sermon 72a, in which Augustine maintains that 'it means more for Mary to have been a disciple of Christ than to have been the mother of Christ'.

[19] Luke 3, 7, with parallel in Matthew.

[20] I Corinthians, 15, 50.

but 'Everyone who calls on the name of the Lord shall be saved'.[21] Kinship is then very thoroughly troubled by this story, but—and this is significant— Christians no more lived 'after kinship' than do (as we shall see) those who find themselves in the infertility clinic. Paul, after all, tells his *brothers* that flesh and blood will not inherit the kingdom. We can imagine a community, perhaps, that dispenses with the categories of kinship altogether, but this particular community does not take its foundational stories to demand the erasure of kinship, but rather its reconfiguration—kinship is to be played out in a new key, but still to be played out.

The reconfiguring of kinship in the New Testament occurs at two related levels, since as Barclay puts it, 'the early Christian movement brought into question not only ethnic, but also family solidarities'.[22] First, as regards the claims of ethnicity, Christianity proclaimed an extension of the privileges promised to one people, namely the Jews, to another and adopted people, inheritors of these promises not biologically but spiritually. The new Israel did not, however, so much deny the privileges attaching to descent as claim spiritual descent for themselves; they were grafted in.[23] Second, the reconception of ethnic kinship is matched by a similar disrupting but also reimagining of familial kinship. The rhetorical equivalent of the 'raising up children to Abraham from the stones', but for familial not ethnic kinship, is Jesus's reply to the announcement that his mother and brothers are at the door: 'who are my mother and my brothers?', and the affirmation, 'whoever does the will of God is my brother and sister and mother'.[24] And the outward and visible sign of the displacement of normal family loyalties is in the call of the first disciples away from their fishing and their father, into a new company.[25]

What should be stressed, then, is that kinship is not erased by these moves but is played out in a different key. As the spiritualizing of ethnic identity leads not to an abandonment of ethnicity, but to its reappropriation as that of the 'new Israel', so also the displacement of familial kinship leads to the appearance of new families—'woman, behold thy son' and to the disciple so named, 'son, behold thy mother' (to cite the most iconic instance of such reconfiguration of the family, in Jesus's words from the cross). Brothers aren't banished from the New Testament, but reappear as brothers of all others within the community of believers: 'The most prominent use of "brother" in the New Testament is

---

[21] Romans 10, 13, quoting Joel 2, 32.

[22] J. M. G. Barclay, 'The Family as Bearer of Religion', in H. Moxnes, ed., *Constructing Early Christian Families* (London, 1997), 73.

[23] Galatians 3–4 and Romans 3–4 and 9–11 indicate something of the tensions involved in making and sustaining these claims—tensions analogous to those involved in relying on the genealogies of Matthew and Luke to do what genealogies so often do, namely to ground claims to authority and status (here the authority and status of Jesus specifically by virtue of his descent from David), even while those genealogies disrupt the line of descent with a virgin birth.

[24] Mark 3, 33–34, Matthew 12, 48–50, and Luke 8, 19–21.

[25] Mark 1, 17 and Matthew 4, 21.

as a metaphor, or fictive kinship term'.[26] This is not, then, an unkinning, but a rekinning—even if the reappropriation establishes what should be regarded as, in the case of the community of discipleship, a 'counter-cultural social structure'.[27]

The two sides of the reconceptualization and reappropriation of kinship (ethnic and familial) are strikingly present in an account of Christianity given by the early second-century apologist Aristides, when he distinguishes Christians from other nations (*ethne*) according to various matters of conduct, and claims amongst other things that:

> if they [Christians] have male or female slaves or children, they urge them to become Christians so that they can hold them in affection, and when they do become such, they call them brothers without distinction...If they see a stranger, they bring him into their own homes and greet him like a real brother—for they call one another 'brothers' not by physical connection but by the soul.[28]

As Meeks points out, 'there is something odd about [Aristides'] starting point: the Christians are obviously *not* a natural *ethnos* like the Babylonians, Egyptians, or Jews. Yet Aristides assumes without argument that observers will consider them in such a way'.[29] Christian discipleship is, here and elsewhere, envisaged as disrupting the continuity and authority of lineage—ethnic and familial—but then as reimagining it.[30]

One immediately pertinent question to pose to Aristides' assertion of an '"ethnic" self-consciousness' amongst 'early Christians' and the supposed 'displacement of the natural family by new relationships and obligations', concerns the 'extent [to which] the radicality' of this imagery 'corresponds

---

[26] H. Moxnes, 'What is Family? Problems in Constructing Early Christian Families', in Moxnes, ed., *Constructing Early Christian Families*, 35.

[27] To cite Moxnes's description in 'What is Family? Problems in Constructing Early Christian Families', in Moxnes, ed., *Constructing Early Christian Families*, 37. The full significance of the countercultural nature of these alternative forms may be lost on us unless we hold on to the point, also made by Moxnes, that the call away from the family is not a call from the 'family as an "emotional unit"' alone, but from the family as a wider and especially economic entity (41); pointedly, at Mark 10, 29–31, when Jesus responds to the claim that the disciples have left everything, he lists as what they have parted with not only brothers, sisters, mother, father, and children, but also houses and fields. 'Since the household was of fundamental importance for economic and social support, and for integration into the local community as well as for participation in religious and cultural life, leaving this community was a much more drastic rupture that it seems in today's world' (37).

[28] W. Meeks, *The Origins of Christian Morality* (New Haven, 1993), 9, citing Aelius Aristides, *Apology*.

[29] Meeks, *The Origins of Christian Morality*, 9.

[30] To cite Peter Brown's formulation of the point, 'The church was an artificial kinship group. Its members were expected to project onto the new community a fair measure of the sense of solidarity, of the loyalties, and of the obligations that had previously been directed to the physical family': in *The Cult of the Saints* (Chicago, 1981), 30.

to the realities of social experience'.[31] It is worth noting two ways in which the Christian imagination of a new kinship took concrete social form and in so doing challenged what we figure in our day as the desperation of child-lessness, and which we take to be answered by the fashioning of a child of one's own.

The first instantiation of this new imagining of kinship is in the remarkable establishment of the practice of sexual renunciation within 'Christian circles as a drastic alternative to the moral and social order that seemed so secure'[32] prior to this innovation. As Peter Brown shows in his important study, *The Body and Society: Men, Women and Sexual Renunciation in Early Christianity*, such renunciation carried diverse and sometimes conflicting meanings. But for our purposes, its chief meaning is as creating, most significantly perhaps for women, a certain freedom for certain women to refuse the role into which not only women (but especially women) were routinely pressed by implicit and explicit social expectations of raising children.

We are not unfamiliar with social worlds in which childbearing is conceived as belonging to a woman's very essence or identity. But in the Roman world with its population 'grazed thin by death' to use Chrysostom's phrase,[33] the social co-option of women to this role was more pressing than in our own:

> Unexacting in so many ways in sexual matters, the ancient city expected its citizens to expend a requisite proportion of their energy begetting and rearing legitimate children to replace the dead. Whether through conscious legislation, such as that of Emperor Augustus, which penalized bachelors and rewarded families for producing children, or simply through the unquestioned weight of habit, young men and women were discretely mobilized to use their bodies for reproduction. The pressure on young women was inexorable. For the population of the Roman Empire to remain stationary, it appears that each woman would have had to have produced an average of five children. Young girls were recruited early for their task. The median age of Roman girls at marriage may have been as low as fourteen. In North Africa, nearly 95 percent of the women recorded on gravestones had been married, over half of those before the age of twenty-three.[34]

Against this social co-option, one crucial meaning in the institutionalization of virginity lay not, I would argue, in any supposed special virtue in continence as such (or not only in that), but in the implicit declaration of the insignificance of childlessness. Childlessness was no longer, individually or collectively

[31] Meeks, *The Origins of Christian Morality*, 12.

[32] P. Brown, *The Body and Society: Men, Women and Sexual Renunciation in Early Christianity* (London, 1988), 32.

[33] In *De Virginitate*, cited by Brown, *The Body and Society*, 6.

[34] Brown, *The Body and Society*, 6; on general demographic patterns and trends in the early Christan period, see B. W. Frier, 'Demography', in *The Cambridge Ancient History*, 2nd ed., vol xi, *The High Empire, A.D. 70–192*, eds. A. Bowman, P. Garnsey, and D. Rathbone (Cambridge, 2000), 787–816.

and socially, tragic. Virginity was a badge, in other words, of Christianity's disbelief in what is constructed in our day as the tragedy of childlessness.[35]

I suggest further that the establishment of dedicated virginity is itself intimately connected with a second aspect of the social outworking of Christian troubling and refashioning of kinship, and that is in the later elaboration of practices of 'fictive kinship' as the anthropologists might term them, to which Aristides is an early witness.

We know that in the early monasteries, avowed celibates took seriously their removal from the worldly configuration of families and kin and made this displacement manifest through their use of the terms 'father', 'mother', 'brother', and 'sister' for fellow members of their communities, thereby voicing the reality of the new kinship which those communities ventured. And we know too, that these ventures in kinship were themselves an elaboration of what was implicit in baptism—since, as Meeks puts it, 'At the earliest stage of the movement' Christians 'created [this] rite of passage to dramatize the separation from one life and one society and the joining of another, leaving the family of birth and the culture of residence and becoming a sister or brother of those who are God's children.'[36] What we must note in addition, however, is that it was not in the monastery alone that this elaboration of the meaning of baptism for kinship was so plainly expressed—indeed, it would be better to say that by far the most important element in the actualizing of this imaginary is found in the history of godparenthood as a history of spiritual kinship. What is perhaps immediately explicit and obvious as a reconceiving of kinship in the appropriation of kinship terms in the parlance of monasticism, is merely, then, the tip of a much bigger iceberg.

The origins of godparenthood itself and more particularly its conceptualization as creative of spiritual kinship, are somewhat lost in the mist and the subject of much dispute;[37] in its full flowering, the rules which governed the practice are highly various between countries and dioceses, and over time, and thus defy any simple accounting.[38] In its residual forms in the modern period, it is the subject of scholarly neglect until quite recently (and possibly of scholarly mistreatment, based on a presupposition of the decline and insignificance of

---

[35] It would also be important, to give the wider context, to relate this renunciation to Jewish attitudes to child-bearing, which continue to 'inform the Israeli embrace of reproductice technology'; see S. M. Kahn, *Reproducing Jews: A Cultural Account of Assisted Conception in Israel* (Durham, NC, 2000), 3.

[36] Meeks, *The Origins of Christian Morality*, 12.

[37] The best and pioneering treatment is J. H. Lynch, *Godparents and Kinship in Early Medieval Europe* (Princeton, NJ, 1986). S. Bailey claims that 'the idea of spiritual parenthood' is 'suggested by Cyril in the *Catechetical Lectures*', and Eric Southworth suggests in turn that he may have Lecture 7 in mind: see S. Bailey, *Sponsors at Baptism and Confirmation: An Historical Introduction to Anglican Practice* (London, 1952), 17.

[38] As J. Bossy's early forays on the subject establish: see, for example, *Christianity in the West* (Oxford, 1985), 9; and further, J. Bossy, 'Blood and Baptism: Kinship, Community and

religion), but now of serious and important research.[39] What matters for moral theology in general, and in particular here for our engagement with contemporary framings of kinship, is, however, that we should notice something of the character of the highly structured and deeply socially embedded practice of spiritual kinship as a bold, profound, and influential attempt to express and realize the theo-logic of Christian kinship.

This is a complex subject, but it is sufficient at this point to observe and reckon with only a central point, namely the startling audacity of this tradition's institutionalization of Christianity's reconfiguration of kinship, such that by the early Middle Ages, 'The ritual of entry of an infant into the Church [and therefore into society] became a ritual of presentation of an infant by the godparents.'[40] The stark nature of this solemn, ritualized displacing of 'natural' kin can so easily escape us—but is evident and underlined in two details of the practice which are worth particular mention: the expected or enforced absence of parents from the baptism in many places; and the (by no means universal but nonetheless common) forbidding of relatives from taking on the role of godparents (since any mere intensification of 'natural' kinship which occurs with the use of relatives in this role was fundamentally at odds with a practice which sought not to intensify existing kinship, but to displace or relativize it). Were anthropologists to report on a people whose rites of welcome for the newborn rigorously exclude biological mother and father, it would be considered worthy of comment—and yet this has been the practice of our own tribe in its recent past and even into the present.

With Wayne Meeks I raised the question whether 'the radicality' expressed in early Christian liturgy and life, in particular in the picturing of the 'displacement of the natural family by new relationships and obligations' (in, for example, Aristides' *Apology*), corresponded 'to the realities of social experience'. And plainly it has to be recognized that certain other social realities bore down on the attempt, in the practice of avowed virginity and of spiritual kinship, to take a step outside the dominant structures of kinship.

The Trojan horse of worldly kinship, we might be tempted to say, is very often property.[41] The family, for most of its history, has been an economic and not merely a social or emotional unit, so that any displacement of the family was of economic significance (and this issue will recur in the next chapter). Certainly, property and kinship in the later classical world existed

Christianity in Western Europe from the Fourteenth to the Seventeenth Centuries', in *Sanctity and Secularity: The Church and the World*, ed., D. Baker (Oxford, 1973), 129–43.

[39] See G. Alfani and V. Gourdon, eds., *Spiritual Kinship in Europe, 1500–1900* (London, 2012), and in particular their introduction for comments on the neglect or misconstrual of spiritual kinship in some anthropological work.

[40] T. Maertens, quoted by Lynch, *Godparents and Kinship in Early Medieval Europe*, 43.

[41] See Bossy on this point.

in a tight nexus,[42] so that for Augustine and Benedict, for example, if the new understanding of kinship disturbed certain patterns of holding and conveying property, so conversely old ways of holding and conveying of property imperilled new patterns of being kin. For this reason Augustine was determined to have his priests living in community. And when Benedict tells us that private property is a wicked vice, its wickedness lies, if only in part, in its power to endanger the new solidarities of which the monastery spoke. Thus when Peter Brown notes that 'In the 370s and 380s, the patterns of inheritance within rich Christian families had been manipulated in such a way as to ensure that the ascetic renunciation of wealth and marriage by one member of the family did not affect the flow of property to other heirs',[43] one can almost hear in the background the weary sighs of the worldly wise Bishop of Hippo and his great monastic successor over the power of natural kinship to threaten the counter-kinship imagined and practised in Christianity.

For now, however, we notice not the counter pressures to which it was inevitably subject, but instead the fact of Christianity's bold and ambitious attempt at the reconfiguration of dominant patterns of kinship.

IV 'CONCEPTION AMONGST THE ANTHROPOLOGISTS'

As mentioned earlier, the rise of the new ARTs has encouraged anthropologists to return with fresh interest to a subject that has been central to their

---

[42] This nexus is well brought out in a funerary inscription from North Africa cited by B. D. Shaw in 'The Family in Late Antiquity: The Experience of Augustine', *Past and Present*, 115 (1987), 20: 'To Sergius Sulpicius, who was just beginning to leave behind his boyish years, and who, to the joy of his father, was obedient to the better side. A loving son, Festus by name, he was good by nature, the great hope of his father, endowed with qualities of total respect (obsequium) and a beautiful honesty. He loved his parents, and obeyed all their commands with wonderful duty. If only his father could have enjoyed such filial piety a little longer! Alas! It was a cruel and unmerited fate, a mournful thing for all, that he perished while not yet having enjoyed his sixteenth year, and ruined and bereaved his father, whose old age is now deprived of its cane.' For all the virtues identified here, 'In the final instance, it was the economic connection that mattered', notes Shaw (20), that this boy was destined to be a supporting cane or prop to his father. '[S]uccession—that is, biological continuity—was inextricably bound up with a hard economic reality'. The links between kinship and property are similarly evident when (in the *Confessions* at II, iii, 6) Patricius celebrates the signs of Augustine's pubescence; the celebration is on account of the securing of his future. This 'was perfectly typical of his class and station in life' suggests J. J. O'Donnell, *Augustine's Confessions*, vol. II (Oxford, 1992), 120, citing in support, Rouselle: a boy 'and his family would watch for the first signs of his sexual maturity. The appearance of pubic hair and his first ejaculations were a cause for celebration for the whole household, particularly the father'. See A. Rouselle, *Porneia: On Desire and the Body in Antiquity* (Oxford, 1988), 59.

[43] P. Brown, *Through the Eye of a Needle: Wealth, the Fall of Rome, and the Making of Christianity in the West, 350–550 AD* (Princeton, 2012), 295.

discipline from its earliest days—kinship.[44] A dominating thought has been that the ARTs challenge or subvert standard understandings of it. (Ironically, as we shall see, it may be the 'biologism' of anthropology's own understanding of kinship that has been most thoroughly disturbed; outside anthropology, biologism may be thought still to be doing quite nicely.)

According to Marilyn Strathern 'New procreative possibilities—fertilisation *in vitro*, gamete donation, maternal surrogacy—formulate new possibilities for thinking about kinship', such that we have entered 'an epoch of sorts'.[45] A sense of epochal change is indicated by the titles of books, articles, and chapters within a field that has emerged from anthropological engagement with these 'new procreative possibilities'. From Edwards's et al. *Technologies of Procreation: Kinship in the Age of Assisted Conception*,[46] to Strathern's *After Nature: English Kinship in the Late Twentieth Century*;[47] from Becker's 'Rewriting the Family',[48] to Charis Thompson's 'Quit Snivelling Cryo-baby, We'll Work Out Which One's Your Mama: Kinship in an Infertility Clinic';[49] from Bonaccorso's *Conceiving Kinship* and 'Making Connections',[50] to Inhorn's *Reproductive Disruptions*[51]—on and on such titles go, each signalling the by now commonplace idea that we live in an era in which kinship is being newly made, remade, or even unmade. Anthropologists' interest in these technologies, especially on account of their supposed effects on understandings and practices of kinship, family, and relatedness, has led to a burgeoning research programme. Inhorn and Birenbaum-Carmeli's review article of 2008, 'Assisted Reproductive Technologies and Culture Change', surveys the work of more than fifty scholars concerned with the role and significance of ARTs in contemporary culture.[52] Since 2008 the number of contributors and contributions has grown further.

---

[44] So it is that the first chapter of Sarah Franklin's important study, *Embodied Progress: A Cultural Account of Assisted Conception* (London, 1997), is entitled 'Conception amongst the Anthropologists', a phrase I have borrowed for this section.

[45] M. Strathern, *Reproducing the Future: Anthropology, Kinship and the New Reproductive Technologies* (Manchester, 1992), vii.

[46] J. Edwards, S. Franklin, E. Hirsch, F. Price, and M. Strathern, eds., *Technologies of Procreation: Kinship in the Age of Assisted Conception* (Manchester, 1993).

[47] M. Strathern, *After Nature: English Kinship in the Late Twentieth Century* (Cambridge, 1992).

[48] The title of chapter 13 in G. Becker, *The Elusive Embryo* (Berkeley, 2000).

[49] Thompson, ' "Quit Snivelling Cryo-Baby, We'll Work Out Which One's Your Mama"— Kinship in an Infertility Clinic', in R. Davis-Floyd and J. Dumit, eds., *Cyborg Babies: From Techno-Sex to techno-Tots* (London, 1998), 4–66.

[50] M. Bonaccorso, *Conceiving Kinship: Assisted Conception, Procreation and Family in South Europe* (New York, 2008) and 'Making Connections: Family and Relatedness in Clinics of Assisted Conception in Italy', *Modern Italy*, 9 (2004), 59–68.

[51] M. Inhorn, *Reproductive Disruptions: Gender, Technology, and Biopolitics in the New Millennium* (New York, 2007).

[52] M. C. Inhorn and D. Birenbaum-Carmeli, 'Assisted Reproductive Technologies and Culture Change', *Annual Review of Anthropology* (2008), 37, 177–96.

The most radical diagnosis of all, is suggested, so it might seem, by Carsten's title, *After Kinship*. Carsten notes, however, that her 'title...is...playful; the message of this book appears to be that "after kinship" is—well, just more kinship (even if it might be of a slightly different kind)'.[53] So what has changed? What does kinship look like after its troubling by the ARTs?

The central thought behind the mention of epochs is just that 'if kinship, as a set of social relations, is seen to be rooted in the natural facts of biological reproduction' in what, since Schneider, anthropologists have referred to as the 'folk theory' of kinship,[54] 'then the nature of kinship itself might be called into question by ARTs, which, in effect, destabilize the biological within parenthood through the assistance of technologies and third parties'.[55]

According to Schneider, the folk theory expresses what everyone knows (or thinks they know): at its core it holds that we are related to one another in two main ways, either by blood or by marriage—which is to say, through sexual intercourse. Thus any child will know that amongst his or her uncles, for example, there are those to whom he or she is related through his or her mother, let's say, and that these can be distinguished as between the mother's brothers and any husbands of the mother's sisters (to whom one is not 'really' related, as it might be said, though they are still likely to be termed 'relatives', as opposed say, to parents' adult male friends or neighbours, who may themselves also be addressed as 'uncle', but are certainly not relatives). What Schneider argued is just that the biogenetic grounding of kinship in the Western folk theory is culturally specific and further that this cultural specificity was occluded from the view even of social anthropologists, who assumed the folk theory in encounter with non-Western peoples—most egregiously, perhaps, in Malinowski's translation of a native term as 'father', thereby projecting a Western view of fatherhood on to a people who did not think of fatherhood as resulting from sexual intercourse alone or even at all.[56]

So, it is not kinship as such which is said to have been overthrown by the new technologies, but only certain versions of kinship. There may still be

[53] Carsten, *After Kinship*, 11.

[54] See D. M. Schneider, *American Kinship: A Cultural Account*, 2nd ed. (Chicago, 1980; 1st ed. 1968), for the classic account and critique of the Western 'folk theory' of kinship.

[55] Inhorn and Birenbaum-Carmeli, 'Assisted Reproductive Technologies and Culture Change', 182.

[56] The assumption of something like the folk theory also lies behind an inclination in some analyses to take less than fully seriously spiritual kinship, dubbed 'ritual' or 'pseudo' or 'fictive' kinship. As Franklin rightly notes (in 'From Blood to Genes', 287–88), as a result of the modern critique within anthropology itself, 'the term *fictive*, like the adjective *pseudo*, is. . . used less often', since both involve 'the essentialist presumption of a biological "base" to the kinship superstructure'. For a recent treatment which turns the folk theory on its head, see M. Sahlins, *What Kinship Is—And Is Not* (Chicago, 2013): 'In contrast to our own native wisdom and an anthropological science that for too long has been indebted to it, kinship categories are not representations or metaphorical extensions of birth relations; if anything, birth is a metaphor of kinship relations' (ix).

kinship after (folk) kinship, so this thought seems to go, but this new kinship, unlike the kinship of the folk theory, no longer takes seriously the supposed natural facts of relatedness of the traditional accounts.

Of course an immediate and cautious response to a question about whether these technologies are 'unseating core notions of kinship and undermining the traditional family'[57]—whether, to quote Carsten again, the 'technologization of nature' and the 'naturalization of technology' have had or 'will have a dramatically destabilizing effect on Western notions of kinship'[58]—would be (as, probably apocryphally, Chou en Lai is supposed to have said when asked whether the French Revolution had been a good thing) that it is too early to tell. But against any too-ready an embracing of the 'epochal view' as it might be termed, I suggest the following argument. The dominant notions and self-understandings which seem to govern the consumption of this technology are expressed in two related ideas we have already mentioned—that of the 'desperateness of childlessness' and of the need for 'a child of one's own'. But the construction of infertility in these terms, which in turn determines or shapes the deployment of the technology, means that the ARTs, for all their supposed subversive potential, are in fact chiefly put to the service of the very notions of kinship, which, on the epochal view, they are set to undermine. Thus contrary to what that epochal discourse might seem to presuppose, but unsurprisingly 'given that Euro-American notions of kinship are biogenetically based', the technology is perhaps most frequently deployed by 'many infertile couples [who] now "chase the blood tie" in a relentless quest to produce biogenetically related offspring through the ART-assisted manipulation of their own gametes. . .', as Inhorn and Birenbaum-Carmeli put it.[59]

According to Gay Becker, 'a wealth of cultural phenomena coalesce to create and foster a desire for the new reproductive technologies',[60] but it is the drive for biological parenthood that could be said to be the crucial mainstay of their use and uptake. The driving force of this desire is nicely (though sadly) captured in a comment made by a woman after the failure of a round of fertility treatment: 'After acknowledging that it was the worst experience of my life, I decided to do it again'.[61]

---

[57] Inhorn and Birenbaum-Carmeli, 'Assisted Reproductive Technologies and Culture Change', 182.

[58] Carsten, *After Kinship*, 30.

[59] Inhorn and Birenbaum-Carmeli, 'Assisted Reproductive Technologies and Culture Change', 182. The resonant phrase 'chasing the blood tie' is taken from the title of an article by H. Ragoné, 'Chasing the Blood Tie: Surrogate Mothers, Adoptive Mothers and Fathers', *American Ethnologist*, 23.2 (1996), 352–65.

[60] Becker, *The Elusive Embryo*, 132.

[61] Becker, *The Elusive Embryo*, 132. As Becker notes, 'When initial efforts to conceive are unsuccessful, the decision to proceed may be viewed by both women and their physicians as a risk–benefit trade-off; and if a baby is a priceless benefit, then almost any risk is worth taking', 97.

The social presupposition and re-enforcement of this 'desperateness' is well captured in an article by Sarah Franklin, which opens with a recitation of headlines of a kind familiar to anyone who even merely glances at newspapers—'New Hope for the Childless, Comfort for the Childless, Joy For Baby Hope Couples, Childless Couples Given Hope, Infertile Couples Get Hope From New Method, Mother's Joy Over 1000th Test-Tube Baby, Test-Tube Boy for Thrilled Parents, Test Tube Triplets a City First for "Ecstatic" Parents'.[62] As Franklin comments:

> The typical description of the infertile is one which emphasises their 'desperation', 'anguish' and 'suffering' and refers to them as the 'victims of childlessness', 'unwillingly childless', 'involuntarily childless' or as 'sufferers of infertility'. Juxtaposed against these tales of 'desperateness' are the stories of 'happy couples' who have won their battle against childlessness by producing a 'miracle baby' with the help of modern medical science. Together, these two sets of stories, of happiness and hopelessness, constitute the major frame of reference for discussions of infertility.[63]

And as she further argues, the hopelessness is in turn given a social and biological explanation. Socially, the childless have lost the hope that their lives will follow trajectories they had imagined for themselves and others expect of them. But this social loss is itself thought of as biologically rooted. Biologically, the childless are supposed to suffer from the frustration of an innate drive; as the *Warnock Report* put it, 'there is, for many, a powerful urge to perpetuate their genes through a new generation. This desire cannot be assuaged by adoption'.[64] Such an assumption, that biology is destiny, reflects popular nostrums such as that women (more than men) have a biological clock that ticks increasingly loudly as fertility approaches its period of decline or loss.

It would be worth trying to characterize more fully the nature of the social diminution or privation which it is supposed the childless experience, and even more, perhaps, to probe the supposedly biological imperative said to underlie the need to have children. For now, I merely notice the general

---

It is the compelling force of such thoughts that Becker captures in a chapter title referring to 'Consuming Technologies'; the point is that the technologies consumed can become consuming, for once the project of overcoming infertility by these means is entered upon, a certain logic combines past losses, the merit of perseverance, and a rhetoric of hope, to make it very difficult to desist. The logic is, of course, commercially important for commercial providers; see the comments of Lisa Jardine at the end of her term as chair of the UK's Human Fertilisation and Embryology Authority: 'The world of IVF is a market, a market in hope'. (www.bbc.co.uk/news/magazine-24652639)

[62] S. Franklin, 'Deconstructing "Desperateness": The Social Construction of Infertility in Popular Representations of New Reproductive Technologies', in *The New Reproductive Technologies*, ed. M. McNeil, I. Varcoe, and S. Yearley (London, 1990), 200.

[63] Franklin, 'Deconstructing "Desperateness"', 200.

[64] Franklin, 'Deconstructing "Desperateness"', 208, citing the *Warnock Report*.

cultural assumption that there is a 'desperation for a child of one's own', that this is a key element in the experience of infertility—and thus, as one might expect and I shall argue, that it plays a central role in shaping the consumption of ARTs.

The pattern of use of ARTs is mixed and complex and varies with various cultural and social factors. My purpose here is not to chart the full extent or shape of that variation, but simply to adduce some of the evidence which supports the view that the technology is very often used in a very traditional way, that this extraordinary and astonishing new technology is put into the service of some regular and familiar patterns of family formation, and specifically is often directed to 'chasing the blood tie'.

It has to be noted as a preliminary that the use of ARTs in general and of IVF in particular is distinctly burdensome, both medically (i.e. as a procedure in itself), but also, in the US especially, financially. The burdens of the medical procedure chiefly falling on the woman will include in all cases: demanding drug regimes to regularize/stimulate ovulation, painful laproscopic surgery and/ or other invasive procedures, and considerable disruption to normal life over the sometimes very extended periods during which single or multiple attempts to obtain and fertilize eggs and then implant embryos are repeated. The financial burdens (where the treatment is not covered by insurance) are also substantial.[65]

The point of mentioning these burdens is to register the fact that the use of IVF involves a willingness to bear very considerable costs, not just monetary. It follows that the significant disincentives to the use of the procedures must themselves be outweighed by a strong sense of the relative undesirability of obvious alternatives for infertile individuals or couples—for some, a use of donor sperm;[66] for others, seeking children through adoption; for all, remaining childless. The strength of the preference for IVF over these other alternatives, as well as the way in which these alternatives are themselves deployed if and when IVF is abandoned, is indicative of the determination to 'chase the blood tie'. We should notice, amongst other things, the following features of the situation:

> Firstly, the general preference for IVF over any alternative means of getting pregnant. This preference is not expressed only at the outset of attempts to get pregnant by other than the regular means, but is often sustained for considerable periods of time, through repeated and gruelling cycles of IVF, and

---

[65] According to the NHS, a cycle of IVF in a private clinic costs about £5000, with extra cost for medicines, consultations, and tests. According to the American Society of Reproductive Medicine, an average cost of an IVF cycle is US $12,400, again with additional costs in different circumstances. Since an average couple may anticipate three or four cycles of IVF on the path to pregnancy or before they give up, the typical costs are likely to be considerable.

[66] In passing it should be noted that the general use of the word 'donor' in these contexts is not unproblematic and may be somewhat misleading, since in many jurisdictions (and in the US in particular) significant financial rewards are available to 'donors'. For a recent discussion, reflecting on the 'gendered framing' of donation, see R. Almeling, *Sex Cells: The Medical Market for Eggs and Sperm* (Berkeley, 2011).

sometimes in the face of any reasonable calculation of the odds, before other alternatives are explored. Ethnographic tales of resolute perseverance in this pursuit of pregnancy by IVF are very striking (and moving) in this regard.[67] The costly pursuit of this option in preference to other alternatives suggests a determination to chase the blood tie untouched by any modern troubling of kinship.

Secondly, the strong preference for the treatment of male infertility by ICSI (intracytoplasmic sperm injection), as against the use of donor insemination. That is, men (whose infertility can now be treated in the female) are generally keen, and their female partners at the least willing, for those female partners to enter a rigorous and demanding programme of IVF treatment (on which ICSI depends), even though insemination by donor is a readily available and alternative solution—though not, of course, one which would produce the desired 'child of one's own'.

Thirdly, the fact that even where the ambivalence about the use of donated material is overcome and IVF or ICSI have been abandoned, homage to a chasing of the blood tie is still apparent in the deployment of alternative means of having a child. In the case of male infertility, for example, a couple can be expected to seek a donor who resembles the male in what are regarded as crucial phenotypic respects (such as hair, eye colour, and height), and can be expected to conceal the use of a donor or to conceal it from all but the most intimate relatives and friends. (An epicycle of irony is added by the fact that the practice of insemination by donor is now rendered less desirable for those for whom the blood tie is deemed significant, by a change which itself pays regard to the importance of the blood tie. This is the provision in the UK, for example, that a donor's details must be available to children at 18. It is the same sense of the importance of the biological that drives the social father to wish to conceal, and regulators to require to be revealed, the origins of the child.) What is striking here, in the choice of sperm (as also in the use of eggs), is that even the use of donated material is governed by the logic of a strongly biological notion of kinship. To state it paradoxically, we might say that we tend to chase the blood tie or try to even when we can't.[68]

---

[67] The point is clear in both Franklin's (*Embodied Progress*) and Becker's (*The Elusive Embryo*) studies.

[68] C. Thompson's *Making Parents: The Ontological Choreography of Reproductive Technologies* (Cambridge, MA, 2005), importantly and powerfully argues that the contemporary crafting of kinship in the infertility clinic involves the strategic deployment of traditional notions of biological kinship in service of what she terms 'procreative intent'—in other words, the biological is not simply repudiated, but is used in the light of an intention to make parents of those who want to be parents. So, 'a combination of intent, financial transaction, and genetics trace maternity through the various bodies producing the baby in commerical gestational surrogacy' (150). Thompson takes further the insights of Ragoné's earlier article, which in spite of what its title may suggest claims that in the surrogacy process 'participants pick and choose among American cultural values about family, parenthood, and reproduction, now choosing biological relatedness, now nuture, according to their needs' ('Chasing the Blood Tie', 363). The important point, then, is that

Fourthly, reports that 'the very presence of ARTs has served to marginalize, to some degree, alternate means of family formation through adoption...once regarded as the "natural solution" to infertility'.[69] It is now very much a least-favoured option of family formation.[70]

The picture here is complex and varied and I have no wish to argue that 'chasing the blood tie', simply understood, is the only important factor in and feature of contemporary use of these technologies in the West. I do suggest, however, that this concern for the blood tie remains one of the main determinants of the deployment of the technologies which are somehow thought to undermine or destabilize any such interest. The supposed desperation of childlessness, to be answered by provision of a child of one's own, are crucial elements in the construction of infertility and in the consumption of these technologies.

The author of a significant ethnography comments that: 'Women and men are using these technologies to undermine the cultural ideology of biological parenthood and to transform the meaning of family. They are introducing new social practices...[which] promise to erode the cultural ideology of the biological child and remake cultural views of parenthood.'[71] There is some evidence to support that claim but equally there is evidence to favour the reading of the situation implied in the title of an article which, though twenty-five years old, has not been proved obviously wrong by the passage of time: 'New Reproductive Technologies: The Old Quest for Fatherhood'.[72]

V CONCEIVING CONCEPTION CHRISTIANLY

At the beginning of the chapter I asked how the representation of conception in the Christian imagination allows us to make sense of and critique the new forms of technological assistance to conception and the new relationships they enable. Where does the imagination of Christ's conception put pressure on the contemporary imagination of reproduction?

I suggest here that the standard Christian appraisal and critique of this technology has sometimes been rather narrowly concerned with the licitness or illicitness

---

there is no simple dichotomy, as if these technologies *either* serve to support biogenetic kinship, *or* don't. In fact they are used creatively and pragmatically to achieve desired ends.

[69] For further references, see Inhorn and Birenbaum-Carmeli, 'Assisted Reproductive Technologies and Culture Change', 182.

[70] Though some infertile men show a preference for adoption over the use of donor sperm, since donor sperm seems to some to intrude a third party into the couple's relationship and furthermore creates a non-symmetrical parental relationship—see Becker, *The Elusive Embryo*, 44.

[71] Becker, *The Elusive Embryo*, 244.

[72] V. Stolcke, 'New Reproductive Technologies: The Old Quest for Fatherhood', *Reproductive and Genetic Engineering: Journal of International Feminist Analysis*, 1.1 (1988), 5–19; see also 'New Reproductive Technologies—Same Old Fatherhood', *Critique of Anthropology*, 6.3 (1986), 5–31.

of various means of becoming pregnant, and has thus typically neglected deeper and more fundamental questions about whether and how technology, the use of which may or may not be licit in principle, should figure within Christian life, thought, and practice. Much of the existing discussion seems unaware of the deep questioning of kinship which we have noticed in the Christian tradition, a questioning expressed in the rites and practices of godparenthood, for example, as well as in avowed virginity.[73]

This tradition denies that the working out of the logic of kinship, understood as a chasing of the blood tie, is either inevitable or desirable. Any discussion unaware of this heritage or unwilling to take a stand on it, will not only cut itself off from important themes in Christian understandings of sociality, but also can only be profoundly conservative, since it is likely to reflect contemporary culture to itself. It will fail to address the deep drives that frame the production and consumption of the new technology, and whether any discussion conducted in these limited terms says 'yes' or 'no' to any or all of the ARTs, it is bound to remain shallow and certainly incapable of the therapeutic engagement with our culture to which an everyday Christian ethics should aspire.[74]

It is striking, to take just one example, how the Congregation for the Doctrine of the Faith's *Donum Vitae (Instruction on Respect for Human Life in its Origin and on the Dignity of Procreation)*,[75] cited with approval in the *Catechism*,[76] seems to have no knowledge of any form of kinship other than biogenetic kinship.

---

[73] Of course, picking up something mentioned earlier in this chapter, the tendency of Christian practice to be co-opted by prevailing cultural norms, in spite of the countercultural tendencies even of its central liturgies, is well attested (and not just in the modern period). A telling example of the resilience of popular notions of kinship in the face of Christian ambivalence towards them is mentioned by Bossy. As he sees it, a source of the popularity of the *Golden Legend* in the later Middle Ages was just in its providing Mary with a host of kin from the apocryphal gospels. These sources enabled 'Mary, and therefore Jesus, to appear in the world embedded in that plausible nexus of blood-relations on which, though satisfying about her cousinage to Elizabeth and John the Baptist, the canonical gospels gave such scanty and contradictory information': Bossy, *Christianity in the West*, 9. He continues: 'According to the *Golden Legend* Elizabeth was Mary's cousin on her father, Joachim's, side: but St Anne, despite her advanced years at the birth of Mary, had married twice again after Joachim's death'—and by these two marriages was mother to the two Marys (Cleopas and Salome), and grandmother to four apostles and to John the Evangelist. St Anne, 'the head of this ramifying kindred', become a subject of a lively cult in the fifteenth century, testifying to 'a general satisfaction that Christ had not come a foundling into the world' (9–10). This is very nicely depicted in the sculpture in the Cloisters collection in New York, labelled 'The Holy Kinship of St Anne', in which a proper family network is plainly on show.

[74] A. L. Hall's, *Conceiving Parenthood: American Protestantism and the Spirit of Reproduction* (Grand Rapids, MI, 2008), is thus a refreshing contribution and an example of the sort of deconstruction needed here—she shows how mainstream American churches have reproduced rather than critiqued dominant cultural (and unChristian) notions of the good family and the good child.

[75] Congregation for the Doctrine of the Faith, *Donum Vitae (Instruction on Respect for Human Life in its Origin and on the Dignity of Procreation)*, (London, 1987).

[76] *Catechism of the Catholic Church* (London, 1994), at §2375, referencing *Donum Vitae*.

As is perhaps well known, the *Instruction* rejects not just what it terms heter-
ologous artificial fertilization (i.e. fertilization by donor sperm), and surrogacy
(whether with or without donated material), but also homologous artificial
fertilization (i.e. insemination by spouse). What interests me is one element in
the argument against the use of donated sperm:

> Heterologous artificial insemination violates the rights of the child; it deprives
> him of his filial relationship with his parental origins and can hinder the matur-
> ing of his personal identity. Furthermore, it offends the common vocation of the
> spouses who are called to fatherhood and motherhood: it objectively deprives
> conjugal fruitfulness of its unity and integrity: it brings about and manifests a
> rupture between genetic parenthood, gestational parenthood and responsibility
> for upbringing. Such damage to the personal relationships within the family has
> repercussions on civil society: what threatens the unity and stability of the family
> is a source of dissension, disorder and injustice in the whole of social life.[77]

The claims here follow one another thick and fast—we get from donated
sperm to dissension and disorder in social life in fairly short order. It is not my
purpose to explicate or to contest these claims, nor to elucidate the precise part
which they play in the *Instructions'* determination of the 'hard cases' of donor
insemination, surrogacy, and the like. Plainly the *Instruction* raises important
questions and is deserving of careful analysis. My present purpose, however, is
to note that the thought world of the *Instruction*, with its central concern over
the 'rupture between genetic parenthood, gestational parenthood and responsibility for upbringing', seems to be very much closer to the thought world, not
of the Christmas season back in 418 or thereabouts when Augustine preached
that sermon, but of the *Warnock Report*.

The *Warnock Report*, in recommending the legal recognition and regulation
of what was then referred to as AID (Artificial Insemination by Donor), came
to a different conclusion from the *Instruction*, and for the sake of addressing 'the distress of childlessness'.[78] But the difference over the conclusion on
this point seems, from a certain angle, little more than a relatively minor
disagreement between parties which share very similar understandings of the
relationship between parent and child. It is just that the *Warnock Report* will
countenance, on balance and hedged about with various caveats, 'a rupture
between genetic parenthood' and social parenthood, which the *Instruction*, in
sharp terms, will not. This difference notwithstanding, there is considerable
irony in finding the *Instruction* vying to outbid the *Warnock Report* in its profound respect for biological parenthood.

In another connection Peter Brown says of a certain and radical hope for the
'dissolving of the household', that its fate was to 'flicker disquietingly along the

---

[77] *Donum Vitae*, 24–5.

[78] *Report of the Committee of Inquiry into Human Fertilisation and Embryology* (London,
1984), commonly referred to as the *Warnock Report*, 4.15.

edges of the Christian church.[79] The words of the *Instruction* suggest that any flicker associated with the hopes involved in the practice of avowed celibacy or in the institutionalizing of spiritual kinship, as a displacing of biological kin, has been well and truly extinguished. Those who 'chase the blood tie' will hear themselves merely seconded by this *Instruction* on this particular point—even if they would not accept other elements of the case made by *Donum Vitae* against the use of ARTs. As for the infertile, they will hear nothing that might contribute to a reframing of infertility itself, when such a reframing belongs to a Christian conception of conception.

The *Instruction* insists that 'whatever its cause or prognosis, sterility is certainly a difficult trial' and that 'the community of believers is called to shed light upon and support the suffering of those who are unable to fulfil their legitimate aspiration to motherhood and fatherhood', and further that 'spouses who find themselves in this sad situation are called to find in it an opportunity for sharing in a particular way in the Lord's Cross, the source of spiritual fruitfulness'.[80] It seems regrettable, however, that the call to 'shed light upon . . . the suffering' of the infertile, is one which the *Instruction* avoids insofar as it does not bring to bear here the radical proclamation implicit in the practices of avowed celibacy, baptism, and godparenthood. Instead, what we have is an echo of modern constructions of parenthood and infertility, just when what is needed is critique. As it is, the infertile are left in a double bind—they are forbidden to make use of technologies that might assist them in realizing their desire for parenthood, fully biological or otherwise, while that desire is left solemnly in place on its contemporary pedestal. (It is perhaps no surprise then, that the most recent Roman rites of baptism have displaced godparents and moved parents centre stage.[81] And lest anyone should think this line of criticism is directed rather particularly at the Roman Church, it should be mentioned that the Anglican Church's very own celebration of blood and soil, otherwise known as Mothering Sunday, would likely provide a rich vein for critical analysis along the very same lines.)

Virginity, godparenthood, and baptism, I suggest, propose a therapeutic and evangelical word in relation to the subject of infertility—and one that would attempt to deconstruct the desperateness of childlessness rather than uncritically to address or console it. Christians do not believe in the desperateness of childlessness—nor indeed, in the possibility of having a child of one's own to overcome

---

[79] Brown, *Body and Society*, 53.　　[80] *Donum Vitae*, 34.

[81] On this point, I simply cite the comments of Alfani and Gourdon, in *Spiritual Kinship in Europe, 1500–1900*, at 28, that 'In 1983, the new version of the Code of Canon Lay (resulting from the Vatican Council, 1962–65), did not include any reference to spiritual kinship and consequently neither to spiritual incest. In the meantime, in 1969, the promulgation of the *Ordo baptismi parvulorum* by Pope Paul VI had established a ritual for infant baptism in which the role played by the child's parents was clarified and explicitly strengthened, to the detriment of godparents who had been the only ones mentioned by earlier rituals'. The rite of Baptism in the Church of England's *Common Worship* follows the same trend.

this desperation. The task for Christian ethics here, then, is to try to come to terms with and narrate the difference which the reality of Christian troubling of kinship should make to our understanding and use of these technologies and the notions of kinship on which their consumption depends. Discussions of the licitness or illicitness of various means of becoming pregnant may be good or bad in their own terms, but they quite simply fail to speak to the childless (who need to hear the proclamation that there is kinship without biology), just as they fail to speak to those with children (who need to hear the proclamation I shall take up in the next chapter, that even biology does not give one a child of one's own).

Of course, it might be said that the practice of spiritual kinship is a somewhat poor token to set against the prevailing cultural construction of the desperation of childlessness. I would agree. But this is only to say that the orthodoxy of thought and practice which proposes and constructs the desperation of childlessness is very widely disseminated and reinforced (so much so that, as we have seen, even the Congregation for the Doctrine of the Faith joins in the hue and cry), whereas the challenge to it seems altogether more fragile and thus in need of powerful explication (as theory) and exemplification (in practice). The presupposition of any such challenge is nicely expressed by the book title *Water is Thicker than Blood: An Augustinian Theology of Marriage and Singleness*[82]—the presupposition being that community and kinship need not be constructed biogenetically, as contemporary norms suppose.

As that title suggests, and as we have already anticipated in a preliminary fashion, we could look to Augustine to supply a critical theory of kin and kinning. But where might we look for exemplification of a critical practice? There are two lines of enquiry here which may contribute to a better description of the theory's embodiment. First, although it is not unproblematic, we might look to practices of adoption as providing different models of making kin.[83] Second, a demonstration of the possibility and nature of alternative kinning would be provided by an ethnography of a Christian community in which a countercultural form of non-biogenetic kinship is plainly and powerfully manifested—a community in which there are no biological ties, but in which the reality of being a mother and father, or brother and sister, or son or daughter, is richly experienced.

Ethnographies of traditional communities of religious may provide such examples, but one of the most interesting and novel experiments in community life and in alternative ways of making kin is found in the L'Arche communities,

---

[82] J. M. Bennett, *Water is Thicker Than Blood: An Augustinian Theology of Marriage and Singleness* (New York, 2008).

[83] Adoption deserves much more careful attention than can be given to it here. I limit myself to mentioning one issue and noting two important studies. Somewhat mysteriously, adoption ceases, so it seems, to have a significant and institutional role in Christian life after the time of Augustine—he at least, following Roman norms, regards it as a recognizable and current practice whereas subsequently it fades from significance; so, for example, Jack Goody claims in *The*

in which those with learning difficulties are invited to live in a shared house with volunteers who contribute to their care. As yet there is no full and careful ethnography of a L'Arche house, though some attempts have been made in that direction.[84]

Whether or not it can commend it descriptively or merely prescriptively, however, Christian ethics looks towards a kinship that does not fall back on 'classic' ways of doing family, which privilege ties of blood. Instead it commends a kinship framed by our conceiving our conception in the light of the conception of Christ, to whom Joseph was truly a father. Christian rites intend to unkin us, only to rekin us with new bonds that dispel childlessness as much as they eliminate orphanhood. And if kinship is a mode of 'organizing alterity',[85] as Faubion puts it, a directing of the self to the other, kinship can hardly be erased but it can be sharply reconceived. The rites of baptism (which displace kin by blood), and of the eucharist (which makes us kin to Christ, and thus to one another by sharing in his blood), are such an enacted reconception—and are signs of the continuing purpose and power of a critical Christianity to fashion kinship amongst strangers.

Development of the Family and Marriage in Europe (Cambridge, 1983). Two important studies are J. Modell's *Kinship with Strangers: Adoption and Interpretations of Kinship in American Culture* (Berkeley, 1994) and *A Sealed and Secret Kinship: The Culture of Policies and Practices in American Adoption* (New York, 2002). One of Modell's central findings is just that American adoption 'not only mirrors biology but also upholds a cultural interepretation of biological, or genealogical, kinship. Every time a child is given up and taken in, the script of "real" relationship is, as it were, written again' (*Kinship with Strangers*, 3).

[84] E.g. K. S. Reimer, *Living L'Arche: Stories of Compassion, Love and Disability* (London, 2009). For an example of a different community but with similar concerns and ideals, see V. Sweet's *God's Hotel: A Doctor, A Hospital and A Pilgrimage to the Heart of Medicine* (New York, 2012); the study is more biographical than ethnographic, however.

[85] J. Faubion, introduction to *The Ethics of Kinship: Ethnographic Enquiries*, ed. J. Faubion (Oxford, 2001), 3. This essay is an important and insightful treatment of the neglected topic mentioned in the title.

3

Being Born and Being Born Again: On Having or Not Having a Child of One's Own

I INTRODUCTION: ON VARIOUS PRONATALISMS

Anthropology's concern for the understanding and analysis of kinship, revivified in recent years by the supposed troubling of kinship by the new ARTs, should serve as an encouragement to moral theology to attend consciously and directly to the theme of kinship. Though somewhat neglected in contemporary moral theological discussions, kinship is an important and foundational theme in Christian thought and practice and must have a place in an everyday ethics. At its very origins Christianity troubled kinship in its conception of the conception of Christ—'troubling' suggesting not a repudiation but a reconfiguring of kinship. And Christianity proclaimed and practised its unsettling most starkly and strikingly in two prominent practices: first, in the institutionalization of avowed celibacy, and second, in the highly structured and deeply socially embedded practice of spiritual kinship—centrally in the invention of godparenthood as the theo-logic of a new kinship. Bossy puts it elegantly: 'In the late medieval centuries the history of the incorporation of children into the community of Christians is a history of godparenthood. The characteristics of this much-appreciated institution were a tribute to the vigour and elegance of symbolic lay theology; they testified to a determination to make sure that on the other side of the waters of baptism the child would find itself received by a Christian kindred or gossip (god-sib) adequate to replace the natural kindred from which he had passed by the rites of regeneration, since flesh and blood could not inherit the kingdom of God.'[1]

Taking the theory of this practice seriously allows moral theology to return to contemporary concerns and debates around conception with a properly therapeutic and evangelical voice. 'Nowhere are the high stakes in procreation

---

[1] Bossy, *Christianity in the West*, 15.

and the cultural meaning of childlessness more evident than in the infertility industry'[2] says one recent commentator. A reconception of conception enabled us, however, to lower the stakes somewhat, specifically through a deconstruction of the 'desperation of childlessness' (understood especially as a desperation for a 'child of one's own'). It is on this desperation that this industry depends, since it is such desperation which drives couples to resort to and persist in the pursuit of conception by IVF in preference to an acceptance of such alternatives as adopting or fostering, or indeed of remaining childless. The consumption of ARTs is typically a way of 'chasing of the blood tie'. It is often predicated on the (culturally constructed) tragedy of childlessness in which Christianity does not (or at least ought not to) believe, as if kinship were only biological.

Of course, Christianity is not wholly alone in denying the tragedy of childlessness. There are plainly a number of different ways of deconstructing the 'tragedy of childlessness', each with its own flavour. As May sees it in her history of American reproduction, perhaps the most influential deconstruction of childlessness in the contemporary scene is in a conscious embrace and advocacy of the merits of being not 'childless' but childfree—the state of being without children, but now presented and perceived not as a lack or deficiency but as a liberty and an opportunity. This celebration of freedom and independence was hatched, as May sees it, in revolt against the baby boom and the 'tyranny of parentism' as it has been described. Such childlessness 'was not a new phenomenon, nor did the stigma surrounding the childless entirely disappear. What changed in the 1970s was the visibility and stridency of the voluntarily childless'. 'Voluntary childlessness', previously stigmatized as selfish and even unpatriotic was now held to represent 'not simply a legitimate alternative to parenthood, but a better lifestyle—better for individuals, better for couples, better for the planet'.[3]

So now we have to notice that if Christianity, properly understood, is incompatible with certain 'pronatalisms'—such as the pronatalism that underwrites the infertility industry by holding up as an object of natural, overriding, and incorrigible desire, 'a child of one's own'—it doesn't follow that it will fall into step with antinatalism. There were voices in the early period of Christianity and later (such as those of the Shakers and Tolstoi, to take some recent examples), drawn to denounce procreation. But these voices did not prevail. Christianity does not find itself, then, in happy company with each and every deconstructor of the 'tragedy of childlessness', for Christianity's own deconstruction must reckon with an element of the Christian tradition unequivocally announced by Augustine. Sounding a clear note above the diverse and sometimes ambivalent voices which

---

[2] E. T. May, *Barren in the Promised Land: Childless Americans and the Pursuit of Happiness* (Cambridge, MA, 1995), 153.
[3] May, *Barren in the Promised Land*, 182.

preceded him, Augustine declared that even 'if there had been no sin, marriage would have been worthy of the happiness of paradise, and would have given birth to children to be loved'.[4] Such a claim meant that even if Christianity did not proclaim the 'tragedy of childlessness'—and therefore cannot be complicit with a simple and robust pronatalism of the blood tie (or at least ought not to be complicit)—neither can it embrace an antinatalism which views children as a burden or an encumbrance and a threat to one's 'lifestyle'. Children belong to the happiness of paradise and are a blessing even outside its boundaries.

But if children are a blessing, the way in which they are so remains to be imagined—for here too, over the meaning and value of children, we find a site of cultural contestation (even amongst those who do indeed value them). We have already identified one attribute of the highly desired child of contemporary longing as revealed by patterns of use of the technologies of assisted reproduction (IVF, ICSI, and so on)—the longed-for child must be a child of one's own. But this, as we might say, is a necessary but by no means sufficient attribute of the wanted child of modernity. Who or what, more fully, is the child of modern desire? How is that child imagined and constructed? And how, if in contrast, is the child imagined by Christianity with its very own stories and rites for imagining and forming the child?

As a reflection on conception allowed us to consider the construction of kinship from one angle in the previous chapter, a turn to birth allows us to consider kinship through another lens. In the last chapter this consideration was conducted principally through construing and contesting the notion of the desperation of childlessness; in this chapter it will be conducted principally through seeking to construe and contest the highly (but conditionally) desired 'child of one's own' of late modernity. The aim will be to encourage Christian moral theology to overcome its primary focus on hard cases in this and other areas, and to develop instead an everyday ethics. It will do this as it turns towards social anthropology in search of the elements of a psychologically and a socio-culturally realistic understanding of contemporary forms of life, with which its own normative account may and must engage.

The path taken here is as follows. Section II looks at some of the rites according to which contemporary births are conducted (as these are explicated in a recent ethnography of the technocratic rites of the modern hospital). It notes that the dominant rites which mark and shape the once-born child of one's own are rites that deprive birth of other than chiefly technocratic meanings. Turning (in section III) to Christian rites, I consider how they mean to construe and construct the twice-born child, briefly contrasting (in section IV) the conditionality of the modern valuation of the child with the representation of the child as gift in Christianity's central rite of reception for the newborn.

---

[4] Augustine, *City of God*, trans. H. Bettenson (Harmondsworth, 1984), Book xiv, chapter 23, 585.

It is vital to stress at the outset that this chapter can only offer very preliminary and partial reflections on the cultural significance of the child of one's own of contemporary imagination. While I have placed this child in the context of ARTs in the last chapter and of rites of birthing in this, a fuller discussion would have to consider the desire for parenthood in a wider context that would include, for example, changing patterns of sexual relationship and marriage. Thus it might be argued that the child has now taken on a significance in cementing relationships that were previously cemented by sexual intercourse—it's a child of *our* own which makes *us* us, whereas once it was the sexual union of flesh which served that purpose.[5]

II BIRTHING THE ONCE-BORN CHILD

Who or what are modern children? Why do we want them? And how are they fashioned or made? These are surprisingly difficult questions to answer—but questions which properly press upon us if we are to understand the making and status of the child who turns out to be such a culturally ambivalent object.

Philippe Ariès famously and controversially claimed that childhood was invented or discovered only sometime from the late thirteenth century onwards—or rather, perhaps he didn't, but based on a mistranslation, was thought to have claimed it.[6] Either way, his work gave rise to a series of rebuttals aimed at showing that childhood really did exist at times and places he is supposed to have said it didn't. The controversial claim was taken to be that it was only from the thirteenth century on that childhood was identified as a stage of life importantly distinct from other stages; previously children had been merely small adults. Like many other daring and dashing scholarly theses, this one did not withstand sustained scrutiny and was moderated to become the still-important point that 'childhood has a history'—which is probably what Ariès meant in the first place.

As well has having a history, childhood has an anthropology—since there not only have been but are many and diverse ways of creating and shaping a child. And the subtitle (*Cherubs, Chattel, Changelings*) of a recent survey entitled *The Anthropology of Childhood* indicates something of the range of currently (as well as historically) favoured constructions of the child.[7]

---

[5] I borrow this important observation from a perceptive report from one of the readers of this manuscript for Oxford University Press.

[6] P. Ariès, *Centuries of Childhood: A Social History of Family Life* (London, 1979), published in French in 1960 and first translated in 1962. For the contention that Ariès indeed meant only that 'childhood has a history' and for an account of some of the controversy, see H. Cunningham, 'Histories of Childhood', *The American Historical Review*, 103 (1998), 1197–99.

[7] D. Lancy, *The Anthropology of Childhood: Cherubs, Chattel, Changelings* (Cambridge, 2008).

The author of that volume, which attempts to provide a survey of recent anthropological work, characterizes the modern child of North America and Europe as the cherub mentioned in his subtitle. He finds the beginnings of modern childhood some 150 years ago, following here V. Zelizer's *Pricing the Priceless Child: The Changing Social Value of Children*.[8] According to Zelizer, it was in late nineteenth-century America that the 'essential condition of contemporary childhood' came into being, laying the grounds for the triumph in the twentieth century of the 'economically useless but emotionally priceless child'.[9] For a whole host of reasons, children were no longer valued chiefly for their labour, but now as emotional and affective assets, treasured for their 'sentimental worth'; as Lancy puts it, 'for their contribution to parents' *emotional* wellbeing rather than to their *material* comfort'.[10] It is this child, the 'sacred child' in Zelizer's description[11]—the child as an essential component in an emotionally and sentimentally satisfying form of life in the family—which we moderns have invented and shaped and to which we have given such cultural significance and value. Something of the nature of the high valuation of the child in this conception is revealed in that perfectly understood, if perfectly loaded question: 'do you have a family?'.[12]

Given the contemporary valuation of the sacred child, we would surely hesitate to accuse another commentator of exaggeration when he remarks that 'Today, as perhaps never before, we are obsessed with kids. We come close to worshipping them in our family photo albums, vacation splurges, holiday giving, and even religious services.'[13] The 'god-like cherubs', as Lancy terms them, of the modern cult of the child,[14] like other objects of worship, receive offerings and sacrifices, regularly made. Most of us could provide examples of such sacrifices, but a glance at a John Lewis catalogue featuring what used to be called 'pushchairs', now denominated 'child transport systems', with price tags of more than £1000, indicates one popular form of the devotion required from the worshippers. But the devotion demanded is not only of material resources, but also of certain forms and levels of ongoing attention—thus in Sweden, to cite one ethnography, 'parents' anxiety concerning their infant's viability and... risks during childhood is much, much higher than "in sub-Saharan Africa and other places where the [actual] risks to infant survival are twenty-five times as high"'.[15] But perhaps the greatest devotion and attention is demanded not by a

---

[8] V. Zelizer, *Pricing the Priceless Child: The Changing Social Value of Children* (New York, 1985), 1.

[9] Zelizer, *Pricing the Priceless Child*, 209.

[10] Lancy, *The Anthropology of Childhood*, 110.

[11] Zelizer, *Pricing the Priceless Child*, 210.

[12] As G. Cross puts it, 'A child makes a couple into a family': *The Cute and the Cool: Wondrous Innocence and Modern American Children's Culture* (New York, 2004), 5.

[13] Cross, *The Cute and the Cool*, 4; cited by Lancy, 25.

[14] Lancy, *The Anthropology of Childhood*, 352.

[15] Lancy, *The Anthropology of Childhood*, 110, citing B. Welles-Nyström, 'Parenthood and Infancy in Sweden', *New Directions for Child and Adolescent Development*, 40 (1988), 75–96.

concern for a child's safety, but for their success: Adrie Kusserow's enthnography of child-rearing in three communities in New York makes for startling reading, especially in relation to the most privileged of the communities, where 'by age three Parkside children were already considered little competitors', directed by their parents to doing and being 'the best'.[16] 'Many parents experienced a great deal of angst over whether their child would perform well during the interview process in the preschool they had chosen'.[17] One father finds distinct parallels between raising a child and the venture capital business.

What the demands and expectations of the New York parents tell us, then, is that however tough life may be for the worshippers, the worshipped don't get off scot-free, so to speak. As Kusserow notes: 'The world the child enters is challenging and competitive'.[18] It can be tough to be worshipped—devotion so easily passes into surveillance, and a willingness to sacrifice to the god transmutes quite smoothly into demanding sacrifice from the god. Or, to put it in other terms, it is not children as such who are worshipped, for this worship is far from unconditional. Perhaps like many forms of worship, this worship rather noticeably has the nature of a bargain, since the child of one's own, merely by being one's own, meets only a necessary but by no means sufficient condition for being wanted.

What any further necessary and sufficient conditions may be, would be a matter for careful and further enquiry, and would surely defy any very simple statement since the construction of the modern child is a complex cultural process. We should, however, notice one crucial factor in determining the nature of the wanted (and worshipped) once-born child of the modern imagination. The construction of the modern child may be highly complex, but if we ask that classic childhood question, 'where do children come from?', one popular answer would surely be, 'from hospital'—and the hospital is indeed the place where that child is very likely born. And, so it has been argued, the technologization of hospital birth plays a central part in fashioning the child of our day.

'The birth process is a universal part of human female physiology and biology, but in recent decades anthropologists have come to understand that birth is almost never simply a biological act: on the contrary, as Brigitte Jordan has written, "birth is everywhere socially marked and shaped"'.[19] So say the editors of a recent collection of essays in the relatively new field of the anthropology of birth. Naturally enough, the marking and shaping of birth is a matter of how birth is practised. How, then, does our tribe practise birth? Judged against other practices and our own recent practice, what is most

---

[16] A. Kusserow, *American Individualisms: Child Rearing and Social Class in Three Neighbourhoods* (New York, 2004), 81.

[17] Kusserow, *American Individualisms*, 81.

[18] Kusserow, *American Individualisms*, 81.

[19] R. E. Davis-Floyd and C. F. Sargent, eds., *Childbirth and Authoritative Knowledge* (Berkeley, 1997), 1.

noticeable in the practice of birth in the modern West is chiefly its medicalization. The form of birthing we practise—which, whether for good or ill
is gaining an 'intensifying hegemony'[20] not only in the West but throughout
the world—is dubbed 'techno-birth' by Robbie Davis-Floyd, the author of an
influential study.

In that study, *Birth as an American Rite of Passage,* Davis-Floyd analyses the
hospital births that have become the norm in the US and in much of Europe,
replacing the tradition of home birth. These hospital births follow a set, highly
regimented, and remarkably standardized routine, which would be familiar
to many:

> The vast majority of women giving birth in American hospitals are dressed in a
> hospital gown, placed in a hospital bed, hooked up to an electronic fetal monitor
> and ordered not to eat; they have an intravenous needle inserted into their arm,
> are anesthetized to some degree, receive the synthetic hormone pitocin if their
> labor is not progressing rapidly and regularly, and have an episiotomy (a surgical
> incision of the vagina to widen the birth outlet.) Nearly one-quarter of all women
> giving birth in this country will do so this year by Cesarean section, perhaps the
> ultimate technological intervention.[21]

As Davis-Floyd sees it, however, the technology here is not mere technology—the use of which, as she says, would hardly merit comment since the
social use of tools and techniques is common to human societies. Rather this
technology has become 'technocratic'—and for Davis-Floyd, 'technocracy'
signifies the 'management of society by technical experts'. 'In hospital, birth
is . . . defined by its management by technical experts',[22] who deploy the technology technocratically, just in the sense of using it as a means to manage the
birthing process by imposing a pattern, logic, and meaning upon it.

According the Davis-Floyd's further argument, the 'pregnancy/childbirth
process in the United States' can be analysed as 'a year-long intitiatory rite
of passage' which serves to enrol the soon-to-be mother into the values and
beliefs of that technocratic model.[23] 'These rituals, also known as "standard
procedures for normal birthing", work to convey the core values of American
society to birthing women',[24] and they amount to 'a proliferation of rituals

---

[20] R. Davis-Floyd, *Birth as an American Rite of Passage* (Berkeley, 1992), 4.

[21] Davis-Floyd, *Birth as an American Rite of Passage*, 3–4. The figure of 25 per cent of births
being by caesarean is presumably for 1992; by 2011 the figure is said to be nearly 33 per cent,
up from 5 per cent in 1970—though there is great regional variation. See B. E. Hamilton, J.A.
Martin, and S. Ventura, 'Births: Preliminary Data for 2011', *National Vital Statistics Report,* 2012,
61:5, 1–20; cited in K. B. Kozhimannil, M. R. Law, and B. A. Virnig, 'Cesarean Delivery Rates
Vary Tenfold Among US Hospitals', *Health Affairs* 32:3 (2013), 527–535.

[22] Davis-Floyd, *Birth as an American Rite of Passage*, 319.

[23] Following the account of the stages and staging of a ritual as outlined in Arnold van Gennep's
early and influential account of rites of passage; see references in Chapter 7 in this volume.

[24] Davis-Floyd, *Birth as an American Rite of Passage*, 2.

surrounding this natural physiological event more elaborate than any hereto-
fore known in the "primitive world".[25]

The details of the argument need not concern us, but Davis-Floyd argues
that such standard procedures as regular cervical checks to monitor progress
during labour are at once 'invasive, disruptive and painful' and yet 'are neces-
sitated by the standardization of American birth, not by the physiological
needs of the birth woman and her child'.[26] And so for many features of the
year-long rite, of which birth is only the final step—these rites serve to teach
the woman to understand herself and her birth according to the meanings
technocracy dictates. These meanings, says Davis-Floyd, derive from the
seventeenth century's ambition to understand and treat the universe and
the human body as machines. Within this world view, the female body is
an especially recalcitrant machine, pregnancy and birth amount to a highly
dangerous pathology, and only technological assistance will ensure the survival of the mother and the delivery of a perfect baby as the end product of
the process.

Notice here—though this is not a central focus of Davis-Floyd's analysis—that technocracy recruits the mother to certain views not only of herself,
but of her child. It works, in other words, not only to control and define the
pregnancy and the birth but also to define and determine the child to which
the pregnancy is directed. And it does so by pathologizing the pregnancy as
risky—both in its progress and as a process aimed at delivering the perfect
child of technocratic imagining.

It is the practice of amniocentesis—powerfully illuminated in Rayna Rapp's
study *Testing Women, Testing the Fetus*—which is perhaps the starkest means
by which such a construction of the child is achieved or furthered. As Rapp
argues, the medical 'common sense' that emerges from the whole drama and
process of amniocentesis is one which treats the bearing of a so-called disabled
child as irrational or even immoral.[27] This is in spite of the genetic counselling,
which is central in this regard, wrapping itself in a myth of its being value-free
or neutral. As Rapp puts it:

---

[25] Davis-Floyd, *Birth as an American Rite of Passage*, 1–2.

[26] Davis-Floyd, *Birth as an American Rite of Passage*, 112: 'Any strategies, from ambulation
to breathing to taking showers, that the mother has developed for coping with her labor in her
own way can be disrupted by the frequent performance of vaginal exams "for her own good".
Brigitte Jordan. . . points out that such exams are only necessary under the technocratic model
that so drastically attempts to minimizes production time. In no other culture have such invasive, disruptive, and painful procedures been performed with such frequency and regularity as
in the American hospital. In Holland, a country whose infant mortality and Cesarean rates are
considerably lower than our own, such exams are considered necessary much less often than in
the United States—women are encouraged to push when they experience the urge to push, not
when and only when they cervix has reached the arbitrary standard of 10 centimeters dilation.'

[27] R. Rapp, *Testing Women, Testing the Fetus: The Social Impact of Amniocentesis in America*
(New York, 1999). See B. Brock's helpful discussion, 'Supererogation and the Riskiness of Human
Vulnerability', in *The Paradox of Disability*, ed. H. S. Reinders (Grand Rapids, MI, 2010) 127–39.

It is hard to argue for the neutrality of a technology explicitly developed to identify and hence eliminate fetuses with problem-causing chromosomes (and, increasingly, genes). The biomedical and public health interests behind the development and routinization of the technology itself evaluate such fetuses as expendable... [T]he very existence and routinization of the technology implies anything but neutrality. It assumes that scientific and medical resources should be placed in the service of prenatal diagnosis and potential elimination of fetuses bearing chromosome problems. In principle, then, counsellors are trained to offer a value-charged technology in a value-neutral manner.[28]

What we might say then, of the technologization of hospitalized birth, is just that it serves to draw not only the mother and her pregnancy but also the child into a logic of risk and danger—where risk and danger are understood in a particular way—and to remove the mother, the pregnancy, and the child from other possible defining logics and narratives, such as those of need, vulnerability, and care.

As this point makes clear and as Davis-Floyd notes, the imposition of technocratic meaning on pregnancy—the notion that pregnancy is a dangerous process which needs to be carefully managed if a healthy baby is to be born—is the denial to it of other meanings. As Davis-Floyd says, the present 'cultural treatment' of pregnancy is 'almost entirely medical. In this medicalization, we see a narrowing of the sets of symbols and meanings that our culture offers to pregnant women for interpreting their experiences.'[29] And the rise of techno-birthing has displaced what she refers to as 'spiritual or humanistic' rites of passage, which construct not only the mother but also the child.[30]

Whatever we make of Davis-Floyd's detailed claims and argument, that her analysis strikes a chord or reflects a general concern is evidenced in the widespread critique of the technologization of birth as threatening to deny

---

[28] Rapp, *Testing Women, Testing the Fetus*, 59.

[29] Davis-Floyd, *Birth as an American Rite of Passage*, 38.

[30] This narrowing or loss of meaning—this de-meaning of birthing—is perhaps most strongly felt during what Davis-Floyd treats as the very last stage of the pregnancy, the phase which 'begins and ends gradually during the newborn's first few months of life' and is sometimes 'experienced as "postpartum depression"' (*Birth as an American Rite of Passage*, 41). Although she includes it in her analysis of the ritualization of pregnancy, there is a strong sense at this point in her narrative, with the removal of the mother from the hospital, that the ritual is petering out. Indeed, she notes the concern of a British commentator, discussing childbirth in the UK, that 'the lack of effective rituals of reintegration in the West may be a major cause of postpartum depression among new parents'. This commentator, we are told, 'points out that after discharge from the hospital or the last visit from the midwife, the new mother often feels "utterly lost and alone". He recommends that a representative of society, such as a health care visitor or social worker, should go to the new mother's home to present her with a bouquet of flowers and a congratulations card, or that her religious institution collaborate with the clinic to provide her with some sort of reintegrative ceremony' (42). The recommendation is obviously well-meaning, but it has to be said that the vision of a health care or social worker armed with a bunch of flowers neither stirs the imagination nor seems to promise a wholly adequate acknowledgment of the experience of birthing and of the arrival of a child.

women an emotionally satisfactory (or 'real') birthing experience,[31] and more sharply still in counter-movements for home birthing. According, for example, to Klassen's study, *Blessed Events: Religion and Home Birth in America,* home births have come to provide a way of avoiding and protesting the technologization of birth which has become the dominant medical model, and a means of reclaiming birth as an ethical or religious events.[32]

Klassen's book is a 'study of a "resistance" movement'[33] amongst religious women, who choose home births and thus not only defy the medical establishment, but also wider social norms and expectations which have come to support the medicalization of birth. 'What these women shared, despite their different sorts of religious and spiritual allegiances, was a desire to situate birth within realms of meaning beyond the biological act itself'[34] and so to experience and frame birth in ways which are forbidden or at least occluded in the obstetrics ward. These women, she says, were looking for a 'deeply quotidian' 'sacrality', 'the everyday sacred',[35] in supposedly 'profane' domestic spaces[36]— and they did not find themselves assisted in this quest, she argues, by often highly problematic religious traditions.[37]

What matters for our discussion are not the details of these two works, but the nature of the general challenge or question which they pose to ethical thought and practice and to moral theology in particular. Birth has largely been removed from spheres in which its meaning is construed humanistically, to use Davis-Floyd's term. And yet the existence of the resistance movement is a sign of a sense of a resulting existential inadequacy, if the term be allowed. Birthing is not, contrary to its sequestration in the hospital, typically experienced even

---

[31] For references, see K. L. Michaelson, ed., *Childbirth in America: Anthropological Perspectives* (South Hadley, MA, 1988), Introduction.

[32] P. E. Klassen, *Blessed Events: Religion and Home Birth in America* (Princeton, 2001).

[33] Klassen, *Blessed Events*, 213.   [34] Klassen, *Blessed Events*, 4.

[35] Klassen, *Blessed Events*, 99.   [36] Klassen, *Blessed Events*, 97.

[37] '[I]n Western religions, women's actual experiences of birth have been sorely ignored and underritualized... [So] I ask not how religious traditions have ritualized birth or used it to make sense of human existence, but how birthing women use religion to make sense of their births, and how in turn they draw on birth to make meaning of their lives' (5). Even those of her informants, then, who acknowledge particular traditions, are driven to what she depicts as a creative and eclectic use of ideas—a 'religious bricolage' (15)—or even to a 'hybrid of perspectives', drawn from religious, 'alternative health', and feminist sources, in attempting to give sense and meaning to pregnancy. It is not to my immediate purpose to explore this interesting study in depth. It would be worth wondering, however, whether some of these or other home birthing protests at medicalization amount to more or less than the religious 'bricolage' which Klassen discerns: less in the sense that the search for a more 'authentic' birth has many analogues in a consumerist society, without needing any religious images or ideas to motivate or structure it; more in the sense that some of the births may make a more thorough and critical use of particular traditions than ideas of hybridity and bricolage may suggest. Klassen tends to rely on a familiar (but not unproblematic) contrast between religion and spirituality. Spiritual responses to and understandings of birth and birthing are 'personal', drawing on 'eclectic sources', whereas religious responses are said to draw on more traditional resources. For some of the difficulties with such a contrast, see C. Bender, *Heaven's Kitchen: Living Religion at God's Love we Deliver* (Chicago, 2003), 3ff.

so as a chiefly medical event, and the home-birth movement seeks to place birth in a context which will acknowledge the moral weight and significance of birthing. The challenge, then, for an everyday ethics is to narrate the moral significance or meaning which is or may be found in birth, notwithstanding the attempt to construe it in solely medical terms. Of course, since religious meanings and rites in birthing have themselves been displaced or pushed to the margins by technocratic meaning and rites, those who seek to resist the de-meaning of birth may not readily find resources for their resistance in a marginalized traditional religion. Moral theology may need, therefore, to connect and reflect explicitly on those resources which may have been eclipsed or occluded from its consciousness, even though they speak of its very own particular concerns.

We have said something of the wanted child of late modernity. That child is not simply the child of one's own, for in a variety of ways the worship of children seems distinctly conditional. And, in noticing the medicalization of birth, we have noted not only one of the most important influences on the shaping and defining of pregnancy and its product, but a key element in the construction of the conditionality that qualifies the wanted child—a conditionality to do here with need and disability. There is much more to be said about the wanted child of modern desire, since we have only stated some of the conditions which that child must satisfy. And there is more to be said about how we form and imagine this child, in countless ways, through schooling, familial socialization, more broadly through advertising and media, and through the general social reception and construction of pregnancy in accordance with certain more or less stringent demands and expectations. But however we finally and fully characterize this child and its formation, the once-born and wanted child of the modern West is especially significant as an emotional and sentimental asset, completing and creating the family, as the site of truly affective relationality.[38]

But let us note an irony here relating to our conditionally wanted cherub. May conjectures a sort of dismay as being fundamental to much contemporary

---

[38] It is striking to me that Lancy sees the hugely desired 'child of one's own' as serving a variety of needs but finally concludes that: 'Cherubic children are so attractive, so much a reflection of our longing for innocence and naivety—while still allowing us the pursuit of sensual indulgence and materialism—that they've become essential components of "the good life"... [For modern Americans and Europeans] "parenting" has become the ultimate hobby, allowing us to indulge our values and tastes in shaping a real live human being' (111). What is notable is the sheer inadequacy of this answer to the explanatory task. It should certainly seem to us curious (but not unprecedented), to find a work of anthropology which is somewhat anecdotal in its use of 'we', and thus less careful than in its use of an anthropological 'they'—but the further point is just that the crude characterization of the desire for children as tantamount to a choice of hobby surely fails to carry the weight it must bear. It is, after all, difficult to see the need upon which the 'tragedy of childlessness' is built—and the more specific 'chasing of the blood tie' which presupposes a need for a child of one's own—as adequately explained by appeal to parenting as even the 'ultimate hobby'.

child-bearing.[39] The family has become the site or at least the hoped-for site of relationships that will have an affective quality, a sentimentality if you like, that has been lost from a social world which is experienced as somewhat bleak. As May sees it, the combination of relatively low birth rates with the widespread acceptance of the tragedy of infertility is not so much paradoxical as two sides of the same coin—a despair at the world on the one side leads some to decline to reproduce, while on the other side it leads others to create for themselves families that will mitigate social isolation, lack of identity, or even alienation. And yet, if the story of amniocentesis tells us anything, it seems to tell us that the wanted child—or rather the conditionally wanted child—is now itself subject to the same harsh logic of the same harsh world which he or she was meant to re-enchant.

III BIRTHING THE TWICE-BORN CHILD

Genealogies must start somewhere—and that somewhere can never be the beginning. But even allowing for that, Lancy and Zelizer's genealogy of the late modern child starts a little late from a certain point of view—as well as ignoring the relatively recently significant fact that the modern child is not only born, but also conceived, so to say, in the hospital.

Lancy, following Zelizer, traces the origins of the modern 'innocent and fragile' child,[40] to some 150 years ago; but the emergence of any mid-Victorian cult of the child itself surely depends in turn on the earlier Romantic movement, and behind that, most obviously, on the reception of Rousseau's imaginings. Nothing amongst Christianity's many offences seems to have offended Enlightenment sensibilities quite as strongly as the idea of original sin, so that we might well say that the archetypal noble savage of eighteenth-century imagination, the one found on our very own shores, was the child, whose nurture and shaping would now be premised on a respect for an original innocence. (And anthropology, by the way, once liked to mix this up a bit by regarding savages as children and children as savages, as Montgomery points out.[41]) Rousseau's relationship to Augustine—or at least to the Augustinianism mediated to him by Pascal and La Rochefoucauld—is by no means simple.[42] What is clear enough, however, is that the generation after Rousseau turned quite

---

[39] May, *Barren in the Promised Land*, 207ff.

[40] Lancy, *The Anthropology of Childhood*, 13.

[41] H. Montgomery, *An Introduction to Childhood: Anthropological Perspectives on Children's Lives* (Chichester, 2010), ch. 1.

[42] Rousseau's account of a child's educational needs (in *Émile*) may be more subtle than has sometimes been allowed, but it doubtless expresses aspects of his complex and ambivalent yet essentially antithetical relationship to Augustinianism.

consciously against the very rite which was taken to express an Augustinian doctrine of the child. As Alfani and Gourdon note, 'At the time of the French Revolution, and particularly during the Thermidor period, an attempt was made by the "enlightened" elite to establish birth ceremonies entirely devoid of any reference to original sin, and structured as rites of acceptance of the infant within the "national community" and the family'.[43] (David Beckham may have been longing for such a service when he told the press that he and Victoria certainly wanted Brooklyn christened, but were not yet sure into which religion.)

Rousseau's heirs were right to turn against this rite—just in the sense that baptism stands firmly between the eighteenth century and the child of late modernity, contending as it does against the construction of the child as an innocent cherub or noble savage. But it contends against other constructions of children too. Put another way, the child who is not just born, but born again, is imagined in such a way as to contest many elements in the construction of the modern child. And this imagining of the child speaks to some of the silences that have been left by the medicalization of birth and birthing. So let us go back to just before Rousseau (though to rites which are still extant), to the Book of Common Prayer of 1662, but not first of all to baptism where we might expect to begin, but to a service entitled 'The Thanksgiving of Women After Child-Birth, Commonly Called, The Churching of Women'.

There is some difficulty over the interpretation of this rite. Keith Thomas seems responsible for some of more jaundiced readings of the service, with his comment that though Radical Protestants in the early seventeenth century came to blame the ceremony as one 'which breedeth and nourisheth many superstitious opinions in simple people's hearts', 'a fairer view would have to regard the ritual as a result of such opinions, rather than the cause'.[44] (This seems somewhat like saying that it is better to regard *Mein Kampf* as arising from anti-semitism than as causing it. As fairness goes, it doesn't help the case for the defence greatly.) The negative interpretation is taken up by Coster,[45] but countered by Cressy.[46]

In broad terms, Coster sees the service as one of purification (as it was so named in the Sarum Missal and in the 1549 Prayer Book, where the service

---

[43] Alfani and Gourdon, eds., *Spiritual Kinship in Europe, 1500–1900*, 'Introduction', 28. Interestingly these rites sometimes preserved roles for godparents even though 'these godfathers and godmothers were no longer considered as actors in a spiritual rebirth of the child'; 29.

[44] K. Thomas, *Religion and the Decline of Magic* (London, 1971), 43, citing J. Canne's, *A Necessitie of Separation* of 1634.

[45] W. Coster, 'Purity, Profanity and Puritanism: The Churching of Women, 1500–1700', *Studies in Church History*, xxvii (1990), 377–87.

[46] D. Cressy, 'Purification, Thanksgiving and the Churching of Women in Post-Reformation England', *Past and Present*, 141 (1993), 106–146. And see further, D. Cressy, *Birth, Marriage and Death: Ritual, Religion and the Life-Cycle in Tudor and Stuart England*, new ed. (Oxford, 1999).

is essentially a translation of the Sarum rite) and highly objectionable,[47] whereas Cressy sees it as chiefly a service of thanksgiving (as it is named ten years later in the Prayer Books of 1559 and 1662), and as one which women valued in allowing them their day in church, so to speak—and a good party afterwards.[48] These modern-day battlelines mark out the divisions in the sixteenth and seventeenth centuries, with Protestants finding elements of purification (which they judged Jewish and/or Popish) even within the service that was named a thanksgiving, whereas its defenders found only thanksgiving.

It seems to have become something of a commonplace in the early to mid-twentieth century that the rite was so irreducibly superstitious—or to use Keith Thomas' words, that so many 'sundry superstitions'[49] had attached to it—as for it to be beyond redemption.[50] To the simple moralist, however, the service is, certainly in the 1662 version, chiefly a thanksgiving (as Cressy holds), whatever associations it may have gathered in popular use. The new mother is directed by the rubrics to come to church 'at the usual time after her delivery',[51] and is there exhorted to 'give hearty thanks unto God' for her 'safe deliverance' and

---

[47] Coster suggests that the rite was essentially one of re-entry into society: 'In the past the ceremony of churching was the only means by which, after childbirth, a woman could return to the community of the Church, and indeed to society in general' ('Purity, Profanity and Puritanism: The Churching of Women, 1500–1700', 377) As such, Coster sees the service as chiefly to do with impurity. He takes in particular the wearing of a veil (which is what 'decently apparelled' in the rubrics was generally taken to mean) as a sign of uncleanness: 'Insistence on the veil seems to undermine the argument that the ceremony was merely a thanksgiving' (384). (Certainly, as he notes, the attempt by Laudians to insist on the veil caused controversy.) Similarly he construes the bringing of an offering and kneeling 'in some convenient place, as hath been accustomed, or as the Ordinary shall direct' (usually near the altar, in a special pew) in the same terms. Thus his negative conclusion—'The need for such a ceremony seems to indicate a very low general opinion of sex, childbirth, and women in early modern England'. It has to be said, that Coster's ability to be affronted by the service is very finely honed—he finds, for example, the use of Psalm 121 (I have lifted up mine eyes unto the hills) 'magical' and otherwise 'offensive'. I've tried reading Psalm 121 many times in an attempt to find it either magical or offensive, but my efforts have been miserable failures. (Coster's sensibilities in this regard rather put one in mind of the woman who calls a policeman to report the scandalous doings at No. 24 just across the road, which she can see from her window. The policeman can see nothing, however. 'You have to stand on a chair', she explains.)

[48] Cressy thinks in the revised services, the woman was not 'a penitent' but a 'celebrant' ('Purification, Thanksgiving and the Churching of Women in Post-Reformation England', 119), offering contrary readings of the details to Coster's.

[49] Thomas, *Religion and the Decline of Magic*, 41.

[50] Though intriguingly Coster mentions ('Purity, Profanity and Puritanism', 386), that 'In the 1950s sociologists working in East London still found over 90 per cent of mothers participating in the ceremony'—referencing M. Young and P. Wilmot, *Family and Kinship in East London* (London, 1957). And interestingly, when I gave this chapter in its earlier lecture form, a number of women came up and shared their recollections of taking part in 'churchings' in the 1960s and even later.

[51] The norm, according to Coster was about a month, though there was much variation either side of that number; see 'Purity, Profanity and Puritanism: The Churching of Women, 1500–1700', 380–382.

preservation in 'the great danger of Child-birth'. The priest then says one of two psalms. The second, Psalm 127, declares:

> Lo, children and the fruit of the womb: are an heritage and gift that cometh of the Lord…Like as arrows in the hand of the giant: even so are the young children. Happy is the man that hath his quiver full of them: they shall not be ashamed when they speak with their enemies in the gate.

Between the mid-sixteenth and well into the nineteenth century infant mortality within the first year of life seems to have hovered around 15 per cent,[52] so on very many occasions this psalm would plainly have been inappropriate. The alternative, Psalm 116, would surely have been preferred:

> The snares of death compassed me round about and the pains of hell gat hold upon me.…Thou hast delivered my soul from death: mine eyes from tears, and my feet from falling. I found trouble and heaviness, and I called upon the Name of the Lord

—and so on. The service concludes with prayers (including the Lord's Prayer and responses)—the final prayer giving thanks again for deliverance from the 'great pain and peril of child-birth'.

The ceremony functions then, as a thanksgiving, either for the mother's survival and for the birth of a child, or simply for the former.[53] I will come back to the nature of the thanksgiving for a child in a moment, but let me quickly note how this rite serves, implicitly at least, to mark and attend to aspects of birth and birthing which are unspoken, overlooked, or discounted by the secular rites of hospital birth, in general cultural consciousness, and even perhaps in much contemporary religious practice.

First, and in all cases, it invites and allows the woman to place the fact of her giving birth in a public context of meaning and recognition, which thereby acknowledges the significance of the experience and endurance of birthing as of social and existential moment. It invites a woman to claim and reclaim the story of the birth of a child as one which can and must be narrated within a wider than medical frame of meaning, as part not of a neutral, profane, or private world, but of a moral, religious, and communal one.

Second, where there has been a stillbirth or a very early death (and therefore no christening and possibly no funeral), the ceremony amounted to a public acknowledgement of a loss which in our day is still very often concealed or

---

[52] See E. A. Wrigley and R. S. Schofield, *The Population History of England 1541–1871* (London, 1981), 249. And notice that the figure for the children of labourers is, even in 1913, much the same; see H. Hendrick, *Children, Childhood and English Society, 1880–1990* (Cambridge, 1997), 51.

[53] As Cressy puts it ('Purification, Thanksgiving and the Churching of Women in Post-Reformation England', 145): 'the cermony celebrated [the woman's] survival, and offered the comforts of religion. It recognized her endurance of the pains and the perils of childbearing, and focused on the woman rather than her baby. It was fundamentally, a thanksgiving. Was it also a purification? Only if she thought herself unclean.'

denied in diverse ways. Until very recently in the UK the standard procedure for dealing with stillbirths was simply to remove the baby as quickly as possible, prior to issuing what was termed 'the stillbirth *disposal* certificate'. (The word has now been changed, after much campaigning, to 'burial'.) In the UK, one in 200 babies is stillborn and 30 per cent of these are born at full term.[54] Again, the cultural denial of the loss of a stillborn child as something more than a merely medical anomaly, is stoutly resisted by this public and communal rite, which could accommodate, acknowledge, and comfort the grieving.

Third, the thanksgiving for survival makes an important point even in the West where (at least for most women) childbearing does not carry the risks it did even quite recently. Globally, according to an analysis published in the Lancet in 2010, some 343,000 women died in childbirth in 2008.[55] There are vast variations between countries and vast variations within them. In whole swathes of Africa the mortality rate is more than a hundred times higher than in most of Europe, and the deaths which give the US its place at number 39 in the table (with a higher death rate than Albania and Lithuania, at 16.7 deaths per 100,000) are plainly not evenly distributed throughout the US, but like infant mortality, fall heaviest on particular classes and ethnic groups. Thus to give thanks for deliverance, as the rite does, remains powerful and appropriate not only for the woman herself, but also socially as a mark of recognition of a world in which maternal survival is not to be taken for granted.

But let us go back to the psalm of thanksgiving, Psalm 127. What precisely is the thanksgiving for? This question is crucial to understanding the child imagined by these rites. The psalm declares—as do other psalms—that children are 'an heritage and gift from the lord' and that 'Happy is the man that hath his quiver full of them: they shall not be ashamed when they speak with their enemies in the gate.'[56]

Over the interpretation of these and the similar verses in Psalm 128 (127 in his numbering), Augustine shows a very noticeable degree of anxiety, determined to insist that we cannot 'refer [such] promises... [that is for many children] to this-worldly happiness',[57] for so to read them would be to show ourselves to be 'carnally-minded, with no sensitivity to anything that concerns the Spirit of God.'[58] Children are 'temporal blessings' but birds have offspring too, and it

---

[54] See the extensive *Lancet* series on stillbirth for full data.

[55] See M. C. Hogan et al., 'Maternal Mortality for 181 Countries, 180-2008: a Systematic Analysis of Progress Towards Millennium Development Goal 5', *Lancet*, 375 (2010), 1609–1623.

[56] The thought that children are a blessing is, of course, something of a commonplace in the psalms—and is taken up again in the very next psalm, 128, which might have served just as well for a thanksgiving: 'Blessed are all they that fear the Lord: and walk in his ways... Thy wife shall be as the fruitful vine: upon the walls of thine house. Thy children like the olive-branches: round about thy table.'

[57] Augustine, *Expositions of the Psalms*, in *The Works of Saint Augustine: A Translation for the 21st Century*, pt. 3, in 6 volumes (Hyde Park, NY, 2000-4), trans. M Boulding, Psalm 127, section 2; all further references will be to Psalm and section number.

[58] Augustine, *Expositions of the Psalms*, Psalm 127, section 2.

is worth remembering that children 'are born to push you aside[.] All new-born children tacitly say to their parents, "Get out of the way, it's our show now"'. Thus if 'we still enjoy the children who displace us' says Augustine, much more should we 'rejoice in the children with whom we shall live for ever',[59] the spiritual children of whom the psalms truly speak.

What, we may wonder, prevented a 'carnally minded' interpretation of the service of Thanksgiving? What prevented the clannish reading of the psalm which Augustine himself means to block? Well, the answer is that the baptism which would typically have preceded the Churching resolutely refuses (as I have previously remarked and now want to note more carefully) any understanding of children as an addition to a tribe whose strength is in numbers and ties of blood.

The rite of Baptism from the Book of Common Prayer, which shares its central features with other early rites, has no recognized place for the parents.[60] The parents, it is true, are to give notice of the baptism, but then they disappear from the rubrics—since the rite intends that 'this child' will receive 'that thing which by nature he cannot have', namely regeneration, naturally the mere generators are somewhat besides the point. Thus the rubrics tell us that 'the Godfathers and Godmothers, and the people with the Children, must be ready at the font'. There is no mention of the parents. It is the godparents who are addressed on the child's behalf and who must answer for the child; there is again no mention of the parents. It is the godparents who are asked to name the child after the 'priest shall take the Child into his hands'—and by implication (and tradition), and most dramatically of all, it will be the godparents who receive the child back from the priest after the child has been dipped in the water, 'discreetly and warily'. And it is the godparents who are addressed by the minister at the end with the solemn recitation of their duties towards the child.

Via the rite of baptism, with its starring role for godparents, the Christian reconception of kinship as spiritual kinship was universalized—it was not left in the monastery or reserved to esoteric sects or factions. It took its place at the centre of Christian life in a rite for the reception of each and every child, creating for them a new kinship of godmothers, godfathers, and of god-siblings, too.[61]

Yes—but what did all this amount to? If the form of baptism is a most remarkable sign of a rather striking and resolute repudiation of the very idea of a 'child of one's own' and refuses any interpretation of the rite as the reception of a new member of a clan, how did that repudiation work itself out, if at all? The

---

[59] Augustine, *Expositions of the Psalms*, 127, 15.

[60] Compare *Rituale Romanum*, 'Rules for Administering Baptism', 34.

[61] I noted in the last chapter, with regret, the insinuation of parents into modern Roman Catholic rites of baptism, as into recent Anglican services. One might also note the trend in certain modern contexts for the 'familialization' of godparenthood, as Alfani and Gourdon term it: 'The movement towards eventually keeping godparenthood within the family, and towards perceiving the ceremony as a celebration of the family, which we call "familialization", is undeniable. A recent enquiry into the Italian case showed, for example, that in the 1980s, three-quarters

title of a certain book, *When Children Became People: The Birth of Childhood in Early Christianity*, may risk over-egging the pudding.[62] The invention of a new sensibility towards what may then be figured as a freshly constituted moral subject is always likely to be an extremely complex matter—Peter Brown's story of the invention of the poor as objects of moral concern during the ebbing of the Roman Empire provides a case in point.[63] But the question very certainly has to be asked whether some analogous story can be persuasively told about the emergence of children as newly morally significant at the very same period of the later empire's decline—and further, perhaps, whether this emergence can be linked to the reconception of the child by means of the rite of baptism as the most significant element in the Christian re-imagining of children.

A full case for the emergence of a newly moralized child could not be made briefly and is beyond the scope of this chapter, but any such case would very likely point to one prominent shift in practice at this time which we may pause to note. In the Roman world where children were valued economically (that is, not only economically but explicitly economically), a child had a changeable, uncertain value. A child could be either a vital contributor to the present and future economy of the family or alternatively (in different economic conditions with too many siblings or simply as the wrong sex), a burden on the household. The practice of *expositio* (that is, the exposure of newborn children), though locally varied in its very practice and prevalence, was nonetheless a 'perfectly legal and socially acceptable'[64] means of managing the size of a family, and is surely the most telling mark of a child's socially insecure valuation, a valuation which was all the more fragile for girls. We should beware of any *post hoc, propter hoc* inference—but a case for a new valuation of children with the coming of Christianity would note that the outlawing of infanticide by Constantine in 318 and the practice of exposing children by Valentinian in 384 certainly did occur after that 'moment' at the Milvian Bridge.[65]

of godparents were selected from close kin, with uncles and aunts of the baptized being the most common choice': *Spiritual Kinship in Europe, 1500–1900*, 30.

[62] O. M. Bakke, *When Children Became People: The Birth of Childhood in Early Christianity* (Minneapolis, 2005).

[63] P. Brown, *Poverty and Leadership in the Later Roman Empire* (Hanover, NH, 2002). For a clear account of the subtleties involved in judging the significance of Christianity on a broad range of matters to do with the family, see A. Giardina, 'The Family in the Later Roman World', 392–415 in *The Cambridge Ancient History*, vol. xii, 2nd ed., eds. A. K. Bowman, A. Cameron, and P. Garnsey (Cambridge, 2005).

[64] M. Corbier, 'Child Exposure and Abandonment', in *Childhood, Class and Kin in the Roman World*, ed. S. Dixon (London, 2001), 66: 'to the question of how common and how wide-ranging the practice of exposure was, we can only respond as follows: over the centuries, whatever its precise legal basis, the exposure of newborn babies in Rome was perfectly legal and socially acceptable'.

[65] See Giardina's summary of Constantine's laws relating to family matters: 'Insofar as the moral code of a minority group can be expected to influence the laws and ancient traditions of a large empire in a short space of time, this set of measures unequivocally shows the mark of Christianity' ('The Family in the Late Roman World', 393).

That is only to note one striking change during the late empire—it is not to begin to make the sort of case, such as Brown makes for the poor, which would indeed need to be made to carry the argument. It is perhaps enough to say that there was something of a change in sensibility; if not a revolution, then certainly a shift. Dixon—whom Bakke judges the most insistent spokesperson for the 'sentimental ideal' of Roman family—admits that 'the modern concern for child welfare had no real equivalent in the ancient world. Depending on their social standing, young children were routinely apprenticed, put to heavy labour, sexually exploited, or beaten by schoolteachers.'[66] We know that not all this changed under Christianity—indeed the woes of the life of the Roman child don't look radically different from the woes of life in an English public school in the mid-1970s perhaps. But something had and did change with the coming of Christianity in its relativizing of the claims of pagan familial bonds—even if those good old family values refused simply to die.[67]

However this may be, we know, as Lancy says, the evidence is that 'for much of human history, children were, and still are in most parts of the world, treated as a commodity. Children...assist with the care of younger siblings, and they do farm work. They may be sold into slavery, sent to urban areas to fend for themselves in the streets, or their wages incorporated into the family's budget'[68]—and they may serve as soldiers. Thus the existence of a rite which denies the existence of the child of one's own is by no means superfluous—not even in our own context, for even if the worthless and priceless modern child may not be a chattel (as simply saleable), the management of the child has something of the character, it must be said, of asset management.

---

[66] Bakke, *When Children Became People*, 54–55, quoting S. Dixon, *The Roman Family* (Baltimore, 1992).

[67] The subtleties here are nicely captured in Janet Nelson's remark that the task of the ecclesiastical historian, in relation to the study of children, is to 'identify within the Christian tradition the contribution of the Church, its personnel, its theorists, its institutions, to the processes whereby childhood was defined, moulded, embodied and used. It was not only for the Church that parents produced children—though churchmen often taught the "order of married persons" to that effect. But the Church did condition the manifestations of parental feeling; and in societies polarized between rich and poor, noble and low-born, the Church preached ideas about childhood which transcended, and perhaps modified, a social reality in which some children (like some adults) were so much more equal than others. For their part, parents, which is to say the vast majority of the laity, exerted a steady pressure on the Church to express, reinforce, sacralize their attitudes to and treatment of children, and hence the process of social reproduction itself. Parents and churchmen acted on each other to construct what childhood should be: generation upon generation of real children constituted the great laboratory in which the work went on.' This astute remark highlights something of the difficulty of isolating causal factors in the midst of complex social change, in which the church in its various guises, may itself function as an effective spokesperson for values which it should, by its own lights, repudiate. J. Nelson, 'Parents, Children, and the Church in the Earlier Middle Ages', in *The Church and Childhood*, ed. D. Wood (Oxford, 1994), 82–83.

[68] Lancy, *The Anthropology of Childhood*, 12.

So in connection with that thought, let us return finally to the service of baptism, with its own solemn final instruction to the child's godparents that 'ye shall provide, that he may learn the Creed, the Lord's Prayer, and the Ten Commandments, in the vulgar tongue'—its solemnity underlined by the immediate and further instruction that the child be brought to the bishop 'so soon as he can say the Creed, the Lord's Prayer, and the Ten Commandments, in the vulgar tongue'.

I use the language of the Book of Common Prayer, which with its 'child...he' does not conform to current patterns of gender neutrality in its language—though it is interesting to find Archbishop Laud declining to instruct a princess royal he baptized on 4 November 1631 to 'fight manfully under Christ's banner', since the phrase, as he said, 'appertaynes not naturally to the female sex'.[69] So let us note, before we mark the significance of the *telos* which these words lay out for the child, that the service is, no matter its lack of inclusive language, wholly indifferent to the sex of the child—and thereby again deeply countercultural in very many cultural contexts, and certainly in its original cultural context. The single rite is provided for each and every child. But on this one layer of counterculturalness it lays another—setting confirmation as the goal and purpose of a child's upbringing. For what is explicit here is the imagining of each and every child, male or female, as first of all a moral and spiritual being, worthy of education in relation to this aspect of their being. When education is in danger of becoming a form of work in preparation for work, the imagining of a child as first of all and above all addressed by the word of God, invites a framing of the child in higher terms than some other readily available and quite popular alternative constructions.

IV 'SERIOUS AND SAD IN THEIR PLEASURES'

According to Tocqueville's celebrated observation, 'In America I have seen the freest and best educated of men in circumstances the happiest to be found in the world, yet it seemed to me that a cloud habitually hung on their brow, and they seemed serious and almost sad in their pleasures.'[70]

I can't help thinking that this remark has a relevance, not only to America, in relation to one of the supposed pleasures of late modernity. For the once-born child, the child of one's own of contemporary imagining, that priceless

---

[69] Cited by B. Cummings, *The Book of Common Prayer* (Oxford, 2011), note to 412, on 776—though I am not entirely sure whether the archbishop would have preferred that she should 'fight womanfully' or rather that she should not fight at all.

[70] A. de Tocqueville, *Democracy in America*, trans. G. Lawrence, ed. J. P. Mayer (New York, 1969), 565.

emotional asset and supposed *sine qua non* of the sentimentally fulfilled life, is a pleasure about which we are remarkably ambivalent, serious and sad. This child, after all, has a curious valence in our contemporary world. A child is at once, though for different people or at different times, the most wanted and the most dreaded of objects. For those taught to believe in the desperation of infertility, children are that without which life lacks meaning and purpose; and yet for the unwelcomely pregnant or for those pregnant with children who are not perfect, they are a most dire threat to their lives, meaning, and purpose, of which they are taught to rid themselves. The modern child is desired but also dreaded. And he or she is also innocent and yet (especially if a she) sexualized to a striking degree; is protected by ever more constraining forms of surveillance and yet abused and exploited not only by random individuals, but systematically and commercially by trades in child pornography and prostitution (and even, most shamefully, within the church); is cosseted and treated as a pet on one side of the globe, while on the other side child labour supplies the goods that sustain the luxury those privileged children enjoy (or from which they suffer); and removed from the world of work in the West, yet placed in a system of education that seems more and more designed to manufacture the highly skilled workers demanded by our economies. The modern child is a very curious thing indeed. De Tocqueville mentions a cloud hanging on the American brow in relation to some of their pleasures; here the cloud looks more like a pall of very dark smoke.

In rural northern Greece, certain funeral laments are the origin and basis of certain wedding songs.[71] Why? The connection is that in weddings and funerals there is a separation—someone is taken from a family; they are removed from their home; they leave their friends and their regular connections; they pass from one place to another. Thus the songs can serve for both occasions.

It is the 'passing over' and 'separation' which provide the common thread—and in baptism, too, there is a separation and passing over, just as in a wedding and a funeral. And it is a moment of high symbolism—even in rites that have insinuated parents into a service from which they are properly displaced. For a brief moment the child is handed over to the minister—who will, in due course, hand the child back, newly emerging from the waters of the font. What godparents and parents are invited to imagine and acknowledge, and here enact, is that a child must and may be received as a gift. The child, so this rite imagines, is never, ever really ours. We do not own them. They are not possessions and they are not property, not ours to be disposed of or shaped as we will. They are not to be fashioned and bent to our purposes, only turned towards the word of God which addresses them. And they are only properly received when they are received as gifts from the hands of God—which is why adoption

---

[71] For details, see L. M. Danforth, *The Death Rituals of Rural Greece* (Princeton, 1982), discussed in Chapter 6.

might have some claim to model an archetype of parenthood for those who are themselves children by adoption.

This and the previous chapter have merely begun to chart some of the highly various personal, social, and technological meanings with which having and not having children are currently imbued. Taken together, however, the chapters suggest that Christianity offers a solemn and challenging and yet, in contrast to our sad pleasures, a joyful scripting of birth in its ritualized and symbolic reimagination of the child. What it denies is both the tragedy of childlessness and the existence of the child of one's own as the answer to that tragedy; what it asks us to imagine and to enact is a kinship beyond biology, in which the child is to be received as gift.

4

Regarding Suffering: On the Discovery of the Pain of Christ, the Politics of Compassion, and the Contemporary Mediation of the Woes of the World

I INTRODUCTION: ON NOTICING THE CROSS

I have been asking how the Christian imagination of certain moments in Christ's earthly life represented (and thus shaped and conditioned) human life. And I have asked how this imagining stands in critical relation to other imaginings and practices of human being. I have turned especially to social anthropology for descriptions and understandings of these contemporary forms of the social, arguing that moral theology finds here a better conversation partner than in moral philosophy, which should largely be left to its own (very curious) devices. In making this turn away from moral philosophy and in encouraging this conversation with social anthropology, we can begin to conceive a slightly different moral theology—not one chiefly of hard cases, but one devoted instead to framing and constructing an everyday ethics that would speak of the quotidian meanings and shapings of and responses to conception, birth, suffering, death, and burial.

In this chapter I ask questions specifically about the imagination of Christ's suffering in the Christian tradition and the role it has played—and may continue to play—in shaping human sensibilities. In particular I ask what significance it may have for what is termed 'the politics of compassion'.

The question of suffering has been a question about many things—including, most famously perhaps, a question about whether suffering is compatible with the existence of a good God. This is not, however, the question here. My concern is with the challenge that suffering poses to the practical, not the theoretical reason— that is, first to our action in the world, not to our understanding. And in considering the role of suffering in relation to human action, I begin by considering the centrality of the suffering of Christ in the Christian imagination and more widely.

The insinuation of the cross into Western life and thought is so thorough that, somewhat paradoxically, we may hardly notice its presence. Its cultural reach into our languages (spoken and visual) is such that it is everywhere and hence, in a sense, nowhere, all at the same time. Thus we may fail to find it at all remarkable that the chief executive of a FTSE 100 company having to announce poor trading figures, or a football manager losing yet another game, can expect, according to the reporters, to be 'crucified' by the shareholders or the fans. We wander through the great galleries of Europe and North America and do not think especially noteworthy the depictions of suffering, pain, misery, torment, and death—though this would be highly remarkable, so I suspect, to, say, Chinese visitors. Similarly, we are barely aware of the incongruity of crosses (the Romans' most gruesome, and for that very reason, sometimes favoured mode of execution) hung nonchalantly from earrings as mere fashion accessories; think of hanging a small electric chair from your ears, and the concealed incongruity should become apparent.[1]

There was a time, however, even in the Christian era, when the cross did not enjoy—or suffer from—its current ubiquity. Its present invisibility is a function of that ubiquity, but for a large part of Christian history the cross and the suffering of Christ which it represents, was itself more straightforwardly absent from view. So, our first question poses itself immediately. When and why was the suffering of Christ discovered?

I turn from that question (in section II) to what we might be tempted to think of as the discovery of suffering in contemporary social anthropology (in section III). This discovery was itself a response to a contemporary anxiety about the adequacy and effectiveness of the representation of suffering—and about the consequent viability of a politics of compassion. In a very recent work by Didier Fassin, however, we find not a concern about the viability of that politics (the politics of humanitarian reason, as he calls it), but about its consistency and moral adequacy. I turn then (in section IV) to consider the nature and possibility of a Christian response of Fassin's highly ambivalent appraisal of contemporary humanitarianism. I suggest first, that the deep appropriation of Christ's suffering in Christian life and thought amounts to what Foucault called a 'technology of the self', and must be distinguished from mere spectatorship; and second, that the proper practice of this appropriation, such as in the L'Arche communities, allows for a more thorough humanitarianism than that which is the object of Fassin's critique. In conclusion (in section V), I simply note that the mere awareness that compassion does indeed have a genealogy, however it is recounted, suggests that an everyday ethics, Christian or otherwise, must take seriously the matter of the cultural representation of suffering to which we now attend.

---

[1] A point made by G. Howes in *The Art of the Sacred* (London, 2007).

II DISCOVERING THE SUFFERING OF CHRIST

Early iconography shows a distinct lack of interest in the suffering of Christ. Certainly the very earliest depictions we have of Christ on the cross do not conform to later expectations. Take, for example, one of four ivory carvings that make up the sides of a small casket now in the British Museum, and probably made in Rome sometime between 420 and 430 (see Plate 2). The immediately preceding scene has Christ on his way to Golgotha—the cross is casually slung across his shoulder, and the sandalled and toga-clad figure with well-coiffured hair could be undertaking a country walk rather than being marched to his death. Consistent with that image, in the crucifixion panel itself a powerful, athletic figure, head held high and eyes open, confidently looks out at us, the halo about his head signalling the dignity of his composed and majestic death, contrasted sharply with Judas's ignominious suicide on the left.[2] There is none of the pain or suffering or grief that we now associate with Christ's death—as it has been mediated to us through later paintings (such as the celebrated crucifixion in Grünewald's *Isenheim Altarpiece*, see Plate 3), but also through passion plays and hymns, through prayers, and through Bach's two great passions, all of which invite and require us to attend very closely to a Christ who knows agony and pain.[3]

The early iconographic representation of a Christ who does not appear to suffer, even in his crucifixion, seems to be of a piece with early theological representations. Thus in sermons near enough contemporary with that ivory casket, St Augustine seems generally uninterested in a suffering Christ.

What may strike us first of all is the relatively small number of the nearly 750 extant sermons[4] directly concerned with Christ's passion. In the occasional sermons, collected according to liturgical season, there are only four on 'The Lord's Passion', compared with fifteen or so on Christmas Day, with very many more on the resurrection, and with some fifty or so on the feast days of diverse martyrs. Even when we add to the total for the passion nine sermons commenting on the relevant chapters of the Gospel of John, and

---

[2] For the ivory panels and their interpretation as pointing to Christ's victory and not his suffering, see e.g. N. MacGregor, *Seeing Salvation: Images of Christ in Art* (London, 2000), 122–25, or alternatively, *The Image of Christ*, ed. G. Finaldi (London, 2000), the catalogue of the exhibition 'Seeing Salvation' at London's National Gallery, 108–109. For a fuller treatment of these images in their wider iconographic context, see R. Viladesau, *The Beauty of the Cross: The Passion of Christ in Theology and the Arts—From the Catacombs to the Eve of the Renaissance* (Oxford, 2006), ch. 2. Of the crucifix panel itself, Viladesau comments (45): 'There is no attempt to portray suffering as such'.

[3] For the history of later iconography, including the *Isenheim Altarpiece*, see R. Viladesau, *The Triumph of the Cross: The Passion of Christ in Theology and the Arts from the Renaissance to the Counter-Reformation* (Oxford, 2008).

[4] That is, not distinguishing between the sermons as they are commonly called, i.e. some 450 occasional sermons (not counting the variants separately), and the sermons, sometimes termed

take account of the Christological readings of diverse texts in Augustine's *Exposition of the Psalms* (such as on Psalm 22, 'My God, my God'), the total number of sermons devoted to or touching on the passion still seems relatively small.

But it is not the frequency of Augustine's attention to the passion but chiefly its nature that has to be noticed. Take those nine sermons on chapters 18 and 19 of John's Gospel. Even when dealing with the passion narrative itself, there is certainly no dwelling on Christ's suffering, and other aspects of the story seem of far greater interest to Augustine. He attends more closely to resolving a seeming conflict between the evangelists regarding the hour of Christ's death, for example, and to establishing at some length that it was the Jews, not Pilate, who pursued Christ to the death, than to the nature of Christ's suffering. But even more than that, any mention of Christ's suffering is very significantly modified by the framing of the entire story as chiefly a display of Christ's power. Augustine's treatment of the beginning and end of the story are representative of his discussion of the whole. The story begins with the soldiers falling to the ground in Gethsemane at Jesus's announcement, 'I am he'. Augustine comments:

> His own single voice uttering the words, 'I am [He]', without any weapon, smote, repelled, prostrated that great crowd, with all the ferocity of their hatred and terror of their arms.... 'I am [He]', He says; and He casteth the wicked to the ground. What will He do when He cometh as judge, who did this when giving Himself up to be judged? What will be His power when He cometh to reign, who had this power when He came to die?... Why, then, did they not seize Him, but went backward and fell, but just because so He pleased, who could do whatever He pleased?[5]

And as it begins, so it ends with Christ magisterially 'giving up the ghost'.

> Who can thus sleep when he pleases, as Jesus died when He pleased? Who is there that thus puts off his garment when he pleases, as He put off His flesh at His pleasure? Who is there that thus departs when he pleases, as He departed this life at His pleasure? How great the power to be hoped for or dreaded, that must be His as judge, if such was the power He exhibited as a dying man![6]

The passion of Christ, as it is treated here, is first of all a display of power, and only rather incidentally it can seem one of suffering.

The tension involved in holding these two themes together emerges somewhat more sharply in Augustine's treatment of Psalm 22 (21 in his numbering of the Psalms)—and in particular in his treatment of the

---

tractates, which form continuous commentaries on a book of the Bible, i.e. 124 on John's Gospel, plus 150 on the Psalms, and ten on the First Letter of John.

[5] Augustine, *On the Gospel of John*, Tractate 112 (on John chapter 18, 1–12), in vol. 7 of *Nicene and Post-Nicene Fathers*, 1st series, ed. P. Schaff, trans., J. Gibb (Edinburgh, 1991).

[6] Augustine, *On the Gospel of John*, Tractate 119, commenting on John 19, 24–30.

text, 'my God, my God, why have you forsaken me'. The sermon to which I refer, his second exposition of the psalm, was preached on Good Friday, the yearly 'liturgical commemoration' of Christ's death, which 'in a sense makes present what took place in time past, and in this way...moves us as if we were actually watching our Lord hanging on the cross'.[7] '[I]t is a time for groaning, a time for weeping, a time for confessing and imploring God's help'. But Christ hangs there not in the manner in which modern day Christians are encouraged to imagine his experience when they are prompted to Passiontide groaning. Thus the so-called cry of dereliction is not what it seems; Augustine asks, 'Why did he say, *My God, my God, look upon me, why have you forsaken me?*, unless he was somehow trying to catch our attention, to make us understand, "This psalm is written about me"?'— for 'God had not abandoned him, since he himself was God'.[8] Christ speaks here in our voice from the cross: 'He speaks consistently in the character of our old self, whose mortality he bore and which was nailed to the cross with him'.[9] He was 'acting as his own body, the Church'. But in his speaking 'to catch our attention', his dereliction is assumed or performed, so to speak, and performed in the context of those 'acts of great power and authority', which include his bowing of his head and his death. Whatever metaphysical and theological ingenuity can do to reconcile such freedom and power with genuine suffering, Augustine's Christ never seems present in the utter abjection of the victim presupposed in subsequent imagining of Christ's death— in the desolate depictions of the high Middle Ages (such as the so-called *Christ on the Cold Stone* figure), as in such recent theological treatments as J. Moltmann's *The Crucified God*.[10]

In a similar way, the suffering of the martyrs is far from being accented in Augustine's sermons—indeed, as Augustine notes, it is the martyrs' seeming lack of suffering which is most remarkable in certain cases. Take the great Roman Saint Lawrence, roasted on a gridiron as the story of his martyrdom, read on his feast day, relates. He bore 'those torments with...calmness',[11] famously quipping 'turn me over, I think I am done on this side'. The only person who gets hot under the collar, so to speak, is the martyr's persecutor, increasingly frustrated that his dastardly antics fail to disturb the saint. The same pattern is repeated in the martyrdom of Vincent, also burnt for his faith: for 'if we consider the agitation of the torturer and the calmness of the one suffering the torments, it is very easy to see who succumbed to the pains,

---

[7] Augustine, *Expositions of the Psalms*, 21 (2nd exposition), 1.

[8] Augustine, *Expositions of the Psalms*, 21 (2nd exposition), 3.

[9] Augustine, *Expositions of the Psalms*, 21 (1st exposition), 1.

[10] J. Moltmann, *The Crucified God*, trans. R. A. Wilson and J. Bowden (London, 1974). For a *Christ on the Cold Stone* of about 1500, see item 48 in the *The Image of Christ*, the catalogue of 'Seeing Salvation', 121.

[11] Augustine, *Sermons*, 303.

and who rose above them'.[12] The overall effect of these stories Augustine puts very well:

> If, in this passion of Vincent's, one only gave thought to human powers of endurance, it begins to look unbelievable...Such hideous cruelty was being unleashed on the martyr's body, and such calm serenity being displayed in his voice; such harsh, savage punishments being applied to his limbs, such assurance echoing in his words, that we would have imagined that in a marvellous way, while Vincent was suffering, it was someone else, not the speaker, that was being tortured.[13]

As with the passion of Christ, these passions are stories first of all of triumph and power. What that early ivory image suggests and what Augustine's sermons confirm, is that although it was a point of orthodoxy that Christ was fully human and could and did suffer, in the early period Christ and his martyrs are imagined as so masterful in their deaths that their suffering is—well—not much like suffering.

How did we get from here to Grünewald's great crucifixion where there is none of the masterful contempt of Lawrence and the other martyrs, none of the imperious impassivity of the early Christian depictions of Christ's passion? How did we pass from the world of seemingly impassible martyrs and regal Christs on the cross, to dwelling on the reality, actuality, and the very details of Christ's suffering? When and why did Christ and the martyrs give up on Stoicism, so to speak? When and why did Christian devotion become, first of all, a devotion to the suffering Christ? Or as Emile Mâle once put it: 'How did it happen that, in the fourteenth century, Christians wished to see their God suffer and die?'[14]

The story of a vast shift in 'a whole imaginative and emotional climate' as Rachel Fulton terms it,[15] is likely to be a very complex story and not one where a moral theologian can claim any knowledge or expertise. Fulton, in her magisterial *From Judgment to Passion: Devotion to Christ and the Virgin Mary, 800–1200*, ranges over a vast terrain of medieval life, thought, and practice in trying to account for this shift. That it occurred, and (roughly) when, is uncontested—at some time shortly after the first millennium, Christians turned from thinking of Christ's wounds in fear to thinking of them in compassion.[16] The causes of the change are more contested, however, and the picture is complex.

Fulton and others agree nonetheless in giving Anselm a pivotal place in the story—owing not so much to his originality, as Fulton sees it, but to his representing and using creatively 'elements available in the tradition' in response

---

[12] Augustine, *Sermons*, 275, 2.   [13] Augustine, *Sermons*, 276, 2.
[14] Cited by R. Fulton, *From Judgment to Passion: Devotion to Christ and the Virgin Mary, 800–1200* (New York, 2005), 5.
[15] Fulton, *From Judgment to Passion*, 5.   [16] Fulton, *From Judgment to Passion*, 465.

to the 'anxieties and preoccupations of his day'.[17] These elements and preoccupations include somewhat earlier reflections on the nature of Christ's human presence in the Eucharist, engagement with Christ's human nature in monastic devotion and prayer, as well as the heightened and disappointed millennial expectations of 1000 and 1033 (which encouraged a search for Christ's interior presence). It also included Anselm's own important contribution to the tradition of prayer to the crucified Christ and furthermore his celebrated account of the reason for Christ's work of redemption in *Cur Deus Homo?*.[18]

In that work, answering the question as to why God had become man, Anselm placed great weight on Christ's suffering—suffering that had seemed incidental in previous tellings of the story of the incarnation, in which the fact of the joining of humanity and godhead had been itself the chief focus. In Anselm's account, however, Christ had come down not simply to join our humanity to the divine person in a cosmic journeying, but had joined the human and the divine for sake of paying on our behalf the debt our sins had incurred but which we could not pay. And in paying this debt, Christ's suffering was vital, for it was this pain and suffering that provided the consideration in the transaction by means of which our sins were cancelled. This theological stress on the suffering of Christ itself chimed with devotional trends which, quite separately it seems, paid attention to the humanity of Christ and brought Christ's suffering to the fore as a focus of thought, reflection, and meditation in new and intense ways.

Whatever the complexity of its causes, the emergence of Christ's suffering as the very crux of the Christian story is plain to see. As one scholar puts it (in an important recent study, *The Modulated Scream: Pain in Late Medieval Culture*): 'if during the early Middle Ages, the Crucifixion was a minor detail in God's human biography, during the later Middle Ages the entire life became a prologue to the Crucifixion'.[19] Christ's suffering was no mere happenstance, but the core of his existence—its very point and purpose. He was born to suffer and rose because he suffered. Christ's suffering became the heart and core of his existence—not just a detail at the end. And it would now be examined from every angle, approached from each and every viewpoint, held up to inspection to reveal its last shades and nuances. What had been an incident in Christ's life, noticed but not scrutinized, would now be unpacked and then re-presented moment by moment, blow by blow. We pass from the crucifixion as a single event to its articulation and elaboration in a manner that will eventually be codified in devotion to the blessed wounds or in the Stations of the Cross: a highly realized, carefully articulated, patiently enunciated, intensely considered, concentrated meditation on the short journey from judgment hall

---

[17] Fulton, *From Judgment to Passion*, 189.

[18] For Fulton on Anselm's *Cur Deus Homo?*, see *From Judgment to Passion*, 177–91.

[19] E. Cohen, *The Modulated Scream: Pain in Late Medieval Culture* (Chicago, 2010), 217.

to death, in which every moment and modality of suffering is the subject of focused attention.[20]

My interest, however, is not only in the when and why of this phenomenon (that is, the development of a new devotional interest in Christ's pain and suffering in his passion), but in its wider moral significance. What did this turn to the passion mean, and what did it mean for our moral sensibilities? The point here is that the new devotions encouraged devotees to enter into 'the imaginary landscape of the Passion.'[21] But the meditations, visualizations, and prayers which allowed participants to enter that landscape and follow Christ's torments step by step, as well as to follow his mother's grief and suffering, intended to facilitate more than the mere recollecting of these events. As Fulton puts it, 'praying to the Virgin and her crucified Son forced medieval Christians to forge new tools with which to feel'. Specifically, she argues, the new devotional practices 'schooled religiously sensitive women and men in the potentialities of emotion, specifically love, for transcending the physical, experiential distance between individual bodies—above all, bodies in pain.'[22] This was nothing less than a schooling in compassion and empathy, and thus, arguably, an important moment in the history of both—though as Fulton recognizes (referring to Morrison's observation that 'The history of compassion is yet to be written'), the telling of this bigger story is an outstanding and challenging task.[23]

The newly discovered suffering Christ, so different from the magisterial and seemingly impassible Christ of the earlier tradition, had become more human we might say and so too his martyrs—their seeming impassibility now 'dissolved into fortitude',[24] as Cohen puts it. But this humanizing of Christ and the once heroically insensible martyrs served to shape new human sensibilities. Mere witnessing of pain was not enough—witnessing and entering into the pain of Christ and his mother was expected to induce compunction, sorrow, compassion, a desire to imitate, resolution to follow, and so on. And the significance and vitality, or otherwise, of this new form of human being may be a matter of some moment, not just historically, but in our day, too.

---

[20] So central does suffering become to the imagination of Christ's life, that, as Cohen notes, in certain devotional elaborations it reaches back behind the actual passion so that Christ's whole life comes to be conceived as a passion. 'What is remarkable about this thread is that it takes every single element in Christ's life and weaves it into a pre-Passion Passion. Gestation was Passion; so was Nativity; exile, ministry, preaching, and miracles were all Passion. Even the authority of his parents and the frigid waters of the Jordan were an insult, a suffering, a burden' (*The Modulated Scream*, 225). And of the crucifixion itself, Cohen notes that 'writers attempted to outdo their predecessors in detailed and vivid imagining of the pain of Christ's Passion' (198).

[21] Cohen, *The Modulated Scream*, 217.   [22] Fulton, *From Judgment to Passion*, 197.

[23] Fulton, *From Judgment to Passion*, 197, citing K. F. Morrison, *'I am You': Hermeneutics of Empathy in Western Literature, Theology and Art* (Princeton, 1988); see now and further K. F. Morrison and R. M. Bell, eds., *Studies on Medieval Empathies* (Turnout, Belgium, 2013).

[24] Cohen, *The Modulated Scream*, 259.

III MAKING SUFFERING COUNT: ANXIETIES ABOUT THE POLITICS OF COMPASSION, ANTHROPOLOGY'S DISCOVERY OF SUFFERING, AND THE TRIUMPH OF HUMANITARIAN REASON

There is a well-known contemporary anxiety that suffering doesn't matter—or perhaps that is doesn't matter enough or in the right way. This anxiety is an anxiety about 'the interrelationship between the social representation of suffering and the cultural politics of compassion', to use Wilkinson's terms for his framing of the problem.[25] Specifically the concern is that the present-day 'cultural dynamics of social sentiment'[26] may be insufficient to sustain such a politics, because the excess of images of suffering in our world render suffering no longer emotionally sensitizing but anaesthetizing. Interestingly, some recent social anthropologists have been moved by this concern to discover suffering, so to speak, even while others judge the concern to be (in a certain sense) misplaced.

Anxiety about attention to suffering has a long history—but in its usual form this anxiety is that an interest in suffering has something morbid and troubling about it, as noticed by Plato (in book iv of *Republic*) and by Augustine (at the beginning of book iii of *Confessions*). And as Burke writing on the sublime comments: 'I am convinced we have a degree of delight, and that no small one, in the real misfortunes and pains of others. There is no spectacle we so eagerly pursue, as that of some uncommon and grievous calamity'.[27] (And we could, of course, raise questions about the darker side of the medieval discovery of the suffering of Christ, which is not, however, our subject.[28]) But in the present day, when such 'spectacles' have become much more readily available, there has arisen a very particular and quite different concern. Susan Sontag puts the point very plainly in her lectures *Regarding the Pain of Others*:

> Information about what is happening elsewhere, called 'news', features conflict and violence—'If it bleeds, it leads' runs the venerable guideline of tabloids and twenty-four-hour headline news shows—to which the response is compassion, or indignation, or titillation, or approval, as each misery heaves into view.[29]

But which will it be? The contemporary anxiety is that our response is often one of merely curious spectatorship—and that far from making a contribution

---

[25] I. Wilkinson, *Suffering: A Sociological Introduction* (Cambridge, 2005), 15.

[26] Wilkinson, *Suffering: A Sociological Introduction*, 12.

[27] Cited by S. Sontag, *Regarding the Pain of Others* (London, 2005), 87.

[28] See, for example, M. B. Merbeck, *The Thief, the Cross and the Wheel: Pain and the Spectacle of Punishment in Medieval and Renaissance Europe*, 2nd. ed. (Chicago, 1999) and R. Mills, *Suspended Animation: Pain, Pleasure and Punishment in Medieval Culture* (London, 2006).

[29] Sontag, *Regarding the Pain of Others*, 16.

to a politics of pity or compassion, the promiscuity of images of suffering serves to undermine it.

As Sontag sees it, the depiction of suffering in the modern period began with the intention of arousing indignation and sympathy—Goya's great etchings *The Disasters of War*, to take her chief early example of this modern tradition, demanded of the viewers that they should deplore what the artist was himself presenting. His captions to those etchings ('This is bad' or 'This is worse', for example), provide a firm direction for our responses, which the horror of the images themselves might perhaps have been expected to provide for themselves. But as the later hunt for more and more dramatic images gained momentum, any confidence that images would 'goad viewers to feel more' has dissipated: 'In a world in which photography is brilliantly at the service of consumerist manipulations, no effect of a photograph of a doleful scene can be taken for granted.'[30]

Sontag's sceptical assessment is echoed, and perhaps rendered more pessimistic, by two contemporary commentators, Arthur and Joan Kleinman, the first an anthropologist, for whom the cultural appropriation of suffering via images amounts to no more than 'infotainment'.[31] We are 'desensitized' by the proliferation of images. They suggest:

> Viewers are overwhelmed by the sheer number of atrocities. There is too much to see, and there appears to be too much to do anything about. Thus, our epoch's dominating sense that complex problems can be neither understood nor fixed works with the massive globalization of images of suffering to produce moral fatigue, exhaustion of empathy, and political despair.[32]

It is directly under the influence of this anxiety that an influential work in social anthropology takes up the challenge which the Kleinmans believe falls to anthropology, in particular, to depict suffering more adequately.

In *Vita: Life in a Zone of Social Abandonment*,[33] João Biehl joins words and highly arresting (and highly aesthetic) photographs to depict the suffering of a certain Caterina. Vita is the name of a community or a colony for social outcasts of many kinds, of which colony Caterina is a member. But 'Vita', as Biehl notes, 'means life in a dead language'[34]—and aptly so, since Vita is a place of abandonment where people come to die, 'a dump site of human beings' as one activist puts it.[35] Caterina, whose story is at the centre of the work, ends up in Vita because her inherited neurological disorder is misdiagnosed and

---

[30] Sontag, *Regarding the Pain of Others*, 71.

[31] A. and J. Kleinman, 'The Appeal of Experience; The Dismay of Images: Cultural Appropriations of Suffering in our Times', in *Social Suffering*, eds. A. Kleinman, V. Das, and M. Lock (Berkeley, 1997), 1.

[32] Kleinman and Kleinman, 'The Appeal of Experience', 9.

[33] J. Biehl, *Vita: Life in a Zone of Social Abandonment* (Berkeley, 2005).

[34] Biehl, *Vita*, 36.   [35] Biehl, *Vita*, 1–2.

mistreated—her family simply term her mad, whereas the state categorizes her as mentally ill. But Vita, this rather squalid privately run institution, is the last resort of those who have been rendered 'ex-humans' in Biehl's terms. It is one of many 'zones of social abandonment', places where the poor, the destitute, the mentally ill, criminals, and others, are discarded by society to dwell in a social no-man's land which is closer to death than it is to life. 'The fundamentally ambiguous being of people in these zones, caught as they are between encompassment and abandonment, memory and nonmemory, life and death',[36] is the ex-human. And yet Biehl does nonetheless find life in Vita and humanity in the ex-human. As he struggles with Caterina's fragmentary conversation and cryptic poetry:

> a life force...emerged to rework thought, social relations and family life. Ethnography became the missing nexus between the real of Catarina's body and the imaginary of its mental and relational schemes, between the abandoned and the family, the house and the city, individuals and populations in Vita'.[37]

Vita is, according to Robbins, 'one of the most celebrated anthropological works of the last decade', in a genre he terms the 'anthropology of suffering'.[38] The anthropology of suffering means to exhibit the 'shared humanity that links us to others who suffer', and it is 'clearly a hope' of this anthropology 'that these lessons might become a motive for change'.[39] Kleinman and Kleinman's paper proposed just such a role for anthropology in discovering suffering, and recovering it from the invisibility to which it has allegedly been consigned by the promiscuity of images; and Biehl specifically notes this challenge as motivating *Vita*: 'How to bring into view the reality that ruins the person?'[40]

There is an irony in the emergence of what Robbins dubs the 'anthropology of suffering'—an anthropology founded on the conviction that suffering needs urgently to be made to count for the sake of a politics of compassion, in an age in which representations of human abjection have lost their power. The irony is that as this anthropology has taken up its mission, another and recent

---

[36] Biehl, *Vita*, 4.   [37] Biehl, *Vita*, 318.

[38] J. Robbins, 'Beyond the Suffering Subject: Toward An Anthropology of the Good', *Journal of the Royal Anthropological Institute* (N.S.) 19 (2013), 447–62. Robbins argues that the 'suffering subject' replaced the 'other' as the 'primary object of anthropological attention' in the late 1980s, but that the shift of subject sacrificed something of the critical ambitions and potential of the earlier anthropology. The anthropology of suffering is 'a way of writing ethnography in which we do not primarily provide cultural context so as to offer lessons in how lives are lived differently elsewhere, but in which we offer accounts of trauma that make us and our readers feel in our bones the vulnerability we as human beings all share' (455). His contention is that an 'anthropology of the good', while not at odds with an 'anthropology of suffering', can be more than mere witness. It might contribute to the ambition of the older anthropology, expressed in the celebrated remark of David Schneider, cited by Robbins: '[O]ne of the fundamental fantasies of anthropology is that somewhere there must be a life really worth living' (456).

[39] Robbins, 'Beyond the Suffering Subject', 456.

[40] Biehl, *Vita*, 42.

work announces the 'triumph of humanitarian reason', in which suffering and compassion have created and shaped a new politics.[41] According to Didier Fassin, simple anxieties concerning the politics of compassion are misplaced or redundant, since in our newly fashioned moral economy, 'humanitarian reason' as he calls it, gives suffering a voice and compassion a practice. But, as we shall see, humanitarian reason is still deserving of critique according to Fassin—and this gives rise to a new and different set of concerns, which we might think of as the 'higher anxiety'.

Fassin's book is about the 'invention and...complications'[42] of humanitarianism—which for him is a form of understanding (reason) and action (politics). The Southeast Asian tsunami of 2004 provides an example of the character of the new political order in which the 'tragedy of ruination and the pathos of assistance'[43] are combined. That is, we live in a world in which 'every situation characterized by precariousness' (disasters, famines, epidemics, wars, poverty, homelessness, exile, and unemployment) calls forth a 'display of succor'. Precariousness 'mobilizes sympathy and technology'—physicians, armies, and relief workers are moved by the spectacle of suffering. 'The moral landscape thus outlined can be called humanitarianism.'[44] As Fassin sees it, 'the distinctive feature of contemporary societies is without doubt the way that moral sentiments have become generalized as a frame of reference in political life. This is the phenomenon I term "humanitarian government".'[45]

Fassin intends, however, to problematize humanitarian government and reason in the two senses indicated in his observation that 'although it is generally taken for granted as a mere expansion of a supposed natural humaneness that would be innately associated with our being human, humanitarianism is a relatively recent invention, which raises complex ethical and political issues.'[46] Humanitarianism, in other words, for all its contemporary political acceptance and seeming naturalness, has a history; and from this history, so he claims, particular problems arise. This brings us back to our beginning, since the origins of humanitarianism and the origins of its problems lie, so Fassin says, in Christianity.

Fassin's genealogy and critique are by no means easily stated, but as I understand his argument its begins with the claim that humanitarian reason is 'embedded in our long modernity',[47] and more specifically, that the 'ethos from which it proceeds has its source in the Christian world—in terms of both the sacralization of life and the valorization of suffering.'[48]

---

[41] D. Fassin, *Humanitarian Reason: A Moral History of the Present* (Berkeley, 2012).

[42] Fassin, *Humanitarian Reason*, ix.

[43] Fassin, *Humanitarian Reason*, ix. Echoing, of course, the judgment of Secretary General of the UN Kofi Annan that the response to the disaster was 'a unique display of the unity of the world'. Cited by L. Chouliaraki, *The Spectatorship of Suffering* (London, 2006), 1.

[44] Fassin, *Humanitarian Reason*, ix.   [45] Fassin, *Humanitarian Reason*, 247.

[46] Fassin, *Humanitarian Reason*, ix.

[47] Fassin, *Humanitarian Reason*, 247.   [48] Fassin, *Humanitarian Reason*, 248.

By the sacralization of life, he refers to the placing 'at the summit of our system of values', 'life itself', bare life, 'the simple fact of being alive'.[49] According to Fassin's statement of Arendt's argument (in *The Human Condition*), it was the promise of immortality that was the key to individual life replacing the *polis* as the ultimate good.[50] However that may be, humanitarian reason values such bare life—and it is this valuation of life 'in the sense of being alive' which explains the:

> relative privilege accorded to the undocumented seriously ill over all other immigrants and even asylum seekers, or the universal consensus regarding the intervention of organizations working in emergency aid rather than social justice programs, not to mention protests or riots. Conversely, it is also what makes policies that prioritize the collective interests of public health over benefits for individual patients, and on a quite different level, the gesture of combatants who sacrifice themselves in suicide attacks against their enemies, simultaneously unintelligible and intolerable to most people.[51]

Humanitarian reason depends also, however, on the valorization of suffering (and specifically in its serving as a justification to action), and for this too, Fassin finds a Christian genealogy. Christianity converts suffering into redemption. As Arendt notes, 'it is by no means a matter of course for the spectacle of misery to move men to pity'.[52] But the specific 'entry of suffering into politics' depends on the thought that 'salvation emanates not through the passion one endures, but through compassion one feels'. This 'moral sentiment' then, 'becomes a source of action, because we seek to correct the situation that gives rise to the misfortune of others'.[53] 'Humanitarian government is the heir to this active protest against the suffering of the world'[54]—it has its own specificity and character, but 'one must emphasize the persistence of the place of suffering in the moral space of Western societies, and still more, its valorization as an experience of individual or collective salvation'.[55]

Fassin's summary conclusion is that the 'constitution of life as sacred and the valorization of suffering thus make contemporary humanitarian government

---

[49] Fassin, *Humanitarian Reason*, 250.

[50] H. Arendt, *The Human Condition*, 2nd. ed. (Chicago, 1998), 313–14, cited by Fassin, *Humanitarian Reason*, 249.

[51] Fassin, *Humanitarian Reason*, 249.

[52] H. Arendt, *On Revolution*, cited by Fassin, *Humanitarian Reason*, 305, note 16. If we want examples, the Roman love of the games and the sacrifices of the Aztecs are cases in point. As I. Clendinnen comments in *Aztecs: An Interpretation* (Cambridge, 1991), 'Powerful emotions must have been stirred by these extravagant and enforced intimacies with death, and more with the decay and dissolution of the self, but there is no indication that pity or grief for the victim were among them' (96).

[53] Fassin, *Humanitarian Reason*, 250.

[54] Fassin, *Humanitarian Reason*, 251.   [55] Fassin, *Humanitarian Reason*, 251.

a form of political theology', framed by the 'diptych of life as highest good and suffering as redemptive ordeal'.

> Humanitarian government, because it establishes these two foundations of Christian thought in the political space, clearly represents the religious aspect of the contemporary democratic order. The dual politics it lays claim to and promotes—of life and of suffering—prolongs and renews the Christian legacy.[56]

So much for the genealogy of humanitarianism, its 'invention'; what of its 'complications', or the critique? The 'complications' are that:

> In contemporary societies, where inequalities have reached an unprecedented level, humanitarianism elicits the fantasy of a global moral community which may still be viable and the expectation that solidarity may have redeeming powers. This secular imaginary of communion and redemption implies a sudden awareness of the fundamentally unequal human condition and an ethical necessity not to remain passive about it in the name of solidarity—however ephemeral this awareness is, and whatever limited impact this necessity has. Humanitarianism has this remarkable capacity: it fugaciously and illusorily bridges the contradictions of our world, and makes the intolerableness of its injustices somewhat bearable.[57]

Or again: 'humanitarian government has a salutary power for us because by saving lives, it saves something of our idea of ourselves, and because, by relieving suffering, it also relieves the burden of this unequal world order'.[58] It allows us to hold onto the 'collective sentiment through which our societies can imagine themselves in solidarity with the weight of the world, whether it be close or distant'. There is, it seems, something illusory in the reassurance which humanitarianism provides—it is as if for Fassin, humanitarianism produces only a simulacrum, so to say, of genuine solidarity.

The exact nature of Fassin's critique is not fully clear to me, but I think it helpful to follow Guilhot's suggestion that Fassin 'alternates between an internal critique... and an external one'.[59]

The internal critique suggests that humanitarianism is not finally true to its own commitments; that it is better at bringing a tear to the eye (and thus allowing us to congratulate ourselves on our fellow feeling), than in holding to its own principles. Thus, to take one example, humanitarianism betrays itself in what Fassin terms its 'double register'. In poor countries it deals with undifferentiated populations. In rich countries it deal with individuals. 'But in order for this double register of humanitarianism to work, both the territorial and the moral boundaries between the two worlds must be sealed as tightly as possible—for example, preventing refugees from the South from claiming

---

[56] Fassin, *Humanitarian Reason*, 251.   [57] Fassin, *Humanitarian Reason*, xii.
[58] Fassin, *Humanitarian Reason*, 252.
[59] N. Guilhot, 'The Anthropologist as Witness: Humanitarianism between Ethnography and Critique', *Humanity*, 3.1 (2013), 99.

the prerogatives granted to asylum seekers in the North.'[60] Or, to take another example—provided by the problems experienced by Médecins Sans Frontières during the Iraq War of 2003 and narrated in some detail in a chapter of *Humanitarian Reason* entitled 'Hierarchies of Humanity'—humanitarianism, in spite of its principles, often accords higher value to the life of aid workers over those to whom assistance is given and even differentiates between expatriate and local aid workers. Thus humanitarianism is often committed, in its practice, to 'an ontological inequality which contravenes the principle of common humanity' on which it rests.[61]

That is the internal critique. The external critique takes exception to humanitarianism for its depoliticizing and dehistoricizing of the contemporary world, and for the nature of the relationship which it presupposes and perpetuates. On the first point, insofar as it construes all recipients of aid as victims, it is blind to political and historical causation. 'Inequality is replaced by exclusion, domination is transformed into misfortune, injustice is articulated as suffering, violence is expressed in terms of trauma.'[62] On the second point, humanitarianism rests on the 'obligation of the giver' not the 'right of the receiver' (to use Simmel's terms to which Fassin refers)—it is 'a grant of consideration' not a recognition 'of right.'[63] Thus:

> Ultimately, what is lacking in humanitarian government is perhaps that, beyond life as sacred and suffering as value, it fails to recognize the Other as a 'face', to use Emmanuel Levinas's term, this face 'present in its refusal to be contained', this face that resists any attempt to possess it even in the name of the good. From this point of view, recognizing a face also means recognizing a right beyond any obligation, and hence a subject beyond any subjection—even to humanitarian reason.[64]

But the compassion of humanitarian reason 'always presupposes a relationship of inequality ... When compassion is exercised in the public space, it is ... always directed from above to below, from the more powerful to the weaker, the more fragile, the more vulnerable—those who can generally be constituted as victims of an overwhelming fate.'[65] So constituted (or constructed), victims may come to perform suffering for the sake of occupying the one place where they are noticed, thereby occluding the fact that their subjecthood (and agency) is far from exhausted by the role of victim.

It was an anxiety about the possibility of sustaining a politics of compassion which motivated the development of an anthropology of suffering. Ironically, perhaps, social anthropology has now provided an account of the triumph of humanitarian reason, which dispels the earlier anxiety but creates another, for humanitarian reason allegedly fails to be true to itself and, in any case, the self

---

[60] Fassin, *Humanitarian Reason*, 253.
[61] Fassin, *Humanitarian Reason*, 227.   [62] Fassin, *Humanitarian Reason*, 6.
[63] Fassin, *Humanitarian Reason*, 253.   [64] Fassin, *Humanitarian Reason*, 254–255.
[65] Fassin, *Humanitarian Reason*, 4.

to which it fails to be true is morally suspect. The case for ambivalence about contemporary humanitarianism is nicely brought out by a headline from *Le Monde*, after 9/11, noted by Chouliaraki: 'We are all Americans'. The headline is revelatory, Chouliaraki thinks, of the conditionality of our humanitarianism and of the nature of that conditionality. Humanitarianism depends, suggests Chouliaraki, on a 'culture of intimacy' in which there is a 'potential for us to pity "our" own suffering', but which 'leaves the far away "other" outside our horizon of care and responsibility',[66] notwithstanding the claims of justice. Humanitarianism finally fails to rise above a sort of narcissistic pitying of ourselves.

According to Fassin (referring to Gauchet):

the contemporary presence of religion is most effectively manifested where it is least identifiable, where it becomes so self evident, that we do not recognize it for what it is any more. In this view, the ultimate victory of religion lies not in the renewal of religious expression throughout the world, but in its lasting presence at the heart of our democratic secular values.[67]

Fassin's genealogy of humanitarian reason claims that the 'new relation to suffering' around which our 'contemporary moral economies have been constituted' is a Christian relation. And since this moral economy is questionable, we are returned to the problem we left some time ago concerning the moral significance of the representation of the suffering Christ and the moral value of the sensibility which it may imagine, intend, or create.

IV ATTENDING TO SUFFERING, TECHNOLOGIES OF THE SELF, AND THE CHRISTIAN LIFE

As discussed earlier, the discovery of the suffering of Christ is arguably a significant moment in the history of human sensibility—though as Fulton recognized, the telling of this history is far from easy. Fassin's assertion that the 'ethos from which [humanitarianism] proceeds has its source in the Christian world'[68] may, then, need careful elaboration or even extensive qualification, but Christianity cannot avoid the charges which underlie Fassin's critique simply by nuancing his rough and ready genealogy.

It is worth noting immediately, however, that ambivalence about the contemporary practice of humanitarianism has a perfectly familiar place within Christianity itself. Thus, in a recent paper by Charles Mathewes referring to 'the scandalous present of Christian ethics', the scandal is evidenced by the 'strange silence' of Christian ethics in the US in relation to extraordinary

---

[66] Chouliaraki, *The Spectatorship of Suffering*, 14.
[67] Fasssin, *Humanitarian Reason*, 249.   [68] Fassin, *Humanitarian Reason*, 248.

increases in inequities in the distribution of wealth and in the size of the prison population.[69] The implicit criticism here is that these silences reveal first, a disregard for the political failings that create and perpetuate many of the problems of modernity (the external critique), and second, the existence of a double register, to use Fassin's term, whereby humanitarianism is extended only to certain human beings and is not the universal humanitarianism which by its own lights it should be (the internal critique).[70]

The question becomes then, not whether Christianity can or should accept the spirit of Fassin's critique of contemporary humanitarianism (it should and does), but whether Christianity has the resources to respond to, or better, to advance from and beyond this critique. Can Christian humanitarianism itself address the charges made against 'humanitarian reason'? Can it understand the critique as inviting a deeper and more adequate humanitarianism?

Plainly the problem of external critique is the more difficult. But I suggest that a developing form of Christian practice seeks to address both sides of the critique and does so insofar as it takes seriously the deep practice of attending to Christ's suffering from which Christian humanitarianism stems. I make two moves then, in seeking to describe a Christian practice of a humanitarianism more thorough and self-critical than the humanitarianism Fasssin finds in 'humanitarian reason' and about which he is understandably ambivalent.

The first step involves noting that the Christian appropriation of the suffering of Christ is founded in a more substantial practice than the mere spectatorship on which 'humanitarian reason' must precariously seek to rely in the contemporary political and moral economy Fassin describes. To capture something of the contrast and to clarify something of the character of the Christian practice, we need to understand the complex appropriation of Christ's suffering within the Christian tradition by means of Foucault's notion of 'a technology of the self'.

The second step suggests that such a practice of appropriation of Christ's suffering is not only the grounds for a more consistent humanitarianism (that is, in answer to the internal critique), but also helps to shape a compassionate gaze which, contrary to the charge of the external critique, sees the face of the Other (to use that phrase from Levinas which Fassin borrows in making his deeper objection). The Christian practice of attending to Christ then, invites not just a more consistent humanitarianism, but one that overcomes the implicit disregard for the Other which construes compassion as a grant and not a recognition. Here I turn to the L'Arche community as aspiring to model a practice of true regard.

---

[69] C. Mathewes, 'The Scandalous Present (and Future Promise) of Christian Ethics', an unpublished paper given in Cambridge in 2012.

[70] Double-register humanitarianism has, of course, become something of the order of the day in relation to prisoners.

Taken together, these steps represent a tentative attempt from within Christian ethics to imagine and describe the practice of forms of attention to suffering that can foster a more thoroughly humanitarian reason.

For the moment, however, let us go back to what Sontag refers to as the 'familiar diagnosis' without endorsing it —'flooded with images of the sort that once used to shock and arouse indignation, we are losing our capacity to react. Compassion, stretched to its limits, is going numb'.[71] The thought is that 'our capacity to respond to our experiences with emotional freshness and ethical pertinence is being sapped by the relentless diffusion of vulgar and appalling images'.[72] But this familiar anxiety encourages the speculation that 'A more reflective engagement would require a certain intensity of awareness'.[73] Perhaps, she suggests, 'certain photographs':

> can be used like momento mori, as objects of contemplation to deepen one's sense of reality; as secular icons, if you will. But that would seem to demand the equivalent of a sacred or meditative space in which to look at them. Space reserved for being serious is hard to come by in a modern society, whose chief model of a public space is the mega-store... [and there is] no way to guarantee reverential conditions in which to look at these pictures and be fully responsive to them.[74]

Sontag's hesitant grasping after the proper conditions for the reception of certain images should encourage us to notice that representations of Christ's suffering, whether visual or verbal, were never bare representations, but were used and deployed, drawn on and received, in contexts which decisively governed or regulated their reception. For all that the *Isenheim Altarpiece* in its central panel depicting the crucifixion has an image of gruesome horror and abjection to rival those from the TV news, it was never merely an image flashing across the mind's eye—'fugaciously' (to use a word given a rare outing by Fassin's translator)—in the manner of TV images with their ephemeral immediacy. That famous crucifixion panel from the altarpiece is only one part of a larger work; it was itself only revealed from time to time, and then in the context of the narrative of the Christian year, in a particular season, in particular services, with particular readings and prayers, and with sermons or addresses aimed at further situating and explicating the image. The same could be said of other representations, visual and verbal, of Christ's suffering—they were rarely bare, fleetingly present images, but in the Stations of the Cross, in prayers on the blessed wounds, even in readings from the Bible, belonged within typically ritual practices which contextualized the images and gave them their weight, significance, and meaning.

I suggest that we might underline this fact by describing the various Christian practices of contemplation and appropriation of Christ's suffering

---

[71] Sontag, *Regarding the Pain of Others*, 96.
[72] Sontag, *Regarding the Pain of Others*, 97.
[73] Sontag, *Regarding the Pain of Others*, 94–95.
[74] Sontag, *Regarding the Pain of Others*, 108.

as amounting to what Foucault terms 'technologies of the self'—though we might prefer to refer to them, to avoid a certain sort of misunderstanding or suspicion, as technologies of the self for the sake of the other.

Whereas in his early work Foucault had been concerned with how the subject was framed or shaped by power, in his later work (and more specifically in volumes 2 and 3 of the unfinished *History of Sexuality*), he began 'to study the constitution of the subject as its own object',[75] and in particular its shaping specifically by 'technologies of the self'. These technologies are the means by which the subject asks and answers the questions, 'What should one do with oneself? What work should be carried out on the self? How should one "govern oneself"?'[76]

The examples of technologies of the self that drew his attention in the classical world were particularly the practices of self-control and discipline characteristic especially of Stoicism. Foucault broke these technologies down into constituent elements by interrogating them on four points, relating to ontology, deontology, ascetics, and teleology, thereby constituting 'an analytic of ethical reason and practice', as Laidlaw terms it in his recent and helpful exegesis, followed here.[77]

Laidlaw's account is of four questions relating to those four points. 'First... what is the part of oneself that is the object of thought and work?'— and the answer might be 'certain kinds of act, or desires, or feelings, or "the flesh", the soul, one's "identity"'. Second, 'what are the ways in which people position themselves in relation to their ideals or injunctions or rules?' That is, do they take up these ideals or rules as obeying the dictates of reason, or as being true to one's nature, on account of an aspiration to excel, or as the commands of God, and so on. Third, 'what form does one's self-forming activity take? How is the ethical substance worked on?'—by meditation, fasting, through the interpretation of dreams, or whatever. And fourth, 'what is the mode of being the subject aims to achieve? What kind of being does the ethical subject aspire to be: pure, commanding, free, master of itself, rational, immortal or self-extinguishing?'[78]

What I suggest, albeit in a preliminary way and without working out the details, is that the suffering of Christ is properly thought of as typically entering into the Christian imagination not fleetingly, but via what amounts to various

---

[75] To cite (at 36) what is probably Foucault's own account of his work in an article by otherwise unknown scholar Maurice Florence, entitled 'Foucault, Michel, 1926– ', and attributed to Foucault himself by G. Gutting, editor of *The Cambridge Companion to Foucault* (Cambridge, 1994), in which this essay appears.

[76] M. Foucault, 'Subjectivity and Truth', 87, in Foucault, *The Essential Works*, vol. 1. *Ethics*, ed. P. Rabinow, trans. R. Hurley (Harmondsworth, 1997).

[77] J. Laidlaw, *The Subject of Virtue*, 103–104. And see also A. I. Davidson, 'Ethics as Ascetics: Foucault, the History of Ethics, and Ancient Thought', in *The Cambridge Companion to Foucault*, 115–40.

[78] Laidlaw, *The Subject of Virtue*, 103–104.

technologies of the self. Practices, some of which we have already referred to, we might think of under the third heading of ascetics.[79] These have included the Stations of the Cross, keeping Lent, reading Scripture, the liturgies of Holy Week, meditation on the blessed wounds, saying the Rosary, reciting psalms, and so on. And perhaps more fundamentally still, they include also such practices as the daily, weekly, and yearly memorialization of Christ in the Christian year, which seek to insinuate Christ's life and time into our life and time. These practices are the form which the self-forming activities take. But what of the other elements making up technologies of the self?

As regards ontology—the part of the self that is the object of thought and work—it might be said to be the self specifically as a self. That is, the ascetic work (of Stations of the Cross or whatever) takes the self as its object, with a view (and this is the *telos* of the practice) to opening that self to the suffering Other such that the self comes to identify with the Other in his or her suffering. The remaining question concerns deontology—the manner in which injunctions or ideals or rules, or here the suffering of Christ, claim the moral subject. It might be said that Christ claims the subject not just as an exemplar, but more specifically on account of his death being for us (following Anselm's explication of his redemptive work). It is the claim of a gift or more specifically, the claim of self-sacrifice.

This is but a preliminary and rudimentary attempt to locate these practices of fashioning a distinctive ethical subject within this analytic; its purpose, however, is to distinguish this form of practised attention to the suffering of Christ from mere spectatorship. The English 'attend' derives from Old French, and in turn from the Latin *ad + tendere*—meaning 'to stretch to'—and, 'hence', as the OED has it, 'to direct the mind or observant faculties, to listen, to apply oneself; to watch over, minister to, wait upon, follow, frequent; to wait for, await, expect'. The rich meanings of 'attend' already suggest that attending to, properly understood, must be a rich practice. At the core of the set of meanings is the idea of 'stretching to'. Attending requires that the mind or person attending be enlarged or extended, both in time and over time. To attend to someone is thus a matter of a quality of attention *in* time, but also of a quality of attention *over* time. Attending thus has two axes—and, in relation to suffering, presupposes a certain epistemology of suffering and the suffering subject: that this suffering is recognized and grasped in or over time and thus only through a particular form of engagement and attention.

Notice, however, in addition, that the practices (or ascetics) of attending to Christ and his suffering in and over time, allow and require some complex shifts of perspective and position. Most obviously perhaps in the use of the

---

[79] For important treatments of related themes, see M. Carruthers, *The Craft of Thought: Meditation, Rhetoric, and the Making of Images* (Cambridge, 1998), and also *The Experience of Beauty in the Middle Ages* (Oxford, 2013).

scriptures during Passiontide (in which congregations take on the voices of the characters in the story, including the voice of the crowd shouting 'crucify him' and so on), the users of these technologies of the self are invited to occupy a range of subject positions: as witnesses to the sufferings, but also in various alternating modes of attention, as causes of the suffering and even as victim. Thus we are required not merely and simply to attend to the other, but through certain shifts in perspective, to attend also to our construction of the other, and of ourselves in relation to that other, and to challenge these constructions through taking and occupying different perspectives upon them.

This toying with identities and their usual boundaries is nicely brought out in an aspect of the iconographic tradition which it is easy to overlook or to take somewhat for granted. This tradition regularly and significantly invites us to see ourselves and others in the suffering Christ and the suffering of Christ in others. In Grünewald's crucifixion, Christ is depicted with the characteristic marks of the disease which afflicted the patients of the hospital for which the altarpiece was painted[80]—so we are to find these sufferers in Christ. By contrast, in Rembrandt's stunning late and damaged canvas, the *Anatomy Lesson of Dr Jan Deejman*, a different perspective is taken (see Plate 4). The dissected corpse—that of a murderer hanged in January 1656—is manifestly depicted in the manner of Mantegna's *Lamentation over the Dead Christ*. Here the invitation is to see Christ in the dead criminal.

This artistic tradition, in other words, troubles notions of the self and other, and in particular estimations of the other which would proceed first of all and only from the perspective of pity—which perspective I take to be the object of Fassin's second line of criticism of humanitarianism. Pity of and towards the suffering Christ certainly belongs in this tradition; but Christ is certainly not only an object of pity, but also of reverence, to name but one mode of viewing Christ, transferred in Rembrandt's picture to the hanged man.

So Christian attention to the suffering of Christ resists any simple placing of those who suffer in a particular frame and provides a link to the second element of what might be Christianity's attempt to respond to but go beyond Fassin's critique of an ambivalent humanitarianism. And here I will make brief mention of the founding of the L'Arche community, as aiming at establishing practices of community which embody such a regard for the suffering other.

The L'Arche communities began in France in 1964, when Jean Vanier and Fr Thomas Philippe invited two men with mental handicaps to live in community with them, in response in part to the neglect and disregard of the mentally handicapped in traditional institutions. From this beginning, L'Arche has become a worldwide association of communities committed to providing a sign against

---

[80] St Anthony's fire.

the rejection of those with mental handicap, to use the language the community uses.[81] But, and this is central at this point, its mission statements see the work of the communities not as one-sided acts of charity, but as resting on the conviction that those who are known as the 'core members of the community' teach and serve those who are their carers, in normal parlance. The work of the community against the rejection of the handicapped is thus a work of the moral imagination, whereby the discounting of the handicapped is displaced by a perspective that sees them as teachers of those who enter into community with them. That is, assistants who enter communities 'commit themselves to accompany their members' and do so seeking 'to be guided by God and by their weakest members, through whom God's presence is revealed'.[82]

For Vanier, this mission takes up the mission of Christ, which was not 'simply to do good to the poor but to discover God hidden in the poor, to discover that the poor have the power to heal and free people'.[83] Thus, and taking up and going beyond the concerns we encounter in Fassin's critique, Vanier has his own critique of regular humanitarianism:

> People often come to L'Arche to assist in the community because they want to help people with intellectual disabilities. Vanier does not want to question their motive to help, but he does encourage the assistants in L'Arche to question such motives themselves. While in itself commendable, the desire to be good to other people can easily become self-serving, particularly when it is fueled by the presumption that one's role in the community is to give. People entering L'Arche with this presumption have to learn something that, according to Vanier, is essential for its community, namely, that the marginalized and the despised—'the poor'—have something to give. This has to be learned because without it, true community is impossible. The virtuous motives that make people want to be good to others often betray a hidden sense of superiority; they assume for themselves the role of 'giver' and assign to the other person the roles of 'receiver'. After all, giving can easily be a gesture of power.[84]

Vanier's critique of humanitarianism echoes Fassin's external critique. But this critique is not, in fact, external to a Christian humanitarianism, but strictly internal to it. What is significant about L'Arche is not the annunciation of this critique, but its translation into the powerful imagination of a more effective practice of a more adequate Christian humanitarianism.

Whether the practice of L'Arche itself achieves a mutuality that does not subject the other is, of course, something on which this chapter cannot pronounce. L'Arche itself must be subject to the critical ethnographic gaze and

---

[81] For references, see D. Ford, *Christian Wisdom* (Cambridge, 2007), ch. 10.

[82] See L'Arche mission statements on its own website.

[83] Cited by H. S. Reinders, 'Being with the Disabled: Jean Vanier's Theological Realism' in *Disability in the Christian Tradition: A Reader*, eds. B. Brock and J. Swinton (Grand Rapids, MI, 2012), 474.

[84] Reinders, 'Being with the Disabled', 474.

deserves to be studied carefully and closely to see whether or not it provides a counterpractice to the ambivalent humanitarianism diagnosed by Fassin.[85] But that moral theology may and must turn to such examples of experimental ventures in the shaping of technologies of the self, is, I hope, firmly established.

V CONCLUSION: THE FUTURE HISTORY OF SUFFERING

There is a widespread thought that human sympathy has no history, but arises as a natural human sentiment. Those who have wondered about the origins of morality, certainly from the eighteenth century onwards, have speculated that its ground and base lies in such a natural sympathy. Hume and Adam Smith (and other sentimentalists), for example, advanced such a claim. Kant sought to found an altruistic morality without it, but Schopenhauer reasserted it (while relying on a Kantian argument to provide sympathy with metaphysical warrant). And while Nietzsche may have genealogized sympathy in a critical spirit, Darwin's gestures in the direction of a different genealogy seem to have been taken by some to have burnished the reputation of the naturalness of sympathy by providing it with evolutionary credentials. It is out of this history that humanitarian reason has been born—and on account of a perspective born out of it that humanitarianism has the *noli me tangere* aura that Fassion attributes to it.[86]

Fassin is right to remind us that humanitarian reason does indeed have a genealogy, and one that needs to be recounted in relation to a history of the discovery of the suffering of Christ, from which we began. As it is, humanitarianism can seem somewhat conflicted, inclined to see compassion and pity as natural sentiments (and not as a socially constructed disposition), while also anxious about the social force of these sentiments and thus about the viability of a politics of compassion.

Suppose we grant for the sake of argument, what is deemed commonsensical by some, that sympathy really is some sort of evolutionary deposit. Suppose there is a certain natural propensity to sympathy and that this propensity lies at the basis of sociality and morality. Even granting this, however, it doesn't follow without more ado that this natural propensity will be shaped and moved and mobilized as effectively or as powerfully in each and every cultural space

---

[85] Patrick McKearney's doctoral work on a L'Arche community promises just the sort of understanding and insight which is needed—and I am immensely grateful to him for discussing his work and a draft of this chapter in some detail.

[86] 'Noli Me Tangere: The Moral Untouchability of Humanitarianism', in *Forces of Compassion: Humanitarianism between Ethics and Politics*, eds. E Bornstein and P. Redfield (Santa Fe, 2011), 32–52.

or time. There may be a natural propensity to music—but not all cultures will nurture a Beethoven. There may be a natural propensity to art, but not every time and place will produce a Michelangelo. It matters then, what we do with any supposed inclination to sympathy—it matters how, culturally, we nurture, shape, sustain, and marshal such a propensity—even supposing the original disposition to be one which all humans share.

What I have referred to as our cultural anxiety regarding the representation of suffering plainly worries about the implicit cultural task—that is, it is anxious on account of the fact that the nourishing of any supposed propensity to sympathy is itself vital to a politics of compassion, and is threatened by our 'promiscuous voyeurism' regarding the suffering other (in which voyeurism, certain aspect of Christian attention to the suffering of Christ may be included). Fassin's recent account of the triumph of humanitarian reason goes some way to allaying those anxieties—but not without providing grounds for what I termed 'the higher anxiety'. 'The cultural dynamics of social sentiment' may be politically effective—but the humanitarianism of our moral and political economies is one about which there may be a certain ambivalence.

Fassin's genealogy of humanitarian reason, which derives it from within Christianity, certainly reckons with the fact that suffering arguably acquired deep, sustained, and lasting 'cultural visibility' as a result of the invention of Christ's suffering—something relatively new in our moral universe and only belonging to the second half of Christianity's existence. The discovery of this suffering invited and demanded of the moral actor a pause—with this discovery we were culturally mandated to take the time to look, observe, to attend upon, and abide with those who suffer. But the challenge of Fassin's and other critiques is whether the tradition has within itself the resources to acknowledge and overcome the internal inconsistencies and external complaints that can be put to humanitarian reason, and to overcome them for the sake of a deeper humanitarianism which would attend to and acknowledge the suffering beyond those boundaries.

El Greco's great canvas, *The Disrobing of Christ* (see Plate 5), by virtue of its specific and original location, poses a very specific question. It was painted for the sacristy of the cathedral in Toledo, to hang over the head of the priest as he vested to celebrate the Eucharist. And what that placing of the picture asked was about the possibility of a particular exchange between Christ and priest. As Christ is about to take off his robe, so the priest is about to put one on— and it is no coincidence that Christ's robe looks like a chasuble, the brightly coloured vestment worn by the celebrant of the Mass. As Christ is divested of his robe, so the priest vests himself in a robe which recalls it—and in the season of Passiontide as it is known, the priest's robe would be deep red in colour in memory of Christ's passion, and thus the colour of the robe worn by Christ in the picture of his passion. This imagined exchange, which the priest undertakes time and again, poses questions, not just for the priest there and then, but for Christians at other places and times. How do we take up or take on Christ's suffering and those in whom he suffers? How does the representation of Christ's sufferings cause us to represent and re-present the suffering of Christ and others to ourselves?

The picture poses a challenge for an everyday Christian ethics, a challenge posed in one way by the worry about the effectiveness of the politics of compassion, and in another way by the worry about the moral adequacy of those politics. How can we imagine and practise a better humanitarianism, and how can the continued appropriation of the suffering of Christ, by means of various technologies of the self, sustain and advance such a practice?

5

Dying and 'Death before Death': On Hospices, Euthanasia, Alzheimer's, and on (Not) Knowing How to Dwindle

I INTRODUCTION: ON IMAGINING DEATH

In this chapter we turn from suffering to death and follow a similar path to the previous chapter, asking about the imagination of Christ's death in the Christian tradition and about its practical significance. How has Christianity conceived Christ's dying and Christian dying, and in turn, what has this imagining of death to say about contemporary dying, and to possibly competing forms of envisaging, narrating, attributing, and performing death?

We will note (in section II) that changes in the Christian imagination of Christ's death, along with changes in the understanding of the nature of the last judgment, allowed for and motivated the development of an influential and culturally persistent Christian art of dying.

We will further note (in section III) that presently the imagining and scripting of death takes two highly visible cultural forms: in the hospice (which consciously or unconsciously appropriates the *Ars moriendi* tradition), and in the practice of euthanasia. These two modalities of dying are typically presented as in deep contention one with the other, but I will note what is common to these two scripts: their critique of medicalization, their concern for the preservation of a self-conscious narrative and agency in dying, and, most importantly, their joint inapplicability to the 'long dying' which is increasingly characteristic of the affluent West. There are two key points to be made about this inapplicability. First, hospice care and euthanasia provide scripts for those who are specifically and identifiably dying, not merely dwindling, when dwindling is the increasingly common form that our new, long dying takes. Second, since a very significant number of those who dwindle to death will suffer from Alzheimer's disease, the shared concern of the two scripts for the preservation of a highly conscious narrative and agency in dying renders them even more inappropriate to our conditions. They are themselves responsible in part, perhaps, for the crude construal of Alzheimer's as 'death before death', which has become a dominant theme in its cultural construction and of the particular horror with which it is regarded.

I note briefly (in section IV), that we have seemingly no viable current script to cover this long dying, but chiefly silence or evasion. I take Hockey's ethnography of an old people's home, which is highly recognizable to most of us, as illustrative of how, in such institutions, this long dying is not creatively conceived, practised, or ameliorated, but is enshrined and concealed in a highly rehearsed ambiguity. Long dying takes a number of different forms—but I suggest that the common falling-out of the elderly from commensality (i.e. table fellowship) is a telling symbol of the construction of a 'death before death' that characterizes the long dying of many even without Alzheimer's as a form of social death. (The irony here is that the 'death before death' we claim to dread in Alzheimer's is mimicked in the social deaths created by the sequestration of the elderly, which is their common lot in the modern West.)

Finally (in sections V and VI), I consider what resources moral philosophy, social anthropology, and Christian moral theology may bring to the problem of 'death before death', both as it is said to occur in Alzheimer's, but also as it is created by our care and neglect of the elderly. I suggest, in line with the wider argument of the book, that in turning away from bioethics and towards social anthropology, moral theology must begin to conceive a new *Ars moriendi* (not of individual virtuosity, but of communal practice), which better imagines the performance of a good death under our particular and contemporary circumstances.

II GETTING DEAD CHRISTIANLY

Christians, like everyone else, have made a habit of dying, but it took some time, to cite the words of Février, before 'the death of a Christian became a Christian death'.[1]

Whatever else Jerusalem may or may not have to do with Athens, over the matter of dying the two cities were not immediately or very consciously at odds—it is quite striking that Socrates (the greatest figure of the classical moral tradition) and Christ met their deaths in somewhat similar fashions. Both died by execution; both, though they did not seek their death, did not avoid it; both provided farewell discourses by which their deaths were to be understood and construed; and both forgave those who carried out the sentences against them.[2] And even if, 'in striking contrast to the ancient classical writers,

---

[1] Cited by F. S. Paxton, *Christianizing Death: The Creation of a Ritual Process in Early Medieval Europe* (Ithaca, NY, 1990), 2, footnote 1.

[2] Points made by R. Kastenbaum, *On Our Way: The Final Passage Through Life and Death* (Berkeley, 2004), 53–62.

the early Christian Fathers are decidedly disinterested in the subject of preparing to die,[3] nonetheless when that interest increased, Seneca and Cicero's counsels on a good death were generally put to use without grave difficulties. Meanwhile, in any case, Christians could happily die without a specifically Christian script.

Most famously, Augustine seems to bring Christian death and classical death into contention in Chapter 17 (and following) of Book 1 of *City of God*. Yet the occasion of this discussion is, as Murray rightly points out, Augustine's conflict with the Donatists and not a live dispute with a (dying or dead) classical tradition.[4] It served Augustine's polemical purposes to present the Donatists' suicidal acts of defiance, which struck against attempts to overcome the nearly hundred-year-old schism, as morally suspect, inconsistent with the Biblical witness, and inspired chiefly by certain classical ideals (although not the best of the tradition). But it is, crucially, against Donatism and not against paganism that Augustine is led to distinguish the good death of a martyr, for example, from the bad death of suicide. Against the pagan tradition as such, Augustine has no very pressing concerns—and certainly he is not concerned to provide a script for Christian dying (nor did Monica enact one). To begin with, then, Christians died *a la Romana*.

The conversion of the death of a Christian into Christian death (or at least, into Christian death as it was conceived at the high water mark of the practice of Christian death in the late Middle Ages), seems to have turned on two principal developments which we may simply touch upon. It depended first, on the reimagining of Christ's death as exemplary, and second, on conceiving the deathbed as a peculiarly fraught moment of great existential weight. Only with those two key elements in place were the twin conditions (of model and motive) realized for the great flourishing of the *Ars moriendi* tradition which scripts Christian death in a culturally particular form.

In the previous chapter, I suggested that the discovery of Christ's suffering itself awaited a certain reconfiguration of the early Christian imagination, and it was as part of this that the exemplary character of Christ's death itself came more firmly into view. Augustine's preaching on Christ's death, not

---

[3] D. W. Atkinson, *The English* Ars Moriendi (New York, 1992), xii, vol. 5 of *Renaissance and Baroque Studies and Texts*, ed. E. Bernstein.

[4] A. Murray, *Suicide in the Middle Ages*, vol. ii, *The Curse on Self-Murder* (Oxford, 2000), 106ff. The Donatist church of Augustine's day claimed its descent from the rigorist side in the schism of *c*.310 which resulted from the disputed election to the see of Carthage, pitting those who had refused, in particular, to hand over the Scriptures in a preceding period of persecution (under Diocletian), against those whom the rigorists regarded as collaborators. By Augustine's time, the official attempts to end the nearly hundred-year-old schism by suppressing Donatism had led the more extreme Donatists into highly strung and dramatic resistance, including acts of suicidal terrorism (as the orthodox saw it).

only in his Good Friday sermons, but also in his sermons on the Psalms, prefers the self-possessed Jesus of the Johannine tradition over any other—but this in principle passible but in practice seemingly impassible figure offered no very immediately imitable model for the dying Christian. It is true that according to Augustine, 'the passion of our Lord and Saviour Jesus Christ constitutes a guarantee of glory and a lesson in patience'[5]—but it is generally more of the glory, less of the patience, that comes out in his exegesis of the stories of Christ's suffering and death. In Tractate 119, *On the Gospel of John*, commenting on Christ's assigning his mother to the care of his beloved disciple and vice versa, Augustine does pause to note that 'A passage...of moral character is here inserted. The good Teacher does what He thereby reminds us ought to be done and by his own example instructed His disciples that care for their parents ought to be a matter of concern to pious children'.[6] But this moralizing of Christ's death and dying is not a line that Augustine follows to any great degree, and is one against which his own presentation of the self-possessed Christ militates. Christ's death would only become manifestly exemplary, in other words, as his passion ceased to be imagined chiefly as something he accomplished, and became something he endured and suffered.[7]

But the emergence of Christian death needed not only a reimagining of the nature and manner of Christ's passion; in addition, it needed the further stimulus provided by a heightened sense of the importance of the death of a Christian. That is, Christian dying is invented only with the consciousness that *in hora mortis*, the deathbed of each and every Christian is itself a scene of high moral significance and moment (for which the death of Christ, newly conceived, could supply the pattern). And this dramatizing of the deathbed occurs when the last judgment is relocated from some point in the future when the world will end, to the here and now of each individual death. Only as eschatological expectations of general resurrection give way to more immediate and individual 'final reckoning' and death and judgement are fused, does the deathbed becomes a scene of a crisis which needs to be confronted and addressed (as is explicitly captured in the persistent and battling demons of the pictorial editions of the *Ars*, intent on winning the soul of Moriens in its moment of grave existential crisis. The calmly imagined death of Monica, by contrast, has none of the high drama of these cartoon capers.) As Ariès puts it,

---

[5] Augustine, *Sermons*, 218c, 1.   [6] Augustine, *On the Gospel of John*, 119, 2.

[7] One may speculate that the invention of the dormition of Mary provided an altogether more serviceable model for the Christian imagining of a good death, not only because it did not have to overcome the problem of the seeming impassibility of the dying subject, but also because it was immediately more promising as a model of everyday and serene dying than is the violent death of the cross. See D. F. Duclow, 'Dying Well: The *Ars moriendi* and the Dormition of the Virgin', in *Death and Dying in the Middle Ages*, eds. E. E. DuBruck and B. I. Gusick (New York, 1999), 379–402.

the drama which used to take place at the end of time, now 'takes place in the bedroom of the dying person'[8]—it is here that the cosmic theatre of judgment is now played out.

With these two elements in place (the reimagination of Christ's death such that it could serve as moral exemplar, and the invention of the death-bed as the site of a final drama in which the eternal fate of the individual would be settled), a motive and a means were in place for the development and flourishing of the various texts of the *Ars moriendi* tradition in the late fifteenth century.

Although its roots can be traced further back (in a long tradition of *momento mori* and in a general early medieval tradition commending Christ's forti-tude in the Garden of Gethsemane and on the Cross), the credit for being the immediate author of the tradition belongs to Gerson.[9] By the late Carolingian period (according to Paxton's account), there emerged distinctive liturgies aimed at assisting the dying to die well.[10] But it was the third part of Gerson's pastoral handbook, *Opusculum Tripartitum*, entitled *Scientia Mortis* of *c.*1408 (which Gerson himself translated into French, as *La Médicine de l'Âme*), which 'provided the structure for the *Ars moriendi* treatise'[11]—more fully the *Tractatus Artis bene Moriendi* of the 1420s. This treatise circulated through-out Europe not only in a Latin version, but also in German, French, Dutch, English, Italian, Spanish, and Catalan translations,[12] and was also abridged in a version that dramatizes 'the moral conflict described in the longer version's second chapter',[13] dealing with temptations to which the dying are especially prone. It was the abridgment, often accompanied by illustrations, that was most widely circulated through block book editions.[14] These texts became

---

[8] P. Ariès, *The Hour of Our Death* (London, 1981), 105.

[9] Gerson's work and the subsequent tradition must itself be placed in the context of what Duffy refers to as the 'expansion of religious provision for lay people' which is associated with Lateran Council of 1215 and the popular Christianity of the friars, and gives rise not only to the demand for assistance 'in the pursuit of a serious interior religious life', but also to a rise in the market for religious books: see E. Duffy, *Marking the Hours* (New Haven, 2006), 6, referring to R. Swanson, *Religion and Devotion in Europe 1215–1515* (Cambridge, 1993), chs. 1 and 5. As Duffy puts it: 'The devotional temperature of the fourteenth and fifteenth centuries was. . . rising steadily, as late medieval Christianity went through the religious equivalent of global warming, inspired in part by the preaching and devotional regime of the Franciscans, and partly by a grow-ing hunger for religious variety and intensity on the part of the lay men and women with time, leisure, literacy, and not least, money on their hands' (63).

[10] See Paxton, *Christianizing Death*.

[11] D. F. Duclow, 'The *Ars moriendi* and the Dormition of the Virgin', 380.

[12] On which, see M. C. O'Connor, *The Art of Dying Well: The Development of the* Ars Moriendi (New York, 1941).

[13] Duclow, 'The *Ars moriendi* and the Dormition of the Virgin', 380.

[14] The original version is most easily cited in two English editions, either the ms. *Crafte and Knowledge for to Dye Well* of *c.*1490 or Caxton's *The Arte and Crafte to Know Well to Dye* printed in the same year—which itself claims to be a translation from the French, and is shorter than the other English version. These two are conveniently found in D. W. Atkinson, *The English* Ars Moriendi, and quotations are from this edition.

veritable 'bluffers' guides', or *Dying for Dummies*, as they would now be called—illustrated self-help manuals for the dying, which were extraordinarily popular[15] and had astonishingly long-standing cultural reach and force, through such diverse and influential inheritors as Perkins, Bellarmine, Taylor, and Wesley.[16]

In this tradition, then, the envisioning of Christian death by reference to Christ's death reached its apogee and is expressed in the simple thought that: 'suche thynges as Cryst dyd dyinge on the crosse the same shulde euery man do att hys last ende'.[17] The longest chapter in the *Ars moriendi* texts and the one most illustrated is chapter two, which treats of the temptations to which the dying are prey and the virtues which are remedies against them.[18] The dying man is exhorted in this and the next chapter to 'remember hym and thynke on the passion off Cryste, for therby all the deuylles temptacions and gyles be moste ouercome and voyded'.[19] This remembrance first of all gives him hope: the very attitude of Christ on the cross is itself, following for example, Bernard of Clairvaux's interpretation of his posture as one of openness, an encouragement to the sinner.[20] But the dying man is also bidden to take Christ as a practical exemplar. And Christ, it is said, 'dyd fyue thynges pryncipally hangyng on the crosse: he adoured and prayd, he wepte, he cryed, he commaunded his soule to God, and he yelded to hym his sperite'.[21] Thus everyman should 'adore and pray'; weep (in repentance); cry 'from the depnes of his

---

[15] Some 20 per cent of surviving block books, i.e. those printed from engraved wood blocks, are *Ars moriendi* texts. For the claim and references, see A. Verhey, *The Christian Art of Dying* (Grand Rapids, MI, 2011), 87, footnote 21.

[16] W. Perkins, *A Salve for a Sick Man* (1595), R. Bellarmine, *De Arte Bene Moriendi* (1619), in Bellarmine, *Spiritual Writings*, eds. and trans. J. P. Donelly and R. J. Teske (New York, 1989), 321–86; Jeremy Taylor, *The Rule and Exercises of Holy Dying* (1651); for Wesley and later Methodism, see S. J. Lavi, *The Modern Art of Dying* (Princeton, 2005).

[17] *Crafte and Knowledge for to Dye Well*, 11, in Atkinson, *The English* Ars Moriendi.

[18] Chapter 1 is a commendation of death, but one might say that the *Ars moriendi* tradition seems not to take this commendation at all seriously—that is, insofar as the texts invariably treat very seriously the temptations to which the dying are prone, they take it for granted that that commendation of death is not going to be believed and thus that death will not simply be welcomed.

[19] *Crafte and Knowledge for to Dye Well*, 11, in Atkinson, *The English* Ars Moriendi.

[20] In *Crafte and Knowledge for to Dye Well*, the dying man is encouraged, following the injunction of Bernard of Clairvaux, to 'take hede diligently of disposicione off Chrystys body in the crosse. Take hede and see hys hede inclined to saue the, and his mouth to kysse the, hys armes spredde to clyppe the, hys hands thrilled to yeue the, hys syde openyd to loue the' (5–6). In Caxton's version, although with no mention of Bernard, one who despairs of the mercy of God is counselled: 'In trouth, the dysposicyon of the body of our Lord Jhesu Criste, hanging in the crosse, ought moche enduce a seke persone paynyng to the deth to haue veray hope & confidence in God, for he hath the hede inclined and bowed to kysse us, the armes stratched a brode for tenbrace us, the handes perced and opened for to gyue to us, the side open for to loue us, and all his body stratched for to gyue hym selfe all to us' (24). The invitation to, and reliance on, a particular picture of Christ's death is a striking reminder of the importance and power of the visual culture.

[21] *The Arte and Crafte to Know Well to Dye*, 27, in Atkinson, *The English* Ars Moriendi.

herte' (to seek remission of sins); commend his soul to God, saying 'in manus tuas'; and so too, he ought to yield his spirit willingly.

The *Ars moriendi* tradition here connects with the tradition of the Seven Words from the cross—it is the gathering and formalization of Christ's final words, different in the different Gospels, into a unified set of sayings, which indicates the urge to display clearly and fully the character and scope of Christ's agency in its moral aspect. In those Seven Words, Christ forgives, exhorts, and sustains the other in need, commends his spirit to God, and entrusts his mother Mary to his beloved disciple, her new son, and this beloved disciple to Mary, the disciple's new mother. These seven words amount to a care of the self and other going beyond a mere Stoic patience to a more fully realized ideal of moral agency in death, notwithstanding its pains.[22] And it was this settling of spiritual, moral, and social affairs (with God and neighbour) which was paradigmatic for the *Ars moriendi* tradition and its later successors.

The tradition's extraordinary and explicit prominence at the end of the fifteenth century was relatively short-lived. Luther's churlish dismissal of the tradition ('Many books have been written...on how we are to prepare for death: nothing but error, and people have only become more downcast'[23]), chiefly expressed his animus towards the late medieval economy of sins, purgatory, and forgiveness in which the *Ars moriendi* literature flourished (and which he attacked more explicitly in the *95 Theses* and thereafter). But the claim that these books only served to make people 'more downcast' leaves their vast popularity and continuing influence more than slightly mysterious—for notwithstanding the repudiation of that trade in sins and forgiveness by all sides, the *Ars moriendi* tradition retained its popularity through various adaptations and developments, not only amongst Catholics, but even amongst Protestants. The utility of these books lay, of course, in their 'practical, everyday life' instructions 'for the dying and those attending them about what to expect and how to practice the rites that produce a "good death"'.[24] Christians may once have managed to die without official instructions and doubtless could have done so again; but in adaptations of one kind or another, the *Ars moriendi*, explicitly or otherwise, continued to prove highly serviceable in instructing and guiding the dying. It is only perhaps in the most modern period that this and other available scripts seem singularly to have failed to provide useful instructions for a newly invented form of dying.

[22] The tradition of the Seven Words goes back to very early Christianity—according to Raymond Brown, to Tatian's *Diatessaron* of the second century with its harmonization of the gospels: *The Death of the Messiah*, vol 2 (New York, 1994), 972.

[23] Cited by A. Reinis, *Reforming the Art of Dying: The* Ars moriendi *in the German Reformation (1519–1528)* (Farnham, Surrey, 2007), 1.

[24] Duclow, 'The *Ars moriendi* and the Dormition of the Virgin', 396.

III TWO SCRIPTS—BUT FOR ONLY ONE SORT OF (OLD-FASHIONED) DYING

In our current context, the imagining and scripting of death takes two highly visible cultural forms: in the hospice (the most plausible heir to the *Ars moriendi* tradition), and in euthanasia. It was a concern for a good death that motivated the modern founding of the hospice movement (with the establishment of St Christopher's Hospice by Dame Cicely Saunders in 1967), and there has been, at least in the Anglophone world, a phenomenal proliferation of the ideals, norms, and practices of the modern hospice movement.[25] It was the same concern for a good death that led to the modern movement for euthanasia, which albeit legally practised in only a very few jurisdictions, has provided for the West an increasingly prominent imagination of dying.

The very use of the word 'hospice' was indicative of that movement's concern to signal a return to previous and better practice—and in the contention between this scripting of death and the seeming counterscript proposed by the euthanasia movement—both sides appear willing to play out the conflict as yet another engagement between a traditionalist and a modern, scientific, and rationalist outlook. To fall in wholly with this familiar narrative is, however, to miss what is common to these two movements, and which may otherwise be overlooked. Three such features are identified, the third of which is the most important, as indicating not simply shared presuppositions, but a shared (and very important) failing.

In the first place, both movements arise from a common critique of modern, (specifically) medicalized dying.[26] From the 1960s onwards, modern medicine was regularly charged with being so gripped by a scientific and technological approach as to fail to see the needs of the dying patient which existed outside this framing. According to Kubler-Ross's writing in 1969, 'dying nowadays is…lonely, mechanical and dehumanised',[27] and, according to Seale, the 'defining characteristics [of many studies of dying from the 1960s onwards] has increasingly become a normative rehearsal of the failings of impersonal hospital routines in providing a humane environment for dying'.[28] The failings of a technologized medicine would typically be thought to take one of two characteristic forms—either overtreatment or neglect. Either medicine would do everything for patients for whom this 'everything' offered no benefit but simply a burden; or it would do nothing, treating such patients with the somewhat embarrassed neglect reserved for those who could no longer benefit from

---

[25] See figures for the number of hospices worldwide, up to 1997, cited in C. Seale, *Constructing Death: The Sociology of Dying and Bereavement* (Cambridge, 1998), 114.

[26] A point stressed by T. Walter, *The Revival of Death* (London, 1994) and Seale, *Constructing Death*, 184.

[27] Cited by Seale, *Constructing Death*, 105.   [28] Seale, *Constructing Death*, 103.

a technological wizardry that was perhaps unwilling to face up to its limits. So the story was told in many critiques.[29] The point for now, however, is that for proponents of both hospice care and of euthanasia, this critique is common ground, and with it the conviction that patients and doctors should be encouraged to a greater awareness and openness about death.

In the second place, both movements are perhaps equally imbued with notions central to projects of self-expression and preservation of identity, characteristic of late modernity. Seale refers to a 'deeply rooted cultural obligation to be free, so that life events are interpreted as a matter of personal choice, given authority by reference to an inner unfolding of the essential self'[30]— and arguably, both hospice care and euthanasia pay tribute to this obligation, though in different ways. Hospice care bids to preserve and maintain the project of the self for as long as possible up until the occurrence of biological death; euthanasia brings death forwards so as to avoid the risk of the death of the self prior to biological death. The hospice hopes to sustain the realm of the personal and social for as long as possible and even in the unpromising, hostile territory of dying; euthanasia counsels us to abandon the territory rather than entering it, moving death forward if need be, to prevent our slipping over a border into that risky no-man's land where the self's projects can no longer be confidently sustained. Viewed from this angle, then, again there does not seem to be a deep difference between the hospice and the euthanasia clinic, but rather a common assessment that the ability of the autonomous agent to direct his or her own story is a precondition of worthwhile life. Thus construed, the difference between the two scripts is empirical and specifically about the conditions under which such autonomy can be sustained. (And the choice between them is a pragmatic one, not a matter of very deep principle, as bioethics textbooks would have it.)[31] On the basis of merely a different calculation then, the two movements battle death on different fronts, but in a mirror image fashion, seeking in the one case to evade the loss of the self by an early exit, or in the other case reckoning on being able to sustain the self even in the harsh regions of dying. In either case, the common purpose could be said to lie in ensuring that we leave the world exercising our agency and individuality.[32]

[29] Such as in B. G. Glaser and A. L. Strauss, *Time for Dying* (Chicago, 1968), cited by Seale.

[30] Seale, *Constructing Death*, 120.

[31] I should stress that it is not my claim here that this is the best way to understand hospice care, only that this understanding may be culturally significant under present circumstances. As Eric Southworth has very properly pointed out to me, chapter 53 of *The Rule of St Benedict* (on the reception of guests and especially pilgrims) provides an altogether more adequate understanding of the work of a hospice.

[32] That this represents a plausible reading of both depends on Seale's wider argument about a dominant cultural script of discovery and quest which provides a 'construction of dying as an opportunity for personal growth'—exemplified in stage theories of dying and grief, as well as by the genre of heroic confessional death loved by the media, in which the sufferer is shown engaged in a 'journey, involving tests of personal qualities of courage and will power, offering a diagram for self-defining heroism': Seale, *Constructing Death*, 106. It is certainly a strength of this reading

Both the hospice movement and euthanasia aim to remove the patient from the clutches of an allegedly overly-technologized hospital ward in which only over-treatment or neglect were available. Both, having released the patient from futile treatments, offer to manage or mitigate the pain and suffering which threaten the self, either by treating them or by ending them with a hastened death. Thus there could be said to be a certain commonality behind the contention in which these two movements are engaged. But the most important commonality is not here, but much more significantly in the inapplicability of either of these scripts to the dying which is perhaps most characteristic of our late modern condition. Albeit in different ways, both these movements fail to take account of the wider social context in which their set piece contention takes place.

The insensitivity to the social landscape goes very deep in the case of advocates of euthanasia, who rarely show any willingness to reckon with the harsh facts of deprivation and inequalities of power that provide the context for the operation of the sort of laws permitting euthanasia which they typically advocate. This landscape is significant in two related ways. First, it may be the harshness of the circumstances in which the elderly find themselves that creates the demand for the legalization of euthanasia in the first place. But put that point to one side, though we will need to return to it, and suppose for now that demands for euthanasia are currently what one might term 'wholly innocent and authentic'. Still, in the second place, any change in the law would plainly amount to more than the mere willing of an individual or personal preference as regards my dying (as say, would be my wanting to die besides the sea or in Jerusalem), which preference would have no wider or general social implications. On the contrary, the legal recognition of medically assisted dying will have implications, possibly quite profound implications, for the dying of all others—since those others will now be doing something they were previously not doing, namely choosing not to die. And in the way of such things, this 'choice' may come to stand in need of justification, and so admit of social criticism. About this feature of the social context, advocates for the legalization of euthanasia seem to show no very profound interest beyond offering an assurance that mechanisms or systems can be devised to prevent abuse. This assurance, however, provides rather more comfort to the educated and privileged (rather good at getting their way in life, and reasonably confident that they will get their way in death, too), than to the most representative figure amongst the dying in the UK at the beginning of the twenty-first century, that is, a single, poor, socially marginalized woman.

---

of the situation that it is consistent with Alzheimer's having become prominent as especially troubling to the modern consciousness of aging. In popular parlance, Alzheimer's is 'a death before death', 'a living death', 'the death of the person', and so on. It is particularly feared as erasing the treasured self—leaving us unable to be the selves we are called to be.

To put the point more fully—the question to be asked and answered is whether the demand for the legalization of euthanasia is just. Suppose we test the proposal against John Rawls' widely regarded and influential *A Theory of Justice*.[33] Rawls requires that we ask of any proposed social arrangement whether it is one we could will from behind 'a veil of ignorance'—that is, without our knowing where we will be positioned in the envisaged social order or hierarchy, and thus in ignorance of whether we will be winners or losers in that order. Thus, to take a seemingly straightforward example, no rational agent would likely will the institution of slavery were that person ignorant of where he or she would stand in the slave-owning society.

There is no reason to doubt that the typical plea for the legalization of euthanasia is heartfelt and indicative of real fears and anxieties around modern dying; but could it, according to Rawls' test, be considered just? An immediate consequence of the legalization of euthanasia would be, as noted above, that not to choose euthanasia would become what it was not before, namely a decision and a choice, and as such subject to comment, criticism, and pressure. Allow the veil of ignorance to fall. From behind that veil, we do not know whether we will be (what most readers of this book quite likely are) occupants of places of privilege in the socio-economic hierarchy, and thus confident social actors who are accomplished in working systems for our benefit—or whether, on the contrary, we will find ourselves at the opposite end of the spectrum and thus (since socio-economic status is inversely related to health), sicker as well as poorer, more debilitated in our old age, as well as less privileged and less powerful social actors. Euthanasia, some surveys suggest, finds more support amongst the better educated[34] (and hence more wealthy)—and advocates of euthanasia may simply congratulate themselves on this state of affairs as indicating the merits of their case. But isn't it equally open to us to wonder whether the educated and the privileged take it for granted that they have nothing to fear even from the introduction of medical euthanasia in which the right to die could so easily become an implicit duty to justify continuing a life against whatever formal or informal metrics of worth and value would soon come to stand in judgment over the elderly and dying? A Cambridge don may, perhaps, view such a state of affairs with (smug) equanimity, but a more socially representative figure amongst the dying may understandably take a different view.

If, however, we critique euthanasia from this particular angle, there is another and perhaps more important sense in which the movement for euthanasia and its supposed competitor, the movement for hospice care, both and together fail to reckon with our current and emerging social circumstances. The issue here is not a failure of justice, but a failure of scope or relevance, in the sense

---

[33] John Rawls, *A Theory of Justice* (London, 1972).

[34] See e.g. D. P. Cadell and R. R. Newton, 'Euthanasia: American Attitudes towards the Physician's Role', *Social Science and Medicine*, 40 [1995], 1671–81.

that both hospice care and euthanasia could provide (whether satisfactorily or otherwise), only a very partial solution to the circumstances of contemporary dying. The point is simply, if you will excuse the statement of the seemingly obvious, that both hospice care and euthanasia are chiefly appropriate for the deaths of those who are dying. That is, the hospice or the euthanasia facility—like the deathbed reckoning commended in the *Ars moriendi* tradition—is for those whose dying is clearly signalled and anticipated, as is often the case for those who will die with cancer. But a lot of dying—and in particular our modern long dying—does not conform to this pattern.

According to current expectations, maybe only 20 per cent of us can expect a clearly heralded death as commonly occurs with cancer—but fully twice as many will experience not a clearly marked dying, but a protracted 'dwindling' of increasing debility.[35] The most likely trajectory of our lives towards death will not allow us to assume the dying role, even though we may very well be declining, dwindling, and dependent.[36] Combine this form of ageing with a demographic profile produced by changing patterns of procreation which significantly reduces the cohort of middle-aged carers on whom the burden of care traditionally falls—what is then created is the so-called 'problem of aging', 'the unintended consequence of our success in preventing, curing, or managing the earlier and more acute causes of death that once predominated',[37] such as pneumonia, flu, kidney failure, septicaemia, and so on. (When the modern pension was introduced in the UK in 1945, male life expectancy was 65.) Saved from these early deaths, 40 per cent of us can expect to 'slip into protracted dotage and feebleness, needing protracted long-term care';[38] our 'trajectory towards death' will be 'gradual but unrelenting, with steady decline, enfeeblement, and growing dependency, often lasting a decade or longer.'[39]

This dwindling is not dying—or at least, it is not dying as provided for by either of the scripts on offer since it does not announce itself as imminent, or even as so many months away. And there is a further difficulty. For very many of the 40 per cent of us who will have a long dying, our declines will also be marked by dementia. Figures vary, but in the older cohorts of the dwindling, perhaps as many as 15–20 per cent are predicted to experience some form of dementia, typically Alzheimer's. Now Alzheimer's 'has likely become the most dreaded disease of old age'[40]—certainly it is commonly pictured in

---

[35] See the analysis referred to in Chapter 1 of the report of the US President's Council on Bioethics, *Taking Care: Ethical Caregiving in our Aging Society* (Washington, DC, 2005).

[36] Again, see the analysis from a study conducted by the Rand Corporation, referred to in *Taking Care*.

[37] The President's Council on Bioethics, *Taking Care*, 11.

[38] The President's Council on Bioethics, *Taking Care*, 14.

[39] The President's Council on Bioethics, *Taking Care*, 14.

[40] A. McLean, *The Person in Dementia: A Study of Nursing Home Care in the US* (Peterborough, Ontario, 2007), 1.

highly charged imagery as an 'unbecoming of the self',[41] the 'loss of self',[42] a 'death in life', 'death before death', 'never-ending death',[43] 'the death of the person', a 'living death'. So not only can we say that whatever problem hospice care—or euthanasia—solves, it is not the problem of our modern long dying, we can also say, with further emphasis, that it's not the problem of dying with dementia.

By way of an aside, we might note that bioethics has certainly not caught up with these developments, and had, in any case, always been pretty much irrelevant to those who were not dying but simply aged. Dominated by an either/or between hospice and euthanasia, bioethics gives the unfortunate impression that the only important question raised by aging has to do with managing one's exit from it. To take a single example, *The Oxford Handbook of Bioethics*, in a section devoted to the 'The End of Life', has as its chief concern the management of key decision points which often occur in the course of medical care in the very last stages of life; thus, it has chapters on the definition of death, 'precedent autonomy', advance directives and end-of-life care', and 'physician-assisted death'. The other side of the debate, so to speak, is represented by the elderly having a chapter in their own right in the section on 'Justice and Policy'. But nothing more is said about old age in general—just when one might have thought that this particular and significant stretch of human life deserves examination to identify the moral concerns that may specifically or especially belong to it.[44]

As Seale comments: 'gradual decline in extreme old age, or dementia, do not offer entry to [the] dying role' which is 'particularly supported by the cultural scripts available for the formation of self-identity in later modern and, particularly, anglophone societies'.[45] Dwindling is not the same as clearly marked dying, and dementia, furthermore, seems to deprive us of the kind of agency which the hospice or euthanasia are intended to preserve—indeed Alzheimer's

---

[41] A. Fontana and R. Smith 'Alzheimer's Disease Victims: The "Unbecoming" of Self and the Normalization of Competence', *Sociological Perspectives* (1989), 32 (1), 35–46.

[42] D. Cohen and C. Eisdorfer, *Loss of Self* (London, 1986).

[43] These last three mentioned as 'well-worn phrases' by Sharon Kaufman, 'Dementia-Near-Death and Life Itself', in A. Leibing and L. Cohen, *Thinking about Dementia: Culture, Loss and the Anthropology of Senility* (New Brunswick, NJ, 2006), 30.

[44] *The Oxford Handbook of Bioethics*, ed. D. Steinbock (Oxford, 2007). *The Oxford Handbook of Practical Ethics*, ed. H. LaFollette (Oxford, 2003), is even more constrained and limits itself to a chapter on 'Euthanasia and Physician Assisted Suicide'. *The Routledge Companion to Ethics*, ed. J. Skorupski (London, 2010), has, as we might by now expect, nothing on aging or the elderly, but solely a chapter on 'Ending Life'. It may be, of course, that the Catholic tradition of casuistry is part of the genealogy of this unfortunate state of affairs, with its heightened focus on and interest in 'difficult questions'. Be that as it may, however, it is striking that a standard Roman Catholic text, B. M. Ashley and K. D. O'Rourke, *Ethics of Health Care*, 3rd ed. (Washington, DC, 2002), seems to have no wider horizon beyond this rather familiar and wearisome 'for and against'.

[45] Seale, *Constructing Death*, 2. Eric Southworth asks a pertinent question, worthy of further enquiry: does Christianity furnish any models of exemplary old age in the stories of the saints?

may well evoke the particular horror it does because it seems so determinedly to defy being scripted in accordance with our currently favoured plot lines for the dying.

IV DYING WITHOUT A SCRIPT

How then does unscripted dying occur? How, typically, do we order the dwindling and dying of those who cannot die in accordance with either of the favoured narratives? Quite briefly, I suggest, and referring to an ethnography of an old people's home, that what is characteristic of our current practice in relation to our long dying is not so much an address to the problem, but its highly practised concealment by ambiguity or evasion. The deep irony here is that behind this evasion we create for the long dying, in effect, a social death that mimics the 'death of the person' and the 'death before death' which renders Alzheimer's so horrifying to us. That is, the social deaths of large numbers of our population in sequestered isolation mirrors the 'death before death' which, so we tell ourselves, is cruelly dealt out by Alzheimer's.

In *Experiences of Death: An Anthropological Account*, Jennifer Hockey describes the management of an old people's home as a complex piece of theatre, a sort of 'stage production', in which the literal meaning of what is going on is concealed by figurative meanings.[46] As Hockey puts it: 'The literal meaning of daily life within the home is that forty-five people have lived so long as to have outgrown their places within the outside world'[47] and have come to a place apart to die. The figurative meanings are achieved by the manipulation of institutional 'space and time' in 'such a way that the approaches of death are masked and the illusion of homely independence is fostered'.[48] Those who come to Highfield House have been 'separated from a past life, and from the roles and relationships through which it was constituted'; all are experiencing a 'gradual physical detoriaration' which 'can only lead to their death'; all will receive various 'domestic and nursing services' as 'a way of managing the practicalities of this process of deterioration'.[49] And yet this reality—of managed decline towards death—is, in various ways, concealed from view and goes unspoken.

The very word 'resident' is itself a concealment—by means of the term 'a fictive sense of stability or permanence is…imposed upon a gradually fading population'[50] which is, of course, anything but resident. But in addition

---

[46] J. Hockey, *Experiences of Death: An Anthropological Account* (Edinburgh, 1990).
[47] Hockey, *Experiences of Death*, 97.   [48] Hockey, *Experiences of Death*, 200.
[49] Hockey, *Experiences of Death*, 97.   [50] Hockey, *Experiences of Death*, 101.

to this concealment, the residents, who are not residents, are residents of Highfield House—which is, however, really a home, but not in the good sense. As Hockey notes, although in general 'the word "home" implies something more [and better] than just a house'—so that developers always build homes, not houses—'the prefacing of the word "home" with the name of a category, "old folks" or "dogs", rather than an individual, "Mr Wilkinson", immediately inverts the more positive meaning of the word'.

> Notions of hearth and home sweet home, of the private and the domestic, then give way to images of a public, rule-bound space into which the individual is 'put away'. Thus, although Highfield House is described as being 'as homely and comfortable as possible', the stigmatized word 'home' is not used to name it.[51]

In common with forty out of forty-one other local and similar institutions, Highfield eschews the word home, exemplifying a 'cultural manipulation of awareness'.

So the residents who are not really residents, in the House which is really a home (but not in a good way), are receiving care—but not really, since the care is not the care of 'caring for someone', for when we 'care for someone', we are tied to them by affection, and possibly by blood too. Here and elsewhere in modern provision, care is bought.

This theatre of concealment is not, however, a matter of words and names alone. According to Hockey, the Matron's role is crucial in managing the manipulation of reality—indeed, in various important rituals (such as serving the meat at lunch-time and selecting a slice appropriate to a particular resident, or seating herself at a resident's breakfast table on their birthday and joining in the opening of cards, and so on), the Matron performs 'care' before 'residents and staff, both of whom are involved more literally in the management of dependency'.[52] The Matron's performance helps to promote the wider 'figurative reality within which "life" and "death" are preserved as rigidly opposed categories, and ageing itself is effectively submerged'.[53]

Strikingly, residents themselves overturn this separation and concealment, often by joking. So Hockey reports that when residents see staff with an empty rubbish bag they will often joke: 'you might as well put me in there'. As Hockey puts it, 'residents' use of rubbish as a metaphor for themselves, though made oblique through humour, nonetheless constitutes a succinct and powerful statement about their marginalized social status, as well as their fragile physical state.'[54] In this and other ways, residents keep death present in a context where it is in other ways denied and unacknowledged.

---

[51] Hockey, *Experiences of Death*, 103.   [52] Hockey, *Experiences of Death*, 106.
[53] Hockey, *Experiences of Death*, 123.
[54] Hockey, *Experiences of Death*, 153. A precedent is set by Kierkegaard, who after he fainted at an evening gathering is said to have said 'leave it for the maid to sweep up in the morning'.

What the jokes suggest is well understood by the residents but is never openly spoken is that the home is really a last resort for those awaiting death, who have 'toppled over the edge of the social "map" ';[55] their social marginality 'is recognized, and contained within a space which is physically, socially and structurally marginal to the rest of society. It is transformed into an institutionalised marginality'.[56] In coming to live with those 'with whom they have no longstanding ties of blood or affection',[57] and in shedding 'possessions, responsibilities and personal space', residents are obliged to relinquish key elements of their social selves—enacting a sort of social death, a death before death, in preparation for death itself.

And what should we say of this space of institutionalized marginality and those like it, which we have created and willed for the elderly? With rather striking understatement, Seale comments that: 'In late modernity it appears that the process of ageing is difficult to incorporate as a meaningful and fulfilling part of social life.'[58] (Or as a friend of mine put it recently and more pithily: 'if this is the £1000 per week home, I'd hate to see what the £500 per week one is like'.) The success of medicine in dealing with the acute conditions that killed our grandparents, has given us the prospect of a much extended span of life. But we have not yet discovered how to make of this longevity chiefly and generally a benefit and not quite often a curse. Alzheimer's only exacerbates the problem—and adds the irony that the 'death of the person' which we take to be the tragic fate of those suffering from the disease is only what, in another sense, we will for a much wider class of the elderly. We might then put it more sharply—we have created an old age which for very many is bleak and lonely and during which their social deaths precede their bodily deaths by a number of years. For very many and not just for those suffering from dementia, their experience of aging (which will include debility, dependence, poverty, and marginalization), will itself amount to a death before death, since even without dementia they may well suffer a severe loss of social connections and bonds, and thus a virtual exile from society. I referred in the previous chapter to Biehl's notion of 'zones of social abandonment'—and we are surely bound to consider whether the experience of protracted dwindling, which is the path towards death followed by very many in our society, is precisely an experience of social abandonment.

Tales of those who die alone and remain undiscovered for months or even years in the loneliness of our modern cities are the stuff of urban myths and will capture headlines from time to time. But no headlines are awarded to the far more emblematic and everyday occurrence of what might be regarded as a stark indicator of the loss of the social for the isolated elderly—and that is eating alone. The shared meal, with its forms and rituals, is one of the great

[55] Hockey, *Experiences of Death*, 109.   [56] Hockey, *Experiences of Death*, 110.
[57] Hockey, *Experiences of Death*, 105.   [58] Seale, *Constructing Death*, 105.

signs of the human transformation of the merely biological into the cultural and social (as Lévi-Strauss famously pointed out). Some time ago we humans converted the taking of fuel into a shared and ordered occasion in which our sociality is reaffirmed, negotiated, enhanced, and celebrated. Nothing more clearly signals the fall away from the social for our elderly than their fall out of commensality (to give the habit of shared eating its proper name), and thereby their joining our primate cousins as solitary eaters. And yet this, we know, is the everyday lot of very many of those elderly who increasingly live alone, without regular familial or other social engagement. But lest we are too hard on ourselves, let us take what comfort we can from the fact that the rise of dementia seems at least to check the rise of depression amongst the elderly— and also, if possible, from the fact that eating alone is increasingly the standard expression of 'family life' even amongst those who don't, technically, live alone.

V THE IRRELEVANCE OF BIOETHICS—AND THE NEED FOR FIELDWORK IN ALZHEIMER'S

The two most influential current scripts for dying are essentially inapplicable to the long dwindling to death which is the prospect for many of us. This long dwindling is often experienced in one or other of two modes of 'death before death': the one dealt out to growing numbers of the aged by the rise of Alzheimer's; the other dealt out by the removal of the elderly from the life course into various forms of sequestered isolation which amount to a social death before death. Our question becomes: how can moral theology, concerned to provide an everyday ethics, address our current circumstances? My suggestion is that moral theology must do better than bioethics, which singularly fails to attend to an issue which ought to be of great concern for ethics. Furthermore and in any case (even if bioethics were not so dismal), moral theology will need to turn towards social anthropology if it is not only to understand the character of the problem, but also to begin to imagine a more adequate social practice of death and dying than is current.

I remarked in Chapter 1 that modern moral philosophy (in its dominant *a priori* strains) has the bioethics it deserves. And something of the distinct limitations of a typical contribution from bioethics to the debate which concerns us is provided by a recent report on the care of the elderly from the US President's Council.[59] The limitations focused on here, however, are not those already mentioned limitations of social relevance; here we are concerned to show how even in dealing with the issues it chooses to address, bioethics is

---

[59] The President's Council on Bioethics, *Taking Care*.

drastically afflicted by its failure to grasp the need for analysis and knowledge beyond its own competencies.

As the President's Council sets up the problem of aging, we are faced with a choice between recognizing or repudiating a moral imperative. The moral imperative is to care for the elderly in traditional ways, and the temptation to repudiate it is put in our way by those who champion a case for limiting, refusing, or even withdrawing care. Having set up the problem in this form, the President's Council launches into a lively 'for and against' (which seems a lot like a recapitulation of the dialetics of pro-life/pro-choice hostilities), arguing that the case for accepting, in particular, assisted suicide as a means of moderating the supposed burden of care is fundamentally flawed and threatens to eclipse the moral imperative of care. Others, as the Council acknowledges, take a contrary view.

Thus far then, we seem to have a reprise of the normal stand-off between those who favour hospice care and those who advocate euthanasia. But I want to note now the deeper inadequacies of this framing, a framing which causes the report to rush to answer a question (the licitness or otherwise of various care decisions at the end of life), which really ought to wait its turn behind some rather more fundamental issues. As it is, the discussion of this question in this manner is bound to take for granted certain presuppositions which shape the debate about 'the crisis of the care of the elderly' but will fail to address the adequacy of those particular starting points and presuppositions.

What we might think of as the pro-choice side, to take that first, might be encouraged to reflect that any simple welcoming of advanced directives, living wills, and assisted suicide, as enhancements of autonomy and freedom of choice is, well, simple—as in simple-minded. As has already been suggested, it should not simply be taken for granted that the exercise of any of these options is unaffected by factors that might render the choice of, say, assisted suicide troubling or even sinister. Such factors range from the relatively subtle influence exercised by limited or questionable conceptions of human well-being, to the less-than-subtle force of fears amongst the elderly where there are distinct asymmetries of power. Thus, the readiness of the elderly and the soon-to-be elderly to turn to living wills, advanced directives, and assisted suicide, may not be an expansion of the realm of human liberty as such, but evidence of the acceptance, by the elderly themselves, of problematic conceptions of human well-being (such as ones that regard receiving care as demeaning). Or they may result from negative and prejudicial accounts of the aged (as a drain on scarce resources), or quite straightforwardly from a fear of neglect or of mistreatment—and so on. Insofar as interest in and advocacy of assisted suicide arises from these attitudes, conceptions, and expectations, simply to accept these options as providing the either in the Either/Or, without more ado, is no more sensible than welcoming an increase in prison suicides as an authentic expression of the liberty and autonomy of prisoners. It always remains possible that one of the reasons for an enthusiasm for various exit strategies lies in the bleakness of the conditions we have created for the elderly, including in those conditions the conceptions and valuations of old age we have fostered.[60]

On the other side, however, of this Either/Or—the pro-life side, so to speak—things don't look a lot better, in the sense that the bioethicists who take this line decline (and as bioethicists lack the tools) to deal with pertinent and pressing questions. Those who wag a finger at recent developments and are content to rehearse reasons against assisted suicide, withdrawl of care, and so on (however good those reasons may or may not be), seem to miss another issue which is occluded when the debate is joined in this way. There is a genuine sense of perplexity amongst carers as to what really constitutes care for Alzheimer's patients in the later stages of their decline. Thus expression of interest in assisted suicide or euthanasia ought not to be met, at least not at the outset, with a simple and stark 'no' (even if that might finally be demanded by regard for justice, for example), as if it should simply be faced down. Instead this interest is better treated as a sign of a need for a fuller understanding of the reality of Alzheimer's for patients and carers, and an exploration of what it might mean to provide care in this context. A reported aside from a doctor—'Treating an Alzheimer's patient is like doing veterinary medicine'[61]—may make the point crudely, but even those who speak less harshly may find it hard to understand what is demanded by a duty of care towards those who, so it is commonly said, are dead before death.

So what has gone wrong here? How can we move beyond the moral Punch and Judy show of bioethics? My contention is that a better and more adequate ethics would need to find a place for and reckon with the sort of moral field-work anthropology undertakes. Only with the aid of social anthropology can the social construction of the experience of aging and dementia be understood and the so-called 'problem of aging' itself be subject to a proper critique.

Of course it will already have occurred to the reflective reader that the consistency and coherence of the dominant discourse around dementia, which pictures it as 'death before death', the death of the person, the loss of the self, and so on, could very properly be subject to a straightforwardly philosophical critique. It is plain, I think, that many of the more lurid characterizations of Alzheimer's (as a disease which 'eradicates the essence of the person', has us 'drifting towards the threshold of unbeing', as the 'self is becoming devoid of content', of Alzheimer's patients as 'shell[s] of their former selves', or simply as husks), are less than careful in properly distinguishing consciousness, self-consciousness, memory (in its various forms), the self, subjectivity,

---

[60] At the least, then, we need some richer contextualization of these 'choices' to match the sensitivity and sophistication of M. Cátedra's important study, *This World, Other Worlds: Sickness, Suicide, Death, and the Afterlife among the Vaqueiros de Alzada of Spain* (Chicago, 1992).

[61] S. R. Sabat, *The Experience of Alzheimer's Disease* (Oxford, 2001), 114.

meaning, agency, autonomy, intention, and personhood. They are also less than careful in seeking to understand the relationship between the loss of any of these attributes and what makes life worthwhile.

To take the most obvious starting point for beginning to achieve conceptual clarity, loss of memory (the early indication of senility and in a severe form the basis for diagnosis of Alzheimer's), is not obviously the loss of any of the other items on the list I have just given. We might at least start to get things straight by attempting to distinguish and map the range of concepts and notions which inform or structure our notions of self and subjectivity, as well as by thinking carefully about the contribution of memory to human flourishing and well-being. Memory is plainly crucial in various ways for the identity of individuals, families, larger social groups, even nations and peoples. Memory and shared memories are important to our sense of ourselves and our flourishing, since memories link us to our past, and through that past, to those with whom we have shared it. But it doesn't follow that loss of memory (which is not, in any case, generally an all-or-nothing matter) is the very same as the loss of other things which matter to us: the self, the person, agency, autonomy, wishes, feelings, wants, desires, self-consciousness, consciousness, continuity, will, purpose, motivation, or intentionality.

So far, so philosophical—and so good. But at this point we surely begin to reach the limits of the contribution which bioethics, as standardly practised, could make. A simple reflection in Jonathan Franzen's memoir of his father's experience of Alzheimer's brings the point home: 'the disease is like a prism that refracts death into a spectrum of its parts: death of autonomy, death of memory, death of self-consciousness, death of personality, death of the body'.[62] His imagery is still of various losses as deaths of one kind or another (and thus conforms to popular discourse and perceptions), but the identification of these losses as separable immediately shows up the need for a discrimination which the straightforwardly apocalyptic imagery denies, and which could only be made empirically. That is to say, once we have entertained the thought that the path of this disease is not necessarily like the path of a tsunami that overwhelms everything in one almighty rush, then some pertinent questions immediately arise. What capacities or attributes are lost to the Alzheimer's patient, in what order, over what period of time, under what conditions, and with what significance? And again—can these losses be averted, their significance mitigated, and so on?

Thus at this point it would surely be natural to feel the need for a new and empirical basis and direction in our enquiries, for any adequate enquiry would have to go beyond conceptual clarification of aspects of the person or reflection on our valuations of those aspects. The clarity we seek here is not, in the end,

---

[62] Cited in Leibing and Cohen, *Thinking About Dementia*, 30; from Franzen's 'My Father's Brain'.

conceptual clarity, nor simply a clarity about our reflective valuations, however important such clarity and reflection may be in helping us see what is at stake. Such clarity would seem to serve us no more adequately here than would, say, an inventory of the species of animals and plants in a particular stretch of rainforest—supposing that is, that we are interested not just in listing the different species in some classificatory index, but rather in understanding how they relate one to another and interact to create certain ecologies. The inventory might serve to encourage us to look out for certain things, but beyond that, it would be of little help. There is no alternative to some careful fieldwork if we wish to discover how the species are related in the field—and so in the matter of the persistence and character of human subjectivity in dementia, only some patient anthropological fieldwork will reveal something of the complex ways in which selfhood is achieved, supported, and sustained (or the opposite).

The analogy of the rainforest, however, deserves a further moment's attention if we are not to miss something else. If we suppose the rainforest to be pristine and untouched by human intervention, we might picture the fieldwork as studying what is (for now at least) simply given. But however that may be for some stretch of rainforest, this does not present a model for the study of old age and Alzheimer's. Any serious critique will need to challenge and contest the rather simple thought that there is one human experience of being old (a thought that seems to afflict the debate we have mentioned), and insist instead that there is no one such experience, only a host of experiences, all different, all critically shaped or determined by the social and moral landscapes we construct and inhabit. There is no such thing as a predetermined life course here—as if the path of old age were like the path of a comet, following a trajectory laid down by the laws of physics. There is no natural history of old age—or at least, the biological trajectory is only one part of how we play out and experience old age. There are, instead, vastly different forms of being old which we construct for ourselves, with and alongside other forms of life in which our humanity is constituted. The stories and scripts of old age, dementia, and dependence necessarily must come to terms with physiological patterns of growing old, patterns that can be scientifically described. But the social stories and scripts of aging and regimes of care that can come to terms with these biological realities are multiple and various. These scripts, in turn, condition and shape the biological and other realities to which they themselves refer such as memory, selfhood, subjectivity, and personhood. It is in this highly complex context that the character and significance of old age is realized or constructed—and this context cannot be revealed by conceptual clarification or by reflective valuations, but only by attention to, for example, vastly different regimes of care.

It is to social anthropology, then, that we can turn for help in understanding whether different forms of subjectivity are or are not maintained or preserved in dementia, under what circumstances, and with what significance or meaning. And such understanding depends on the sort of ethnographic fieldwork which attends to the construction of the moral landscape by the routines, discourses, and practices of daily life. To illustrate something of the contribution which comes from social anthropology, I will briefly consider three particular anthropological studies: Pia Kontos's 'Embodied Selfhood: An Ethnographic Exploration of Alzheimer's Disease',[63] Athena McLean's *The Person in Dementia: A Study of Nursing Home Care in the US*,[64] and Lawrence Cohen's *No Aging in India: Alzheimer's, The Bad Family, and Other Modern Things*.[65] These studies directly challenge the simple association of dementia with the loss of self, and invite a rethinking of the pessimistic picture of dementia with the uncritical associations on which it depends. Together they illustrate the critical contribution that social anthropology makes to moral thought, and specifically indicate that social anthropology is a vital precondition to adequate critique.

Cohen's study—*No Aging in India: Alzheimer's, The Bad Family, and Other Modern Things*—turns on the contrast suggested by the title, between Alzheimer's and 'the Bad Family', and reflects the quite different master-narratives that govern the perception and construction of senility in the US (and the West more broadly) and in India.

In the West, senility is subject to a totalizing medicalization via a diagnosis of Alzheimer's, whereas in India, senility is taken to indicate that personal and generational relations have gone awry in the 'Bad Family'. Cohen makes this contrast in sharp terms (tangles in the brain in the West versus bad families in India), only to render it more subtle as his narratives become more encompassing—but in any case, he does not make the contrast in favour of one or the other side, but rather draws attention to the fact that the experience and reality of the aged body in time is not a matter of biology or family, but of biology and family and sociality and politics and culture in their complex configurations. Thus Cohen, notwithstanding his title, is cautious of 'a parceling out of styles of embodied old age along simplistic cultural lines'.[66]

Although Cohen seeks to render more complex the simple contrast suggested by his title, it remains the case that the reception of the ideology of Alzheimer's in India creates a conflict—and a particular story about the meeting of these different framings in India reveals something of what is at stake between the two competing master narratives. In this incident:

> With the diagnosis of Alzheimer's, mediated through the fortuitous appearance of the drug salesman and the visualizing power of expensive machine technology, the family could shift the locus of pathology from themselves onto Somita's brain [that of the elderly mother-in-law]...Sharmila's [the daughter-in-law] considerable pain at

[63] P. Kontos, 'Embodied Selfhood: An Ethnographic Exploration of Alzheimer's Disease', in Leibing and Cohen, *Thinking about Dementia*, 195–217.

[64] McLean, *The Person in Dementia*.

[65] L. Cohen, *No Aging in India: Alzheimer's, the Bad Family, and Other Modern Things* (Berkeley, 1998).

[66] Cohen, *No Aging in India*, 297.

the rigours of putting up with Somita and the added insult of being seen as the cause of her own suffering was healed by the understanding that she was not to blame.

Thus, 'Alzheimer's', 'rather than responding to the critical issues of familial interdependence and the maintenance of a familial self... isolates the body of the old person and denies her intersubjectivity... [I]n locating the problem solely in the old person's brain, Alzheimer's denies these multiple frames of difference in the constitution of the senile body'.[67] It allows 'families to move the locus of aging from transactions between family members onto the old person or onto larger social processes'.[68] This is not, says Cohen, to deny the usefulness of the notion of Alzheimer's:

> But invoking Alzheimer's within the globalizing discursive milieu of Alzheimer's hell asserts that the cognitively organized clinical syndrome it represents is in every case the most real and relevant representation of what might be at stake... Alzheimer's ideology posits normal aging against total and unremitting pathology; in so doing, it both denies the complex experience and the person-hood of the old persons it would represent and shifts attention away from the social origins of much of the weakness of the old.[69]

It ignores the fact that old age as it is experienced under the sign of Alzheimer's, for example, is not a universal life stage, but is complexly constructed from diverse elements of ideas of health and society, from the form and function-ing of families and wider social groups, and so on. There may indeed be an afflicted brain at the centre of all this, but its presentation and meaning is a function of a much wider social and political economy.

Part of this economy—or ecology—has to do with the regimes of care in which the afflicted brain is placed, and these can differ very widely not only between countries, but also within them. The meaning, but also the actual pres-entation, of the afflicted brain is specific to its context, as is suggested by Kontos's paper, based on an ethnographic study of an Orthodox Jewish care home in Canada serving chiefly those suffering from Alzheimer's. The purpose of the paper is specifically to explore and test some of what I have termed the apoca-lyptic imagery around this condition, and in particular its implicit assumption that the loss of cognitive functions is immediately a loss of self. As Kontos notes, 'while Alzheimer's is usually described and analyzed in terms of the cognitive dysfunction it produces, there is as well, a presumed existential outcome: the loss of the self with the concomitant erosion of individual agency'.[70] Her study sug-gests, however, that this presumed outcome is not always confirmed by observa-tion. Against the assumed loss of self, Kontos cites certain occasions of selfhood, as we might put it, revealed in ordinary settings, and reported in what she terms vignettes.

[67] Cohen, *No Aging in India*, 300. [68] Cohen, *No Aging in India*, 301.
[69] Cohen, *No Aging in India*, 303. [70] Kontos, 'Embodied Selfhood', 195.

In the first of these, a patient attends to her appearance just when one might have expected 'indifference from a woman who had lost the ability to feed herself'. 'Molly's insistence on adhering to the social graces and her attention to neatness suggested a strong and continuing presence in the world'.[71] In another case, a woman's creative capacities are revealed in spite of her protested 'I don't remember' in response to an invitation to take up a needle and thread: 'The rhythm with which she was weaving demonstrated a proficiency that was in striking contrast to her previous proclaimed inability'.[72] In a third story, Jacob, who 'was unable to put a sentence together', 'when…called forward, moved firmly and with upright posture to the platform. Without any prompting, he leaned his body over the Torah and recited the prayer with absolute coherence and precise pronunciation'.[73]

According to Kontos, 'the ethnographic data…clearly demonstrates that the residents of Chai Village exhibited selfhood *in the face of even severe cognitive impairment*'.[74] She further claims that 'selfhood resists the ravages of Alzheimer's disease precisely because it resides in corporeality',[75] arguing on the basis of a 'proposed theoretical framework [drawing on the work of Merleau-Ponty and Bourdieu]. . .[which] brings a new and critical dimension to the challenge of the presumed loss of personhood in Alzheimer's and, more broadly, to the Western representation of personhood that hinges on cognition and memory'.[76]

We may, I think, feel somewhat sceptical about 'the Western representation of personhood', as a rather sweeping category by which to understand the range of theoretical conceptualizations which may or may not inform or precondition assumptions about the selfhood of the person with dementia. Be that as it may, what Kontos's stories seem to tell us is that these individuals remain in a certain sense the people they were, with their particularities expressed through learnt behaviours (or embodied memories), seemingly unmediated by self-reflective cognition or consciousness, and that scepticism about selfhood in these cases may very well be dependent on some prior and unexamined notions of selfhood, but untouched by knowledge of how things go on the ground.

Athena McLean's *The Person in Dementia* is a longer and more substantial study than Kontos's, but like Kontos she is concerned to contest the 'dominant imagery of Alzheimer's "victims"…[which is resistant] to the idea that there is any richness or capacity for agency in their subjectivity'.[77] As McLean sees that dominant construction, we are asked to 'agree that the self depends on memory [and thus that]…once memory is lost so is the self'.[78] But McLean thinks that we need to ask, 'Can there be self or identity without memory?', and her ethnographic study of two nursing homes on the East Coast of the United States leads her to insist that there can be

---

[71] Kontos, 'Embodied Selfhood', 197.   [72] Kontos, 'Embodied Selfhood', 199.
[73] Kontos, 'Embodied Selfhood', 201.   [74] Kontos, 'Embodied Selfhood', 203.
[75] Kontos, 'Embodied Selfhood', 203.   [76] Kontos, 'Embodied Selfhood', 196.
[77] Citing E. Herskovits, 'Struggling over Subjectivity: Debates about the "Self" and Alzheimer's Disease', *Medical Anthropology Quarterly* 9 (1995), 146–164, at 157.
[78] McLean, *The Person in Dementia*, 52.

selfhood without the sort of consciously ordered and recoverable memory which is memory's paradigmatic instance (in other words, in cases where there are the sorts of 'embodied memories' to which Kontos refers). But, and this makes a second and very important point, according to McLean's findings the survival of the self, identity, or personality, is a function of the nature of the provision of care, and not only a matter of the course of the underlying pathology. In particular she argues that the discounting of agency or selfhood is itself a major factor shaping the decline of the Alzheimer's patient, since this discounting itself determines or at least shapes regimes of treatment which are likely to produce the losses that are diagnosed.[79]

'It is', she notes, '…easy for a caregiver to disregard the statements and actions (the *agency*) of someone with dementia under the assumption that the actual *person* is gone and that it is the disease that is meaninglessly acting or uttering'.[80] But as Rubinstein puts it in his foreword, in McLean's portraits of demented individuals, 'persons emerge clearly as having distinctive characters, motivations, and selfhoods that are visible despite the disease process'.[81] The discounting of their agency, however, tends to create or extend the behavioural disturbances (agitation, repetitiveness, wandering, hitting, and screaming), which are associated with dementia—and which are in turn used to justify 'warehousing of the elderly'. Attempts are made to eliminate or control these behaviours (often by medication), since they cause trouble and inconvenience to others. But according to McLean, the disturbed behaviours can be seen, in accordance with other research, to represent 'efforts on the part of…elders to communicate and function in their cognitively altered world'. That is to say, that what has been classified as disturbed is 'actually nonverbal communication…or expressions of purposeful activity'.[82] As McLean sees it:

> intentionality continues, even when understanding may be compromised by dementia. 'Disturbed behaviors', whether verbal or physical, are part of the

---

[79] See also Sabat's discussion (*The Experience of Alzheimer's Disease*) of the 'pathological cycle': a negative assessment of the Alzheimer's patient as a result of some tests of some rather arbitrarily identified capacities, shapes engagement and treatment of the patient in such a way as to further his or her decline.

[80] McLean, *The Person in Dementia*, 3. It is, of course, easy for this assumption to determine the response to any seemingly contrary data: thus Fontana and Smith ('Alzheimer's Disease Victims') describe the Alzheimer's patient as engaged in 'routinized social rituals devoid of any unique individual … [because] when the individual self undergoes an unbecoming process, due to the mental deterioration caused by the disease, it is largely social practices that allow the self to continue to exist in the eyes of others' (35). Against any thoughts that the carers continue to recognize or sustain the self, they insist that 'the self has slowly unraveled and "unbecome" a self, but the caregivers take the role of the other and assume that there is a person behind the largely unwitting presentation of the self of the victims, albeit in reality there is less and less, until where once there was a unique individual there is but emptiness. Witnessing, as the "other", the "unbecoming" of the self, creates a feeling of emptiness in the caregivers' hearts. Thus, they act as agents for the victim and impute to him or her the last remnants of self' (45).

[81] R. L. Rubinstein, 'Foreword' to McLean, *The Person in Dementia*, ix.

[82] McLean, *The Person in Dementia*, xi.

continuum of efforts by elders attempting to communicate their needs, feelings and wishes. When persons can no longer verbalize or adequately organize their thoughts and intentions, or when they have difficulty interpreting the intentions of a caregiver or communicating their intentions, they use their bodies to communicate need, distaste, or fear...The use of the body...may in addition signal protest or resistance...against their conditions of living or perceived relations of powers...with caregivers and others. However, when such communications are medicalized as individual pathology, they lose their force.[83]

Where efforts are made to understand the underlying meaning of such behaviours, their causes (in anxiety, fear, confusion, or whatever) can be addressed. And there is, McLean concludes, 'promising evidence that the ways in which the person with dementia is regarded and her behaviors are interpreted and treated will profoundly impact her outcome *even in the absence of medical interventions*'.[84]

Of course, the tendency to respond to the Alzheimer's patient in a particular way is part of larger patterns and configurations of social and medical thought and practice. McLean refers to a 'biomedical model', favouring certain ways of viewing and conceptualising disease, and thus responding to it—including in that model 'The culture of institutional caregiving, with its premium on time and its biomedicalized emphasis on the body,... [which] supports a caregiving culture that is attentive to body task-centred care over person-centred care'.[85] Against the model and the culture, McLean promotes what she calls 'a communications perspective that respects the agency of persons with dementia, regarding them as potentially meaningful communicators who negotiate their environment with the limitations of their impairments', whose behaviours are not, as they are often regarded, 'pathological, meaningless, or ill-willed'.[86] McLean's findings, then, challenge not only particular theories of the Alzheimer's patient, but just as much practices of care which, however motivated, serve to eradicate what selfhood might continue to exist.

Each of these ventures in fieldwork bears further attention and discussion—and my purpose here is not to erect a grand theory regarding dementia or Alzheimer's on the basis of these tentative samplings. The reason for drawing attention to this fieldwork is far more modest—simply to indicate the particular contribution to serious critical enquiry which anthropology makes through ethnographic fieldwork. If we are to escape the moral Punch and Judy show of contemporary bioethics, we need more than mere conceptual clarity combined with a few principles delivered by reflection. Conceptual clarity and principles, admirable as they may be, will not allow us to challenge and contest the rather simple thought that there is one human experience of being old, and to insist instead that there are a host of experiences, all critically shaped or determined

[83] McLean, *The Person in Dementia*, 38.   [84] McLean, *The Person in Dementia*, 5.
[85] McLean, *The Person in Dementia*, 34.   [86] McLean, *The Person in Dementia*, 37.

by the social landscapes we construct and inhabit. It is in this complex context that the character and significance of old age is realized or constructed—and the character of this context cannot be revealed by conceptual clarification and reflection alone, but only by patient anthropological fieldwork.

VI AGAINST 'DEATH BEFORE DEATH'; OR NEW (SOCIAL) SCRIPTS FOR DWINDLING TO DEATH

In my brief discussion of the *Craft of Dying*, I overlooked one element of it, and that is the sense of dying as a communal task.

> Let no man wonder, nor think it inconvenient that so great charge and diligence and wise disposition and providence, and busy exhortation should be had and ministered to them that be in point of death, and in their last end...for they be in such peril and in so great need at that time, that, and it were possible, all a city should come together with all haste to a man that is nigh to the death or dying; as the manner is in some religious [i.e. houses], in which it is ordained that when a sick man is nigh the death, then every of the brothers shall, when they hear the table smitten—what hour that ever it be, and where that ever they be—all things being left, hastily come to him that is a-dying. Therefore it is read that religious people and women—for the honesty of estate—should not run but to a man that is a-dying and for fire.[87]

For those who cannot die by the favoured scripts of modernity—those whose long dying, possibly combined with dementia, is not capable of being conceived or framed by either of its two models—their scriptless deaths seem fated to be preceded by 'death before death', whether that death is decreed by a supposed medical necessity (Alzheimer's), or by current patterns of social exclusion (as in the old people's home). But since, as it turns out, that medical necessity is itself socially conditioned, the dying in either of these categories must have the same hope—that we may recover some sense of a social responsibility towards the dying which the *Ars moriendi* itself commended, even while it spoke first of all to the dying subject.

The modern hospice movement, founded on Cicely Saunder's Christian convictions and commitment, addressed fifty years ago the problem of the terminally ill, imagining and creating the conditions for a good death for a significant class of patients in the face of deeply inadequate medical and social provision. The same commitment and imaginative and practical insights need now to be brought to bear on our own current problem of the social no-man's land in which many of the dwindling elderly dwell. We need nothing less than

---

[87] *The Book of the Craft of Dying*, Comper, 38–39.

a practical reimagining of our social space in such a way that the zones of social abandonment in which our long dying is currently destined to take place, are themselves colonized by new forms of social inclusion, solidarity, and fellowship—as they would be if we thought that we should run to the dying just as we still run to a fire!

Christianity has at its heart a rite which is meant to serve as a programme. Rites and rituals, at least living rites and rituals, are not self-contained or empty—they are enactments of an imagined sociality in schematic and idealized form, and as they are enacted they exert pressure on what is the case for the sake of what should and might be.[88] As Christians solemnly share bread and wine round a single table, in a meal that is open to all and from which no one is excluded, they hope that this rite becomes, as it wills to be, a general social form—and here it should inspire a ministry to the bitterness and despair and loneliness of many of the long dwindlings to death which mark our late modern dyings.[89]

[88] Following J. Z. Smith, *Imagining Religion: From Babylon to Jonestown* (Chicago, 1982), where he defines ritual as 'a means of performing the way things ought to be in conscious tension to the way things are in such a way that this ritualized perfection is recollected in the ordinary, uncontrolled course of things' (63).

[89] In imagining a better future practice, there is much in Christianity's past to provide material for thought and discussion; J. McManners' *Death and the Enlightenment* (Oxford, 1981), remains an immensely rich source.

6

Contesting Burial and Mourning: On
Relics, Alder Hey, and Keeping the
Dead Close

I INTRODUCTION: ON BURYING CHRIST
(PROPERLY)

A close acquaintance of mine, newly arrived from Ireland, gave me clear
instructions that should she die suddenly I had a single duty—and that was
to put her on the first Ryanair flight to Dublin, since 'you Brits', she said, 'don't
know how to do death'. (It seems to me to be a considerable tribute to the
strength of the disdain for our competencies in this matter that my informant was willing, even in imagined death, to endure a flight with Ryanair.)
Jennifer Hockey, in the preface to her *Experiences of Death: An Anthropological
Approach*, recounts a personal want of 'death-related knowledge', revealed by
the sudden and untimely death of a young man in a head-on crash. The ineptitude was shared by her friends: 'While some were able to approach his widow,
many failed...Similarly the offering of funeral wreaths was a gesture fraught
with uncertainty about what to give and where and when to give. Letters of
condolence too were attempted, re-attempted, and then abandoned.'[1] Julian
Barnes, in a recent work that relates to the death of his wife, refers to a group of
his friends as 'The Silent Ones', those who thought the best thing to do under
the circumstances was not to mention her at all.[2]

There is a neat story about the genesis of a British 'least said, soonest
mended' attitude to death. The Victorians did it quite differently, of course,
but huge losses endured in the First World War led to the capping of no longer
sustainable, highly formalized, and effusive displays of grief. In its place, we
put an awkward silence and ritual uncertainty—albeit supplemented in recent

---

[1] J. Hockey, *Experiences of Death: An Anthropological Account* (Edinburgh, 1990), 2.
[2] J. Barnes, *Levels of Life*, (London, 2013).

years by an efflorescence of alternative practices and sites of mourning (most obviously perhaps, in the roadside shrines which have sprung up worldwide) to meet persisting emotional demands.[3] Many other factors are relevant, but whatever the genesis of current attitudes and practice, we now have to reckon with an ambivalence and uncertainty towards mourning, and with its deep opacity to much current understanding (including to a certain extent, to the current understanding even of social anthropology as it will turn out).

But let us begin by going further back. I have been asking in these chapters about the way in which representations and imaginings of certain moments in Christ's life have engaged with and shaped and conditioned the imagination and practice of human life—and how this imagining and practice might stand in critical relation to other imaginings and practices of the human. Here then, we turn to the imagining of Christ's burial in the context of wider Christian attitudes towards mourning the dead.

Christ's burial,[4] according to the Gospels, was somewhat summary. We have essentially two versions, but on the seemingly cursory nature of the burial both are agreed. In the Synoptic Gospels, Joseph of Arimaethea requests and is granted the body and he alone deals with its disposal in a simple, hasty, and minimal fashion—'having taken him down, with the linen cloth he tied him up and put him away in a burial place that was hewn out of rock: and he rolled over a stone against the door of the tomb'.[5] In John, however, notwithstanding the same seeming haste, we get slightly more: Joseph is joined by Nicodemus in the preparation of the body, and the latter brings with him an utterly astonishing amount of spices: enough to 'do honor to a king'.[6] The disciples and women contribute nothing to the proceedings—the women are always at a distance, and as far as we are told, the burial takes place without either the washing of the corpse (which would almost certainly have been customary), or the lamentation (which quite probably was, too).[7]

---

[3] The neat story represents the core event in a history as told more fully by P. Jalland, *Death in War and Peace: A History of Grief and Loss in England, 1914–1970* (Oxford, 2010). Jalland traces the beginning of a decline in mourning ritual to the moves for a simplification of funerary practice sponsored by the National Funeral and Mourning Reform Association from 1875 onwards. The 'process of simplification was accelerated by the Great War': in the first place, undertakers and gravediggers had been conscripted and thus customary practice was necessarily pared down; second, it was argued that national morale would suffer from mass mourning and 'a pageantry of funeral gloom'; and third, 'grandiose funerals' in England came to seem inappropriate when so many soldiers were being buried 'with little or no ceremony' in mass graves overseas (101). For moves in our day to invent rites more adequately expressive of mourners' feelings, some making use of the internet and virtual remembrance, see J. W. Green, *Beyond the Good Death* (Philadelphia, 2008).

[4] The term 'burial', though generally used, refers in Christ's case to an entombment; but since the contrast with pagan practice, discussed below, is a contrast with cremation, I follow normal usage in not distinguishing entombment from placing in or below the ground.

[5] Mark 15, 46 in Brown's translation in *The Death of the Messiah*, vol. i.

[6] Brown, *The Death of the Messiah*, vol. ii, 1267.

[7] Brown, *The Death of the Messiah*, vol. ii, 1244.

Brown thinks there is a direction of travel between the two accounts, with John being concerned to add somewhat to the dignity of the proceedings. (It seems a stretch, however, to claim that 'John's [only very slightly extended] account clearly envisions a customary and, therefore, honorable burial.'[8]) If there is such a direction, however, it has to be said that John did not go anything like far enough to satisfy the later Middle Ages, which foreswore the cursory burial rites that Christ received according to the canonical sources in favour of providing him with the rites he deserved. Van der Weyden's great *Deposition* in the Prado (which might be contrasted with the Reichenau deposition and entombment of *c.*980[9]), serves as indication of the weighty solemnity of the proceedings around Christ's death and burial as they were imagined by this complex and florid tradition, which recruits to the task a considerable cast of mourners. They will be deployed not only at the deposition that must necessarily have occurred, but in the highly imagined sequence that fills the space between that deposition and the sealing of the tomb, and which includes mourning at the foot of cross, as the body is taken from the cross towards tomb, and over the body as it is placed in or lies near, on, or in the tomb.[10]

---

[8] Brown, *The Death of the Messiah*, vol. ii, 1244.

[9] Manuscript illumination, *c.*980, Reichenau, Codex Egberti, Trier.

[10] The elaboration of the passage of Christ's body from deposition to its sealing in the tomb into a series of discrete moments, though it mirrors the tradition of the Stations of the Cross, is the more remarkable because it is almost wholly a work of creativity judged against the sparse account of biblical sources. Without this creativity, the movement from cross to tomb would be over very quickly indeed, as the very simple Reichenau deposition and entombment indicates. In its place, the high Middle Ages and later provided a much more satisfying, highly articulated pictorial sequence in which we can identify at least the following discrete moments:

(i) A general deposition from the cross, with body in motion, with many people—as in van der Weyden's Prado picture or in Fra Angelico's cooler *Deposition* of *c.*1437–40 in Florence, or Rubens' *Descent* in Antwerp of *c.*1611–14.

(ii) The placing of the body at or near the foot of the cross, over which there is a lamentation. This may be a general group lamentation (as in Dürer's *Lamentation of Christ* of *c.*1500 in Munich), or Mary may become manifestly the chief mourner (as in Geertgen tot Sint Jans's *Lamentation* of *c.*1485 in Vienna), and in some cases the principal mourner in a very small group (as in El Greco's *Lamentation* of *c.*1565–70 in Philadelphia), in which case the scene is on the way to becoming a pietà (to which we will come back).

(iii) The body on the way from cross to tomb—as in Raphael's so-called *Borghese Deposition* (also known as *Pala Baglione* or *Entombment* of 1507 in the Gallery Borghese)—with a crowded lamentation going on around the body as it is borne along. (The visual uncertainty of the point in time at which this body is in motion may explain the difficulty that people have had in captioning this picture.) Holbein's *Passion* (an altarpiece of 1524–25 in Basel), in its right wing gives us the same movement of the body, but closer to the tomb, and with a smaller number engaged in lamentation.

(iv) The body at or on the tomb with lamentation—as in Giotto's fresco in the Arena Chapel of 1304–5; Botticelli's *Lamentation over the Dead Christ* of 1490–92 in Munich; Bouts' *Lamentation* of *c.*1460 in Prague; Fra Angelico's *Entombment* of 1438–1440 in Munich; and many other examples.

(v) The laying out of the body on or near the tomb prior to its burial with no obvious lamentation—as in Carpaccio's so-called *Lamentation* in Berlin of *c.*1510, where the body is not attended. This scene is related to the anointing of the body, which is relatively infrequent

Such a vivid and creative imagining of augmented grieving for Christ was surely not without its critics—and Ambrose's aside, '*Stantem illam lego, flentem non lego*' (that Mary 'stood there I read; that she wept I do not read'),[11] could have provided a handy slogan for any who wished to insist on an austere fidelity to the biblical account of the proceedings around Christ's death and burial. But the tide went in the other direction and pictorial austerity was overwhelmed—at least until the Reformation. (Trent's bid, at the close of the Middle Ages, to assert unembellished biblical propriety within the Roman Catholic tradition was much too late to counter images deeply embedded in popular thought and piety.[12]) The context of Ambrose's remark, however—in a funeral oration—suggests that even in his day there was contestation over the representation of the burial of Christ, which was also a contestation over the practice of mourning. The fault lines of the issues are best revealed by the decisive intervention of Ambrose's most significant convert, Augustine—himself more given to tears, as we shall see, than Ambrose's Mary. In the contestation and controversy around burial and mourning at the turn of the fourth century, Augustine provides and vindicates a particular Christian imagination

in Western painting, it seems (but see, for example, Miraillet's [?] *Anointing of Christ's Body* of c.1450–1500 in the Musée Massena, Nice, and Allori's *Body of Christ Anointed by Two Angels* of c.1593 in Budapest), although the carrying of jars of ointment or spices by those engaged in lamentation hints at an anointing to come. These scenes relate to the much more common Epitaphios image in Byzantine art.

(vi) The placing of the body in the tomb, with or without lamentation, and with smaller or larger groups in attendance—as in Giotto's *Entombment* of c.1320–25 in the Villa I Tatti, Florence, van der Weyden's *Entombment* of 1450 in the Uffizi, or Caravaggio's *Entombment* of 1602–3 in the Vatican.

(vii) The body in the tomb, with or without lamentation—the first represented, for example, by Mantegna's *Lamentation over the Dead Christ* of 1478–81, in Milan (although if Christ is on an anointing stone, the scene may be prior to his entombment), the second by Holbein's *The Body of the Dead Christ in the Tomb*, 1521, in Basel.

In addition to this articulation of the moments from cross to sealing of the tomb in a series of events, it is worth noting that the highly favoured representation of the specific mourning of Mary over general lamentation (that is, in scenes where Mary is either very plainly the chief mourner, as in Quarton's *Pietà* of Villeneuve-les-Avignon, before 1457, in the Louvre, or the only mourner, as in Tura's *Pietà* of c.1468 in the Museo Correr, Venice) often gives us scenes which are difficult to place in any specific moment between the deposition and the closing of the tomb. The location of the pietà is often uncertain or vague or, perhaps more interestingly, very obviously an idealized or imagined space, as in Perugino's *Pietà* of 1494–5 in the Uffizi. The seeming weightlessness of the body in this and other pietàs adds to the sense of this being an imagined ahistorical moment, and thus indicates something of a counter impetus to the invention of an historical sequence, in the conversion of specific and located mourning into a timeless and thus eternal lament. (The movement is a parallel to a tendency whereby narrative images of the suffering of Christ are transformed into the non-narrative image of Christ as a man of sorrows, standing outside any actual sequence of historical events.)

[11] Ambrose, *De Obitu Valentiniani Consolatio*, PL 16, 1371—in translation as *Consolation on the Death of Emperor Valentinian*, trans. R. J. Defferrai, in *The Fathers of the Church*, vol. 22, *Funeral Orations of St Gregory Nazianzen and St Ambrose* (Washington, DC, 1953), 283.

[12] On these matters, see J. O'Malley, *Trent: What Happened at the Council* (Cambridge, MA, 2013).

of burial and mourning, and does so in decisive contention with other competing imaginaries—and in a way that is relevant to our more contemporary concerns regarding our partings with the dead.

Our path will be as follows. I find it striking and compelling (in section II) that, notwithstanding possibilities and pressures the other way, Augustine's vindication and justification of 'the care to be had of the dead' in mourning and burial is a justification which eschews any 'superstitious' assumptions (a notion which will be become clear, I hope). The point of noting this feature of Augustine's argument is that when we turn (in section III) to the contemporary contestation around burial and mourning highlighted by the story of Alder Hey, we will find that certain practices of burial and mourning are socially opaque and are very readily deemed superstitious or irrational or emotional. The perhaps surprising supplement to this point will be (in section IV) that social anthropology has itself rather too readily joined in the construal of mourning as an expression of superstition. I argue (in section V), however, that moral theology, instructed by Augustine and repudiating any such assumption, should draw from the more constructive findings of ethnographies of mourning an appreciation of the moral significance and character of the work of burial and mourning. This work should be explicated in an everyday ethics, and such an ethics would thus provide an account of the 'care to be had of the dead' that would comprehend and permit a performance of grief somewhat less anaemic than is allowed for under the current dispensation.

II AUGUSTINE ON BURIAL, MOURNING, AND RELICS (IN WHICH AUGUSTINE LEARNS TO WEEP)

In understanding early Christian thought and practice in relation to death and burial we suffer from the disadvantage that, to quote Brown's assessment, 'we lack a study of the meaning of death in the early Christian world, and its expression in burial practices and attitudes to mourning', apart from a small work by Pelikan that Brown cites (but which is distinctly limited in its range and decidedly intellectualist in its concerns).[13] In Augustine's work, however, we can immediately observe something of the controversy over these matters within the Christian tradition, and between it and the surrounding pagan culture—and thus observe something of Augustine's contribution to the invention of Christian orthodoxy. In particular, Augustine's careful scripting of mourning

---

[13] Brown, *The Cult of the Saints*, 158. See J. Pelikan, *The Shape of Death: Life, Death and Immortality in the Early Fathers* (London, 1962).

and burial in his telling of the story of Monica's death in *Confessions*, alerts us to a contestation in which a new Christian sensibility is being imagined and shaped. We can hardly fail to notice that whereas Augustine provides no very obvious script for dying (which had to wait, at least for its formalization, for the development of the *Ars moriendi* tradition in the fifteenth century, as noted in the last chapter), he provides a very definite script for mourning and burial, in contention with Christians to his left and right so to speak, and with paganism lurking on all sides.

The story is complex and nuanced, but we might sum it up as follows—that notwithstanding certain of his own Stoic predilections, themselves seconded by early Christian reserve towards or even disapproval of grieving, Augustine learns to mourn and provides a vindication of such mourning. Augustine endorses a certain 'care to be had of the dead', even while resisting certain tendencies towards a heightened concern for bodies and their disposal which the cult of the martyrs and their relics fostered. The dialectic is subtle—Christians had held, against pagan polemics, that the integrity of the body is not necessary for resurrection, while also maintaining that the body was owed some care even in death. The pagan polemics did not come from nowhere and were plainly directed at a care for bodily remains characteristic of a Christian (but somewhat perplexing to a pagan) sensibility. But even in the face of what he would come to see as certain possible Christian excesses, Augustine would commend the moderate care of the dead as consistent with the goodness of our bodily life, while insisting that we can do nothing for the dead and they can do nothing for us (at the same time allowing a certain validity to the cult of relics). His justification relies not at all then, and in modern terms, on any 'superstitious' elements.

In considering the construction of Augustine's thought here, we must reckon with three elements: his endorsement of decent and customary burial as being fitting, without mattering greatly; his vindication of mourning; and his response to the pressure exerted on Christian practice of burial and mourning by regard for the relics of martyrs. Together these three elements add up to what would become paradigmatically Christian emotions, sensibilities, and practices in relation to mourning and burial, emerging from a 'debate around the grave'[14] in which Augustine was engaged and caught up. And he was nowhere so caught up as by an event that stands at the very centre of his *Confessions*, namely the death of his mother Monica. In the wonderfully told narrative about the 33-year-old Augustine, written when he was approaching the very great age of 45, traces of significant shifts in Augustine's thought become evident—and so too, the tensions around death and burial in early Christian life and thought.

---

[14] Brown, *The Cult of the Saints*, 26.

II.i Burial

'While we were at Ostia by the mouths of the Tiber, my mother died.'[15] 'I pass over many events because I write in great haste', but here he lingers over an event which stands at the centre of his *Confessions* and is one of the most vividly realized moments in a book that is not short of such moments. And characteristically, Augustine is not as interested in Monica's death as in his own reaction to it.

On either side of this central death there are others that have considerable weight. Before it (in Book IV), there is the death of a close (but unnamed) childhood friend for whom Augustine 'wept very bitterly'[16] and mourned very intently, if somewhat theatrically.[17] On the other side of Monica's death, tellingly present by its absence in its proper narrative place, there is the death of his much-loved son by a mistress—the son called Adeodatus, 'gift of God'. Augustine, the sometime professor of rhetoric, unsurpassably eloquent on almost any subject, surpasses himself here with the excruciating eloquence of his silence in relation to a death that he merely mentions in an aside and not again.[18] But about the death of his mother and his reaction to it, Augustine shows no such reserve, and tells a long and involved tale which shows that his early tendency to mournful melodramatics has been rather firmly overcome.

On the way back to North Africa Monica becomes ill and loses consciousness. When she comes to, she gives Augustine and his brother a straightforward instruction: 'Bury your mother here'—here being Ostia, the port of Rome and thus far from the grave of her husband Patrick, besides whom she had once expressed a wish to be buried.

> I kept silence [says Augustine] and fought back my tears. But my brother, as if to cheer her up, said something to the effect that he hoped she would be buried not in a foreign land but in her home country. When she heard that, her face became worried and her eyes looked at him in reproach that he should think that. She looked in my direction and said 'See what he says', and soon said to both of us, 'Bury my body anywhere you like. Let no anxiety about that disturb you. I have only one request to make of you, that you remember me at the altar of the Lord, wherever you may be.'[19]

---

[15] Augustine, *Confessions*, trans. H. Chadwick (Oxford, 1991), IX, viii, 17.

[16] Augustine, *Confessions*, IX, vi, 11.

[17] 'There was no rest in pleasant groves, nor in games or songs, nor in sweet-scented places, nor in exquisite feasts, nor in the pleasures of the bedroom and bed, nor, finally, in books and poetry. Everything was an object of horror, even light itself; all that was not he made me feel sick and was repulsive—except for groaning and tears.' Augustine, *Confessions*, IV, vii, 12.

[18] 'Early on you took him away from life on earth'—in 389, two years after Adeodatus's baptism alongside Augustine. Augustine, *Confessions*, IX, vi, 14.

[19] Augustine, *Confessions*, IX, xi, 27.

Augustine expresses his delight that her 'vain thought' about being buried with her husband had been abandoned. He had not known of a conversation she had had with some of his friends, when she had expressed her lack of concern about being buried at home, at which they asked 'whether she were not afraid to leave her body so far from her own town. "Nothing", she said "is distant from God, and there is no ground for fear that he may not acknowledge me at the end of the world and raise me up".'[20]

Monica's carelessness regarding the place of her burial is exemplary, for a general insouciance regarding the disposal of the body (and not just its location), was characteristic of early Christian life and thought, even while in the early period there was a preference for burial (over the prevalent pagan practice of cremation),[21] presumably in imitation of Christ's being placed in a tomb. But notwithstanding this difference, there was no such thing as Christian burial even in that early period in the sense of a practice consciously in contention with non-Christian alternatives—and from AD 200 onwards in any case, Romans in general started to favour burial.

The Christian preference for burial did, however, provide material for pagan ridicule which claimed that that preference was on account of a belief that resurrection depends on burial—and the same explanation for the preference is given by some historians.[22] But this, says Rebillard, is to confuse things. It is true that 'belief in the resurrection has often been connected with an obligation to bury the dead' and that 'the manner of disposing of bodies adopted by Christians, at a moment when it was far from being the norm, aroused controversy'. But it was pagans who:

> attributed to Christians…a belief that cremation, or any other form of corporal destruction, would suffice to prevent resurrection. Nothing, however in the Christian responses to these attacks confirms that they had any such belief.…Christians very clearly rejected any connection between the preservation of the body in a tomb and the resurrection as a simplistic argument on the part of pagans to ridicule their doctrine.[23]

Thus grinding to dust the bones of the martyrs of Lyon and scattering them in the Rhône was, as Eusebius tells the story, motivated by a supposed Christian sensitivity in relation to the treatment of corpses,[24] 'but no Christian testimony

---

[20] Augustine, *Confessions*, IX, xi, 28.

[21] The pagan norm derived, according to Pliny the Elder, from a fear of desecration of the corpse and replaced the earlier custom of burial, which became the norm again by the fourth century, as attested by Macrobius. For references, see E. Rebillard, *The Care of the Dead in Late Antiquity*, trans. E. Trapnell Rawlings and J. Routier-Pucci (Ithaca, NY, 2009), 79.

[22] By both Y. Duval and D. Kyle, according to Rebillard, *The Care of the Dead in Late Antiquity*, 84.

[23] Rebillard, *The Care of the Dead in Late Antiquity*, 82–83.

[24] Eusebius, *The History of the Church from Christ to Constantine*, trans. G. A. Williams, rev. and ed. A. Louth (London, 1989), book v, 1, 61: 'Thus the martyrs' bodies, after six days' exposure to every kind of insult and to the open sky, were finally burnt to ashes and swept by these wicked

attests the belief that burial is a condition for resurrection.'[25] Plainly more than two hundred year after the events recounted by Eusebius, pagans thought that Christian beliefs regarding burial remained a useful basis for a touch of ridicule or polemic. Augustine responds to pagan taunts that the Christian God should surely have spared those of his followers who were, in fact, left unburied after the sack of Rome in 410, with the comment—and the exemplary Monica would surely have said the same—that lack of burial is not suffering and that burial is not essential to resurrection, even though one should not neglect to bury the dead, which Scripture counts as a good work.[26]

But how should this good work be performed? What is fitting in a Christian burial? Rebillard claims that in the fourth and fifth centuries there is very little interest in or commentary on the burial of Christ—though he notes that the campaigning Chrysostom, in one of his homilies on John, insists that the fact that Christ arose naked should teach an unconcern about funerals and burial. (Indeed, far from commending the work of Joseph and Nicodemus, Chrysostom actually criticizes their action—these two who lavished attention on burial did so because they did not believe in resurrection and were merely following the custom of the Jews. None of apostles were there: 'And so you will know that he valued none of all that, Christ said "You saw me hungry, and you fed me; thirsty, and you gave me drink; naked, and you clothed me", but nowhere did he say, "you saw that I was dead, and you buried me".'[27]) Augustine, too, is critical of the extravagance of funerals (but not of any extravagance in Christ's), contrasting the grandness of the exit from the world made by the rich man of the parable and by poor Lazarus who ended in Abraham's bosom: 'A great deal of pomp and ceremony...tarted up with worldly trimmings, could have been lavished on that rich man as he lay dying. What troops of ululating menservants and maidservants there could have been, what a procession of retainers, what a splendid funeral, what an expensive tomb! I presume he was smothered in aromatic spices.'[28] And yet it did him no good.

---

men into the Rhône that not even a trace of them might be seen on the earth again. And this they did as if they could defeat God and rob the dead of their rebirth, "in order", they said, "that they may have no hope of resurrection—the belief that has led them to bring into this country a new foreign cult and treat torture with contempt, going willingly and cheerfully to their death. Now let us see if they'll rise again, and if their god can help them and save them from our hands".

[25] Rebillard, *The Care of the Dead in Late Antiquity*, 84, although it would be interesting to consider whether some of the early stories of the martyrs might provide hints of a more lively concern for the preservation of bodily remains; thus, for example, while the fact that the body of St Vincent, dumped into the sea by his persecutors, miraculously reappears on shore, could be read as signalling a simple delight in frustrating pagan wiles, it might suggest something a bit stronger than a mild preference for burial wherever possible.

[26] Augustine, *City of God*, 1, 12—13. As he says elsewhere, 'Let proper care be taken, according to one's means, over burying the dead and constructing their tombs, because the holy scriptures count these things too among good works...' (*Sermons*, 172, 1.)

[27] Chrysostom, *Homily* 85, 5, cited by Rebillard, *The Care of the Dead in Later Antiquity*, 106.

[28] Augustine, *Sermons*, 102, 3.

Monica is scrupulously indifferent to the nature of the disposal of her corpse: 'As the day of her deliverance approached, she did not think of having her body sumptuously wrapped or embalmed with perfumes or given a choice monument. Nor did she care if she had a tomb in her homeland. On that she gave no instruction; she desired only that she might be remembered at your altar, which she had attended everyday without fail'.[29] But if this indifference to the where and how of burial is exemplary, certain counter pressures, well known to Augustine, were already extant—and these exerted a shaping influence on current practice, as we shall see. If we revert to Augustine's narrative, however, we can leave the matter of the location and manner of burial for the moment, and turn to the far more vexed question of mourning. Burial should not be done ostentatiously or lavishly, but it should be done customarily.[30] What custom demanded in mourning was, however, more contested.

II.ii Mourning

The facts of Monica's end are tersely stated—'On the ninth day of her illness' she died. What interests Augustine, as I have said, is not Monica's death so much as his reaction to it.

> I closed her eyes and an overwhelming grief welled into my heart and was about to flow forth in floods of tears. But at the same time under a powerful act of mental control my eyes held back the flood and dried it up.[31] The inward struggle put me in great agony. Then when she breathed her last, the boy Adeodatus cried out in sorrow and was pressed by all of us to be silent. In this way too something of the child in me, which had slipped towards weeping, was checked and silenced by the youthful voice, the voice of my heart. We did not think it right to celebrate the funeral with tearful dirges and lamentations, since in most cases it is customary to use such mourning to imply sorrow for the miserable state of those who die, or even their complete extinction. But my mother's death meant neither that her state was miserable nor that she was suffering extinction.[32]

Here—with this 'we did not think it right to celebrate the funeral with tearful dirges'—Augustine witnesses to a strong tendency in early Christianity. Brown refers us to a fragment (now in the Louvre) of an epitaph of the later fourth century: 'While her parents bewailed her death at every moment, the voice of [God's] majesty was heard at night, forbidding them to lament for the

---

[29] Augustine, *Confessions*, IX, xiii, 36.

[30] For much fuller and important treatment of the background to these matters, see C. W. Bynum, *The Resurrection of the Body in Western Christendom, 200–1336* (New York, 1995).

[31] The contrast with the overflowing tears of the newly baptized Augustine is striking: 'How I wept during your hymns and songs. . . Tears ran, and it was good for me to have that experience' (IX, vi, 14).

[32] Augustine, *Confessions*, IX, xii, 29.

dead child'. This 'inscription', says Brown, 'is a reminder of the force of the tensions latent in early Christian attitudes to death and the afterlife'.[33] The early church, he writes, 'tended to leapfrog the grave' and mourning was 'repressed by a heady belief in afterlife'[34]—hence in the epitaph, the mention of the voice of majesty enforcing a strict control on displays of grief.[35] Rebillard finds in Augustine's response to Monica's death, with his valiant attempts to contain his grief, not only a witness to the power of this norm but an endorsement of it: 'The new meaning of death in Christianity completely transformed manifestations of mourning; joy and hope prevailed over sorrow and tears'.[36] Contrary to Rebillard's claim, however, I suggest that the narrative does not naturally bear his interpretation, for the story is concerned to endorse not Augustine's endeavours to control his sorrow, but rather his final acceptance of the propriety of expressing it.

To begin with Augustine follows best practice and no tears are shed (not at the deathbed, nor when the body is carried out, nor at the graveside)—even though 'I had lost the immense support she gave, my soul was wounded, and my life as it were torn to pieces, since my life and hers had become a single thing'.[37] But, as he tells the story, Augustine was already debating with himself concerning the conflict between the prohibition of tears and dirges, and his feelings. If tearful dirges were out of the question since Monica's state in death was not worthy of such dirges, 'Why then', he asks, 'did I mourn?' But he asks this question, not as Cyprian did—'why do we mourn and grieve for our departing ones as if they were lost?'[38]—as a rhetorical rebuke to those who mourn, but as inviting an enquiry as to whether there is a rationale and apology for a practice of mourning otherwise judged questionable.

To begin with then, Augustine's mourning remains restrained and subject to that 'mental control' which held back his tears. Thus when, 'after the boy's tears had been checked', sympathizers arrived and arrangements for the funeral were put in hand, Augustine 'went apart' with some others and 'discussed subjects fitting for the occasion', and 'They listened to me intently and supposed me to have no feeling of grief'.

> But in your ears where none of them heard me, I was reproaching the softness of my feelings and was holding back the torrent of sadness. It yielded a little to my efforts, but then again its attack swept over me—yet not so as to lead me to burst

---

[33] Brown, *The Cult of the Saints*, 69.   [34] Brown, *The Cult of the Saints*, 69–70.

[35] Jerome's description of the funeral of Fabiola likewise conforms to this expectation: 'Psalms were chanted and the gilded ceilings of the temples were shaken with uplifted shouts of Alleluia'; cited by J. F. Baldovin, 'The Empire Baptised', in G. Wainwright and K. B. Westerfield Tucker, eds., *The Oxford History of Christian Worship* (Oxford, 2006), 123, as evidence, along with Augustine's account, of early Christianity's 'tendency to disallow outward mourning'.

[36] Rebillard, *The Care of the Dead in Late Antiquity*, 101.

[37] Augustine, *Confessions*, IX, xii, 30.

[38] Cyprian, cited in Pelikan, *The Shape of Death*, 71.

into tears or even to change the expression on my face. But I knew what pressure lay upon my heart. And because it caused me such sharp displeasure to see how much power these human frailties had over me, though they are a necessary part of the order we have to endure and are the lot of the human condition, there was another pain to put on top of my grief, and I was tortured by a twofold sadness.[39]

The torture of this tortured soul continues, for:

When her body was carried out, we went and returned without a tear. Even during those prayers which we poured out to you when the sacrifice of our redemption was offered for her, when her corpse was placed beside the tomb prior to burial, as was the custom there, not even at those prayers did I weep. But throughout the day I was inwardly oppressed with sadness and with a troubled mind I asked you, to the utmost of my strength, to heal my pain. You did not do so.[40]

Still at a loose end, Augustine decides to go to the baths because he had 'heard that baths, for which the Greeks say *balaneion*, get their name from throwing anxiety out of mind'. The etymology was erroneous[41] and so too the expectations it aroused: 'I confess this to your mercy, father of orphans, that after I bathed I was exactly the same as before. The bitterness of sorrow had not sweated out of my heart'.[42] And so Augustine sleeps, and on waking finds his suffering relieved, and remembers Ambrose's verses (from his hymn, *Deus creator omnium*) about the restorative value of sleep.[43] So he is brought back to his 'old feeling' about Monica. And now:

I was glad to weep before you about her and for her, about myself and for myself. Now I let flow the tears which I had held back so that they ran as freely as they wished. The heart rested upon them, and it reclined upon them because it was your ears that were there, not those of some human critic who would put a proud interpretation on my weeping. And now, Lord, [very solemnly] I make my confession to you in writing. Let anyone who wishes read and interpret as he pleases. If he finds fault that I wept for my mother for a fraction of an hour, the mother who had died before my eyes who had wept for me that I might live before your eyes, let him not mock me but rather, if a person of much charity, let him weep himself before you for my sins.[44]

---

[39]   Augustine, *Confessions*, IX, xii, 31.

[40]   Augustine, *Confessions*, IX, xii, 32. Augustine's explanation of his continued suffering is, to me, slightly perplexing: 'I believe that you gave me no relief so that by this single admonition I should be made aware of the truth that every habit is a fetter adverse even to the mind that is not fed upon deceit'.

[41]   See Chadwick's explanation at footnote 31 to *Confessions*, IX, xii, 32—*balaeneion* was taken to be formed from *ballo* (to throw or eject) and *ania* (grief).

[42]   Augustine, *Confessions*, IX, xii, 32.

[43]   He might also have recalled Ambrose's words about the restorative value of crying: 'Tears often both sustain and relieve the mind; weeping cools the heart and consoles a sorrowful affection'. Ambrose, *Consolation on the Death of Emperor Valentinian*, 283.

[44]   Augustine, *Confessions*, IX, xii, 33.

Who would find fault? Chadwick mentions the reproach as coming from Plotinus who 'says that the truly rational person does not grieve at the death of relatives and friends and will not allow himself to be moved; that part which is grieved is deficient in intelligence'.[45] The sage philosopher, it was said, should exhibit the mental tranquillity of knowing that to die is as for a chrysalis to become a butterfly. But surely Augustine has not only the reproach of the philosophers in mind, but also the reproach of that earlier Christian tradition, expressed in that forbidding epitaph, in the rhetorical question put by Cyprian, and in Mary's dry eyes as remarked upon by Ambrose.[46] (And Augustine had himself once said, in the early *Morals of the Catholic Church*, that the wise man should act with tranquillity and that 'There is no harm in the word compassionate when there is no passion in the case'.[47]) But the story of the *Confessions* surely reports and accepts a new sensibility—'I was glad to weep'.

When Augustine preaches on 1 Thessalonians, 4.3 (the text being, 'so that you should not be saddened like those without hope'), he insists that 'the apostle did not advise us not to feel sad', but only '*not like the rest who have no hope*'.[48] Since we were made to live, we

> cannot help being sad when those we love abandon us by dying. Because even if we know that it is not forever that they are leaving us while we stay behind, but that it is only for a short time that they are going ahead of us, and that we are going to follow; still, when death, so abhorrent to nature, overtakes someone we love, our very feeling of love for that person is bound to grieve.[49]

So, 'Grief on the one hand, consolation on the other; there we are affected by human weakness, here restored by faith; there we feel pain according to our human condition, here we are healed by the divine promise.'[50] Thus 'it is perfectly in order for loving hearts to grieve at the death of their dear ones', as long as it is with 'a sorrow that will let itself be assuaged; and to shed the tears

---

[45] Chadwick's footnote 33 at *Confessions*, IX, xii, 33, citing Plotinus, *Eneads* I, 4, 4, in which Plotinus criticizes Aristotle and says that the Stoics are not, as it were, stoic enough.

[46] In the context of a sermon, however, which gives fulsome expression to an altogether less restrained grieving. Here and elsewhere, Ambrose, like Augustine, speaks on behalf of grieving even though 'our dead do not seem to be lost but to be sent on before us, not to be swallowed up by death but to be received by eternity'. See *First Oration On the Death of his Brother Satyrus*, section 71; in *Funeral Orations of St Gregory Nazianzen and St Ambrose*. And see his defence of weeping, itself indicative of controversy: 'we have not committed a serious fault by our weeping. Not every display of sorrow is a sign either of lack of trust in God or of weakness in ourselves. Natural grief is one thing, sorrow which comes from lack of hope is another. . . I frankly allow that I, too, have wept, but the Lord also wept. He wept for a stranger; I weep for my brother' (Section 10).

[47] Augustine, *On the Morals of the Catholic Church*, trans. R. Stothert, ch 27, section 53 in *The Nicene and Post-Nicene Fathers*, 1st series, vol. 4, Augustine's *Writings against the Manichæaens and Donatists* (Edinburgh, 1989).

[48] Augustine, *Sermons*, 172, 1.   [49] Augustine, *Sermons*, 172, 1.

[50] Augustine, *Sermons*, 172, 1.

that suit our mortal condition' as long as we are 'also prepared to be consoled'.[51] His dictum in another sermon on the same text has none of the sangfroid of that line from the *Morals of the Catholic Church*: 'It is possible for the human heart not to grieve for a dear one who has died; it's better, though, that the human heart should feel grief and be cured of it, than by not feeling any grief to become inhuman.'[52] And that has the feeling of a last word on the matter.

II.iii Burial Again—the Trouble with the Holy Dead

Augustine's nuanced vindications of mourning and burial would, however, come under pressure, not chiefly from those who wanted to 'leapfrog' over the first, but from those who wanted to attach particular importance to burial of a certain kind—wondering whether special value lay in burials which placed the ordinary dead close to the very special dead. The immediate cause of Augustine's consideration of this matter was Paulinus of Nola's enquiry on just this point (in 421 or 422) on behalf of a mother who had had her son interred near the body of Nola's very own home-grown martyr, Felix. Paulinus had already buried a number of his own children near the martyr in question, perhaps on the basis of a supposition that such burial was indeed advantageous—and certainly the archaeological records of crowding of cemeteries across the Mediterranean world suggest that martyrs' burials were as magnets to other burials.[53]

Paulinus's enquiry arises in the much wider context of the veneration of the holy dead. At one significant moment in the story of the rise and rise of relics, Augustine himself was present: at the discovery in Milan in 386 of the bodies of previously unknown martyrs Protasius and Gervasius, whose remains were swiftly and cannily translated to Ambrose's cathedral as part of his power struggle with the Arian Empress Justina. Augustine recalled this much-celebrated event many times[54] and the miracles that accompanied the translation:

> some people vexed by impure spirits were healed, the very demons themselves making public confession. Moreover, a citizen who had been blind for many years and was well known in the city, heard the people in a state of tumultuous jubilation and asked the reason for it. On learning the answer, he leapt up and asked his

---

[51] Augustine, *Sermons*, 172, 3. Again (at 173, 3): 'It's unavoidable, after all, that you should be saddened; but when you feel sad, let hope console you. I mean, how can you not feel sad, when the body which lives by the soul becomes inanimate, as the animating soul departs from it?'

[52] Augustine, *Sermons*, 173, 2.

[53] See on this point, and in general, F. Van der Meer's excellent *Augustine the Bishop: Church and Society at the Dawn of the Middle Ages* (New York, 1961), ch. 17.

[54] For example in Sermon 286 ('I was in Milan, I know about the miracles that occurred'); in Sermon 318 from 425; in *Confessions* at IX, vii, 15; and again towards the end of *City of God*, book 22, chapter 8 (1034ff).

guide to lead him there. When he arrived, he begged admission so that he might touch with his cloth the bier on which lay your saints... When he did this and applied the cloth to his eyes, immediately they were opened.[55]

No wonder one might have hopes in, and want the dearly departed close to, such powerful relics.

But Augustine had a certain anxiety, however, about the hopes that might be placed in relics. The anxiety is clear, for example, in a sermon in which he recalls the discovery of the bodies of those somewhat shadowy figures, Protasius and Gervasius, while celebrating the reception of relics of the far-from-shadowy Stephen (the very prototype of Christian martyrdom) to a shrine or chapel newly built to receive them.

The body of Stephen had been discovered in the approved fashion (after a tip-off in a dream to a priest named Lucianus), in a village about twenty miles from Jerusalem, in December of 415. The Bishop of Jerusalem vouched for the body and had it brought to his city, where it was broken up, again as was customary, and relics were taken all over the Roman world. Evodious (Augustine's pupil, friend, and fellow bishop) acquired what one commentator refers to as 'the lion's share'[56] of Stephen's body—but some of the leftovers, if I can put it like that, made their way to Augustine's own church in Hippo, where in 425, ten years after the body was found, he preached a sermon welcoming 'the relics of the first and most blessed martyr, Stephen' which, remarkably, have come 'as far as here'.[57]

The reception of the relics was an occasion for celebration. And if many have received relics it is because, as Augustine says, 'that was God's will'. But its being God's will doesn't entirely reassure Augustine. Against a particular risk he insists that 'We haven't built an altar in this place to Stephen, but an altar to God from Stephen's relics',[58] warning, in other words, against the too-enthusiastic honouring of Stephen slipping into worship. The basis for the warning is that such worship would make perfectly good pagan sense—and pagan attitudes and practices are plainly very near the surface of Augustine's world as he sees it.[59] Just how near the surface is plain in the moral he draws on the occasion of the reception of the relics. Those listening to his sermon on Stephen may not expect persecution such as the great martyrs endured, he says, but still they must fight and conquer in 'the daily temptation of human life'. His example of this temptation is, tellingly, of a temptation to pagan superstition:

Sometimes a believer falls ill... An unlawful sacrifice is promised him for his recovery, some harmful and sacrilegious amulet, an unholy spell, a magical

---

[55] Augustine, *Confessions*, IX, vii, 16.

[56] Editor's notes to Sermon 318, with the historical background.

[57] Augustine, *Sermons*, 318, 1.   [58] Augustine, *Sermons*, 318, 1.

[59] Recall the would-be convert who has to check with an astrologer on what day it would be best to become a Christian—as noted by H. Chadwick, *The Church in Ancient Society* (Oxford, 2001), 477.

consecration is promised him, and he's told, 'So-and-so and what's-his-name were in much greater danger than you are, and they escaped it by these means. Do this if you wish to live; you will die if you don't do it'.[60]

'Isn't that the same', he asks (obviously not considering the comparison melodramatic), 'as "Sacrifice, and you will live"?' So, 'you're in bed, and you're in a stadium; you're lying flat on your back, and you're engaged in a contest'.[61]

His final exhortation to his listeners ('Let the martyr Stephen be honored here; but in his honor let the one who crowned Stephen be worshiped') makes a clear enough distinction. But the relics of Stephen—his 'worthy bones'— would very shortly be implicated in a highly charged and emotional drama in which such careful distinctions might very readily be overlooked. It is drama worth recounting because it gives us some indication of the excitable atmosphere in which Paulinus was posing his question.

The story (which could have been written as a mini-drama for daytime TV) unfolds over Easter Sunday, Monday, Tuesday, and Wednesday, in 426.[62] On Easter Sunday, a man who had been suffering from terrible 'trembling of the limbs' is cured. He, along with his eight siblings, had been very effectively cursed (at the very font at which they had been baptized) by their distraught mother, a widow in Caesarea, who herself had been abused by her eldest son and vexed by the failure of her other children to protect her. The effectiveness of the cursing (in producing the tremblings and other assorted maladies) drove her to despair and suicide. The children meanwhile had wandered the world, going from one holy place to another in search of a cure, visiting especially sites associated with Stephen; and two of the troubled siblings, a brother and sister, found themselves eventually at the shrine at Uzalis near Hippo. A grey-haired old man appeared to both in a dream and assured them they would be cured. When they saw Augustine they recognized the old man of the dream, and they made for Hippo to pray at Stephen's shrine there (and sent word to their brothers and sisters to join them). They were not disappointed. On Easter day the brother, seemingly in a fit, fell unconscious near the altar, but arose to great acclaim, cured. Augustine foregoes preaching a sermon on that Sunday—noting that the congregation which is accustomed to hearing accounts of miracles performed 'through the prayers of most blessed martyr Stephen' read from official depositions, can today read the story in the person of the man cured. On Monday he nonetheless promises the normal leaflet for the following day; but after it has been read out on the Tuesday and as he begins to preach, a wild clamour from the nave indicates that the still-afflicted sister has been cured too. Augustine concludes his sermon abruptly and completes it

---

[60] Augustine, *Sermons*, 318, 3.   [61] Augustine, *Sermons*, 318, 3.
[62] Five sermons (320, 321, 322, 323, and 324) preached over those days provide an outline of the story recounted again in *City of God*, xxii, 8.

on the Wednesday, when, presumably, a degree of calm has returned. Thursday was, as far as we know, just a regular Thursday.

In the interrupted sermon on the Tuesday, as if there were not enough excitement already, Augustine had been recounting a story about the even more remarkable effects of the 'powerful presence of the divine majesty' at nearby Uzalis. A son had died in his mother's arms, while yet a catechumen. She wept on account of her unbaptized son being 'irretrievably doomed' and carried him off to implore Stephen to give him back. The son returned to life and she handed him over to the presbyters, at whose hands he received a set of sacraments and died: 'She, for her part, conducted his funeral with such a tranquil expression that it seemed she was laying him, not in the silence of the grave, but in the lap of the martyr Stephen'.[63]

And there's the rub—for in that casual aside, Augustine voices the thought that gives rise to the enquiry addressed to him via Paulinus, some four years previously: who would not want to lay their dead child in or near the lap of such powerful servants of God as Stephen or one of the other martyrs? If martyrs seem to do the living good in life, why not the dead in death? The epitaph mentioned earlier—the one in which the 'voice of majesty' is heard forbidding parents 'to lament for the dead child', also records of that child that 'Her body was buried in its tomb in front of the doors of the shrine of the martyrs'. Thus the parents were consoled—and thus we are reminded of those 'tensions' in early Christian attitudes to death and the afterlife mentioned by Brown.[64]

But for all that Augustine shows little scepticism about the association of relics, prayers, and even cursings with some remarkable events, the distinctly measured little treatise known as *On the Care to be Taken for the Dead* is intent on damping down expectations regarding the efficacy or instrumental significance of funerary rites, howsoever or wheresoever practised. Into the fevered and highly charged emotional maelstrom around martyrs and their relics, Augustine proffers a sober critique of any great concern for these rites, but— and here is the very important point—without discouraging them (except insofar as they are based on the mistaken assumption that we can do the dead good, or they us). In other words, notwithstanding his very ready fears of the possibilities of pagan superstitions, especially in connection with the bodies of the holy dead, Augustine ends up vindicating regular practices of burial and mourning as making good sense and as in no way reliant on such superstitions.

To the principle that we can do no good to the dead, Augustine admits one very modest exception—put in a formula which he uses on other occasions.[65]

---

[63] Augustine, *Sermons*, 324. [64] Brown, *The Cult of the Saints*, 69.

[65] E.g. in Sermon 172, on 1 Thessalonians 4, 13, and repeated in *Enchiridion* and in *Reply to Eight Questions of Dulcitius*; for references see Rebillard, *The Care of the Dead in Late Antiquity*, 168.

When relatives and friends piously commend the dead by their prayers, 'there is no doubt that they [i.e. the dead] are benefited by these devotions, if when they were living in the body they merited such things to be to their advantage after this life'.[66] It is a very small concession, and one that allows Augustine to bless prevalent practices of prayer for the dead even while attaching the very least instrumental significance to them.

But what of the question of whether burial at a particular location is advantageous? Again, Augustine admits that it is, while offering a purely natural account of the advantage. The association of the mortal remains of our dead with the memorial of a saint serves to incite us to prayer. In response then to the very specific case which Paulinus has raised, Augustine's generous, sensitive but restrained judgment is that:

> When ... a faithful mother desired the body of her faithful son who had died to be placed in the church of a martyr, if she truly believed that his soul was being aided by the merits of the martyr, this, because she so believed, was a kind of prayer, and as such of advantage, if anything was of advantage. And the fact that she frequently returns in spirit to the same sepulcher and there commends her son by prayers more and more aids the soul of her dead son. It is not the location of the dead body, but the living devotion of the mother out of memory of the place which affords this aid. At the same time, the love for the one who is commended, as well as for the saint to whom the loved one is commended, has a beneficial effect on the devout soul of the one who is praying.[67]

If we can do the dead no good after their deaths, nor they us (or other dead), why should we have a care for the dead at all? Augustine here repeats his argument (indeed the very words) from the opening book of *The City of God*: the wish to care for the dead, notwithstanding that the care carries no ultimate importance for the dead themselves—nor, since 'the dead of themselves have no power to intervene in the affairs of the living', no instrumental significance for us either[68]—expresses a perfectly proper sentiment. Though a lack of decent burial does not matter to the dead, yet the bodies of the dead, especially of the just and faithful, are not

> to be scorned and cast away ... For if such things as a father's clothes, and his ring, are dear to their children in proportion to their affection for their parents, then the actual bodies are certainly not to be treated with contempt, since we wear them in a much closer and intimate way than any clothing. A man's body is no mere adornment, or external convenience; it belongs to his very nature as a man.[69]

[66] Augustine, *The Care to be Taken for the Dead*, trans. J. A. Lacey, in *The Fathers of the Church*, vol. 27, Augustine, *Treatises on Marriage and Other Subjects*, ed. R. J. Deferrari (Washington, DC, 1955), 359.

[67] Augustine, *The Care to be Taken for the Dead*, 359–60.

[68] Augustine, *The Care to be Taken for the Dead*, 378.

[69] Augustine, *City of God*, 1, xiii, repeated in *The Care to be Taken for the Dead* at iii, 5.

As he says, there is, just because of this closeness, 'a natural love which every man has for his own flesh', and naturally too, a love for the bodies of those who have been dear to us; thus the love which makes us wish for certain things for our own bodies, makes us wish to provide those same things for others. 'Hence the funerals of the just men of old were cared for with dutiful devotion, the processions solemnized, and a fitting burial provided'[70]—and just as the Lord commended the work of the woman who anointed him as for burial, so (contra Chrysostom) 'they are highly commended in the Gospel who took His body down from the cross and prepared it with reverent care for burial'.[71]

The contention that regard for burial is a simple matter of natural love alone, is not, however, unqualified—for Augustine does mention specifically Christian reasons for the practice, though he does so quite lightly. '[C]are for the bodies of our dead indicates a strong belief in the resurrection' he says[72]—even if resurrection does not depend on the well-being of the body. And again—it is fitting that one should exercise care for the body of a relative; it is 'in some way a testimony of one's faith'—for 'if they do this who have no faith in the resurrection of the body, how much more ought we who have faith that a duty of this kind is due to a dead body which shall rise again and live forever'.[73]

There is perhaps, a certain disingenuousness in Augustine attributing care for the dead to a natural love—even while he pleads the resurrection as providing supplementary grounds. Augustine is very well aware that the natural love he commends is not culturally universal, as we might say, even if it is not uniquely Christian. Heraclitus's comment that 'Corpses ought to be thrown away as worse than dung' (cited with approval by Celsus and rejected by Origen in *Contra Celsum*[74]) should be regarded as merely the expression of an austere philosophical viewpoint, with no necessarily popular purchase. And yet, Augustine's entire and immense intellectual endeavour can, in large part, be seen as an attempt to fashion an understanding of the created order which would subtly but decisively alter the meaning and valuation of the body, across the board. He finds himself in contention with Manichees, but also in contention with Platonists and neo-Platonists, and equally in contention with a Christian tradition that for Augustine had not always fully embraced the goodness of the created order. Anyone with the stamina to reach the very last book of the *City of God* will find there Augustine's eloquent hymn of praise to the rational and aesthetic beauty of the human body (including in the latter the male nipple, which serves an aesthetic but no practical purpose, Augustine

---

[70] Augustine, *City of God*, 1, xiii, repeated in *The Care to be Taken for the Dead* at iii, 5.

[71] Augustine, *The Care to be Taken for the Dead*, iii, 5, repeating *City of God*, 1, xiii.

[72] Again from *City of God*—in *The Care to be Taken for the Dead*, 357.

[73] Augustine, *The Care to be Taken for the Dead*, 383.

[74] Origen, *Contra Celsum*, v, 24.

notes[75]), and even more importantly and radically, his unambiguous assertion that women will retain their sex in the resurrection.[76] And then one might be even more inclined to take the view that the 'love of the body' which he commends is far from being wholly and simply natural, but is crucially shaped and deepened by a rather particular and Augustinian (which is to say, for those who came after, Christian) way of looking at the world.

II.iv Caring for the Dead without Superstition

The complex story we have followed touches on subjects of great moment—bodies, mourning, death, and keeping the dead close. We took Augustine's learning to weep for Monica as a centre around which to narrate the other elements of the tale—holding back tears at Monica's death, Augustine hadn't quite parted with the sensibilities that seem to belong to his earlier convictions. But if the body is part of God's good creation, death cannot be a cause for celebration or even for simple and unambivalent acceptance—it is certainly not the point of life, nor the goal to which we are travelling. It can only be a punishment or a curse—not a good. Augustine never quite turned his back on rather more severe attitudes—and we can find him saying Stoic-like things even after he has become critical of the limitations of philosophy. Thus after a particular massacre, in a remark that certainly has a Stoic ring to it, he comments: 'As far as I know, no one died who wouldn't have had to die at sometime anyway'.[77] But if he didn't simply repudiate such realism, as we might call it, it didn't fit well with the world as seen from within the Church. There was, in particular, no way that the philosophers could accommodate the stories of Christ's very bodily resurrection; and Augustine rejected not only the cosmology of the philosophers, which saw salvation in rising above and parting from the material realm, but also the particular sensibilities of the Stoics that accompanied this intellectual picture—or rather perhaps their particular insensibilities. He came to think them cold, inhuman, and impractical. In *The City of God* he asks a question which he implicitly posed to himself thirty or more years previously when he moped around tearless in the days after Monica's death. If the lives of the dead

> brought us the consoling delights of friendship, how could it be that their death[s] should bring us no sadness? Anyone who forbids such sadness must forbid, if he can, all friendly conversation, must lay a ban on all friendly feeling or put a stop

---

[75] Augustine, *City of God*, XXII, xxiv, 1074.

[76] '[W]hile all defects will be removed from those bodies, their essential nature will be preserved. Now a woman's sex is not a defect; it is natural'; Augustine, *City of God*, XXII, xvii, 1057.

[77] A comment which I can't, however, locate in Augustine's writings, though it seems likely to be from correspondence. The remark is quoted by Eric Voegelin, but without a reference.

to it, must with a ruthless insensibility break the ties of all human relationships, or else decree that they must only be engaged upon so long as they inspire no delight in a man's soul. But...this is beyond all possibility.[78]

So, if freedom from the emotions that make death bitter to us is neither possible nor desirable nor appropriate, what is left in the face of death, except that moderate mourning and moderate concern for burial which he commends? With his profound conviction at the goodness of the world, the human body, and our daily life within it, Augustine came to insist that we shouldn't celebrate death as a release of the spirit with the Manichees, nor brush it to one side with the Stoics. Finally Augustine taught: 'It is not possible to love death, only to bear it', or in the more poetic and heart-felt formulation of the *Confessions*, won from bitter experience: 'I was glad to weep before you about her and for her, about myself and for myself'.

III ALDER HEY AND THE MODERN OPACITY OF CARE FOR THE DEAD

In 1999 a Parliamentary Inquiry was instituted to investigate the removal, retention, and disposal of organs and tissues following post-mortem examination at Alder Hey Children's Hospital in Liverpool. The Inquiry was initially concerned with the actions that had preceded the Inquiry and had led to its being established: that is, with the many cases where some or many body parts from a deceased child had been removed and retained without the prior consent of or even subsequent reporting to the parents. (The organs or tissues retained included heart, brain, spleen, kidney, adrenal glands, bladder, reproductive organs, diaphragm, trachea, larynx, oesophagus, stomach, intestines, lymph nodes, thyroid, pancreas, liver, tongue, bones, and muscle.) But the Inquiry also had to concern itself not only with the conduct that had led to its being set up, but also with the conduct of the hospital after the Inquiry was itself established. Why?

When, subsequent to the establishment of the Inquiry, parents discovered that body parts from their child had been retained, they commonly sought the return of those parts, either to be buried with the rest of the body or to be cremated and placed with the existing ashes. In some instances they also sought the return of tissue blocks or slides (i.e. tiny samples of tissue, preserved for clinical examination), placing these beside coffins, or alternatively having them cremated and deposited with the other remains. And here is the moment in the story that demands particularly to be noticed—as the hospital

---

[78] Augustine, *City of God*, xix, 8. See discussion of *apatheia* in *City of God*, xiv, 19.

was returning organs and tissues obtained without consent and held without parental knowledge, 'small samples of these organs. . .' were taken, '. . . without obtaining any further consent, or indeed even telling the parents'.[79]

The story of the events at the hospital prior to 1999 raise many questions (and a satisfactory history has yet to be written), but what I want to note is that the events at the hospital post-1999 (i.e. after the establishment of the Inquiry), pose a particular problem since what now needs to be understood is how medical practitioners and hospital administrators *under investigation for removing and retaining organs and tissue without seeking the consent of parents and without informing them*, should, in returning them under the spotlight of investigation, take samples *without the consent of parents and without informing them*. A wholly adequate explanation would doubtless draw attention to a highly complex range of factors, motives, and influences, but what this fragment of the story suggests, interpreted with other confirming evidence, is that one key element lies in the opacity of the parents' concerns to the understanding of the hospital and, as it turns out, to the wider medical establishment—and even to bioethics in its dominant forms. The original and subsequent actions of the medical practitioners and hospital administrators in relation to the retention of tissue, suggest that the wishes and feelings of the parents were not only unexpected or unanticipated, but somehow inexplicable to official thought and discourse. For even when the parents requested the return of body parts or tissue in response to news of the original incidents of unauthorized removal and retention, the depth and significance and weight of this request was blankly repudiated in a repetition of the original unauthorized removal and retention.

The Human Tissue Authority was set up by the Human Tissue Act of 2004, partly in response to the events of Alder Hey. I served as a member of the Authority from its inception, and was thus party to the many discussions the Authority conducted with a wide range of interested parties as it sought to implement the legislation, chiefly by developing codes of practice in accordance with the Act's underlying principles and spirit. These discussions often referred to the original events at Alder Hey and elsewhere, which had prompted the new statutory structure. On very many occasions I heard expressed the view that the parents' responses to the retention of tissue were, in effect, to be treated as negligible. It was said that the parents, in seeking the return of organs and body parts (even more so in the case of tissue blocks and slides), were merely emotional or sentimental, or even that they were confused or making a mistake. The depth of professional perplexity in the face of parental distress is conveniently and neatly displayed in a submission from the President of the Royal College of Paediatrics and Child Health in written

[79] *Report of the Royal Liverpool Children's Inquiry* (London, 2001), 36.

evidence to a meeting organized by the UK Chief Medical Officer, prior to the passage of the legislation:

> It is perhaps a paradox that in an age when we have more understanding than ever before of the nature of human life and the biology of the human body, we are more distressed than at any time in human history about what is perceived as inappropriate disposal of the whole human body or part of it… This is a philosophical puzzle.[80]

The authors of the article in which this comment is cited, refer to the 'bewilderment' among physicians and surgeons at the parents' distress. The quite common thought, suggested in the previous comment, that the parents were confused and their attitudes a 'puzzle' or a 'paradox', served to excuse the practitioners' bewilderment, which might then take a harsher turn and become something darker than a mere expression of puzzlement—as in the comment to me by a consultant that the only mistake made by the doctors at Alder Hey was in letting the parents know that they possessed their children's body parts.

As mentioned in the opening chapter, blank incomprehension in relation to the parental perspective was not generally relieved by bioethics as again those same authors, Campbell and Willis, point out. They cite the comments of John Harris: 'preoccupation with reverence and respect for bodily tissue' which 'has come to dominate discussions of retained tissues and organs in the wake of the Alder Hey revelations' is 'quite absurd, if understandable'.[81] Insofar as this incomprehension is representative (as I argue it is) of leading forms of bioethics, it is a token of the fact that bioethics is generally incapable of making a contribution to overcoming the scientistic perspective and assumptions of current policy debates (inclined as they are, for example, to use 'emotional' as a pejorative). Bioethics, if this is indeed characteristic of it, shares the presuppositions of that debate, and hence can have no heuristic role or therapeutic value in relieving the social misunderstanding which confronted the Alder Hey parents. The opacity of parental concerns and attitudes will remain intact if there is no better heuristic tool than this.

The Alder Hey parents, it seems, would have been heard only had they learned to express themselves in terms approved by official discourse—though what they wanted to say was probably not expressible in the terms which were on offer (since even the notion of a 'natural love' for the body was probably beyond official or bioethical comprehension). Failing that, it was only too likely that those who dealt with them would treat their views and wishes as morally negligible.

To complete this story of social misunderstanding, we need to note that what can seem like the vindication of the Alder Hey parents by subsequent

---

[80] Cited in Campbell and Willis, ' "They Stole My Baby's Soul": Narratives of Embodiment and Loss', *Medical Humanities* 31 (2) 102.

[81] Campbell and Willis, 'They Stole My Baby's Soul', 102.

legislation and codes of conduct is only very superficially so, and in fact displays no greater social comprehension of what the parental concerns signified than did the discounting of these concerns—albeit that a practical respect for these concerns is to be preferred to their being simply set aside. This is not to criticize the legislation and current practice as such—but simply to indicate that practical respect is compatible with a deeper incomprehension.

Legislation and practice has certainly gone some way towards meeting parental concerns, and in particular aims to ensure that the events of Alder Hey should not be repeated, and that the dead should be protected from the lack of respect which caused the scandal. But a dominant way of understanding the new regulations—that is, as enshrining the importance of consent— can plainly be seen as inadequate in capturing the nature of those concerns. In fact, it seems very like an attempt to translate the parental concerns into the sort of approach with which bioethics is most comfortable. This translation fails, however, almost at the very first hurdle—since it overlooks the fact that the case for the necessity of consent in relation to the use of body parts is far from being simply self-evident, but is plainly reliant on a further rationale (which typically remains mysterious to this approach). I suggest further that it is just the failure to locate the importance of consent in a wider framework which explains this supposedly crucial principle being treated quite lightly in other contexts. In other words, its being treated lightly outside the sphere in which it is trumpeted is the scant homage that current medical practice shows towards a principle poorly understood or vindicated even on its home ground. What emerges, I suggest, is ambiguity and equivocation around the supposedly foundational principle of consent, leaving tensions in practice that threaten another Alder Hey.

First of all then, note the inadequacy of the thought that consent is somehow fundamental in a self-explanatory way. As I have mentioned, the HTA regularly refers to consent as a bedrock of the legislation and as the principle which governs existing and developing regulation. It is plain, however, that the principle of informed consent (however we elaborate it) is not fundamental in the sense that we can dig no deeper. In fact we can very well reflect on when consent is and is not important, and thus probe something of why the giving or withholding of consent matters. To put it another way, we cannot understand why the events at Alder Hey are referred to as the Alder Hey 'scandal' by saying that there was no consent, without thinking further about why the giving or withholding of consent matters. Thus if we are to understand or explain concerns about the handling and use of human tissue, we need to go beyond or behind 'consent' to other values and attitudes.

We can get at this point easily enough by asking why consent is necessary in relation to the use of the body and body parts, but not simply necessary as such. Suppose a photo has been taken of me during my lifetime. Do you need my consent to display it either before or after my death? Now, of course, a photo may depict me far more effectively than certain body parts. And your possessing and using certain photos may cause me far more distress, embarrassment, or concern than would be caused to me by your using or possessing certain tissues or body parts. Thus your use of certain photos, in certain ways, could be thoughtless or unkind or even malicious—and we might say just the same of a diary. And for this very reason we are certainly open to the idea that our use of photos should be governed by certain norms, and even that some of these norms should have to do with consent. But in practice, however we might chose to regulate the use of photos, no one has yet suggested the establishment of a Human Photo Authority or a Human Photo Act, to 'make provision with respect to activities involving human photos'. And no one, as far as I know, has suggested that consent is the fundamental and bedrock principle in relation to the taking of photos. Indeed, if anyone told us that in taking family portraits one should ensure consent and specifically, for example, consent to their display after someone's death, we would be somewhat perplexed or suspect a joke. Naturally, the contrast I am suggesting could be denied either by insisting that there should indeed be a process for the giving or withholding of consent in relation to photos, or that it already exists in the sense that those who are photographed give implied consent to reasonable uses of the photographs. I doubt that either point is persuasive, but my concern with the example, however, is not to establish an absolute difference, but simply to point to the generally different sensibilities which exist in relation to bodies and photographs. (To put it another way, to understand the consent provisions in the Human Tissue Act, it is its being my *body*, not its being *my* body that matters—which is why requiring consent to the use of photos after my death might seem heavy-handed, no matter that they are indeed photos of me.)

One can't then *explain* the importance of consent in relation to the use of bodies and body parts by pointing to the general importance of consent—there is no such thing. We don't demand consent to everything that may be done to us or our bodies, but only to some things—consent is not always and everywhere necessary, but only sometimes and somewhere. Hence appeal to consent is not self-explanatory, but implicitly refers to a more fundamental set of concerns which would have to explain why consent is necessary here and not there. In the case we are considering, the insistence on the need for consent relies on some assumptions about the human body which are hidden, not revealed, by that mere insistence.

I suggest then, that the importance which policy-making and discussion accord to consent in relation to the use of body parts is neither well understood nor well articulated, and, for all that codes which require consent serve to check the excesses and abuses associated with Alder Hey, the principle of consent is likely to exert a somewhat ad hoc influence rather than being able to govern medical practice and policy in any thorough-going way. That this is indeed so is a point that might be made by reference to the matter of organ transplantation. What is striking here, so I suggest, is that the supposedly cru-cial principle of consent is treated rather lightly. (And is treated even more lightly still, to say the least, where the notion of presumed consent is relied on, as in Wales, to increase the supply of organs.)

Crucially, consent to removal of organs can amount to little more than ticking a box on an online form—suggesting a standard for informed con-sent that falls below what is needed to take out a credit purchase agreement. A further difficulty lies in the fact that the most important source of organs for transplant is from those who are categorized as 'brain dead'. The consent to be obtained in such cases will be the consent of the donor if the donor's wishes are recorded, probably with the additional consent of relatives, or the consent of the next of kin alone if there is no record of the donor's wishes. Now the giving of this consent (either the prior consent of the donor or the contemporaneous consent of the relatives) is significantly dependent on the use of the notion of 'brain death'. It is the fact that the potential donor is said to be 'brain dead' which provides the rationale for seeking to remove their organs before their death, simply understood. And it is to the removal of organs after brain death to which donors consent.

The notion of 'brain death' is, however, highly problematic, and so too any reliance on it in seeking consent. The recent report from the US President's Council on Bioethics on *Controversies in the Determination of Death*, said of the UK standard for brain death that it was 'conceptually suspect [and] clini-cally dangerous'.[82] In fact, this concept of brain death is arguably best regarded as resting on a stipulative definition of death, stipulated for the very reason that it provides a permission for what would otherwise be problematic, namely the removal of the organs.[83] And the problematic nature of such an action is not a matter of lay perceptions alone, though it is certainly the case that 'brain death' does not equate with death as normally understood, which is associated with the cessation of breathing and of the beating of the heart. It is rather that, for example, no pathologist would currently think it acceptable to perform an autopsy on someone who is 'brain dead', even though their being brain dead is cited as a justification for the removal of heart, lungs, kidneys, or other organs before their becoming very dead.

It follows, I would contend, that it is hard to regard the consent which is currently obtained as fully informed, since the questionable character of the category 'brain death' is not something to which attention is directed. Indeed, it might be better to say that appeal to brain death is something of a sleight of hand. For policymakers to entertain a shift in these circumstances, as some

[82] Report of the US President's Council, *Controversies in the Determination of Death* (Washington, DC, 2008), 66.
[83] See the history recounted by L. A. Sharp, *Strange Harvest: Organ Transplant, Denatured Bodies, and the Transformed Self* (Berkeley, 2006), 16.

have done and continue to do, to presumed consent to organ donation, seems somewhat extraordinary, even without the rhetorical centrality of consent in policy developments over the last ten years. If presumed consent has any validity, it can only be in cases where, to mention just one condition, there is a high degree of understanding of that to which consent is sought. It is such a degree of understanding and knowledge which alone might serve to warrant the presumption that the absence of objection is evidence of acceptance. Where there is no such understanding and knowledge, such a presumption seems highly dubious. So if the formal gaining of consent as currently practised seems problematic, just because of the ambiguity around 'brain death', the practice of presuming consent must be much more so. And this all goes to show that for all its supposed importance, the principle of consent gives way very easily under certain pressures.

The attitudes of the Alder Hey parents are still mysterious to much public debate and discourse even though the legislation, regulations, and practices which have emerged after Alder Hey may seem to protect their concerns. The question that the scandal might be said to have posed—what was the moral sense or meaning of parental wishes which were the subject of official disdain—remains unanswered in official discourse. (And there are, of course, a host of other such questions here. Why was it that the *prima facie* opacity of the parents' responses and requests did not elicit efforts to understand these responses and requests, but simply and without more ado seemed to suggest to many of the key actors and commentators the existence of confusion, error, sentimentality, or emotionalism, which could be managed or corrected, but didn't need to be respected? How was it furthermore, that there was not only medical and administrative failure, but that a discipline which might have been expected to provide some help, served too often to warrant the disregard?) Answering this and other questions would require a full treatment of the history and context of the events of Alder Hey, which is outside the scope of this enquiry. But we are bound to ask one pressing question: where might we go to gain even some initial understanding of the moral sense and meaning in the parental wishes to keep the dead close?

My claim, in line with the argument of this book, is that we should turn for assistance to social anthropology which from Frazer to Durkheim, and from Van Gennep to Hertz, has had death and burial at the centre of its concerns—and more recently has produced such powerful ethnographies of mourning as the wonderfully titled *The Sorrow of the Lonely and the Burning of the Dancers*.[84] We shall, indeed, find assistance from social anthropology in the task of giving an account of the place of mourning in social life—but we shall also find a regrettable enthusiasm, even amongst anthropologists, for discovering superstition in exotic and less than exotic graveyards. I will note this fact to underline

---

[84] E. L. Schiefflin, *The Sorrow of the Lonely and the Burning of the Dancers* (New York, 1976).

just how very deep is the opacity of mourning in contemporary society. That it is opaque to bioethics is perhaps no surprise; but that it is subject to misconstrual even by social anthropologists is altogether more noteworthy.

IV ANTHROPOLOGY AND MOURNING (IN WHICH SUPERSTITIONS ABOUND)

I propose to look briefly at two ethnographies which are interesting on two grounds. First, they throw light on the practice and grammar of mourning. Second, they both nonetheless find superstition in practices which make sense without any such thing. They serve then, to assist us in the task of trying to conceive and explicate the practice of mourning, while also witnessing to a degree of cultural pressure and readiness to misconstrue such practices.

Loring Danforth's *The Death Rituals of Rural Greece* provides a compelling description, but not a wholly compelling explanation of the rites surrounding death in a village in northern Greece (given the fictional name of Potamia). The description is accompanied by thirty-one photographs (by Alexander Tsiaras), and photographs and text together depict rites which, by our stand- ards, are intensive and extensive, and highly scripted.

Some of the elements in the performance of the duties of mourning we will find exotic and yet perhaps beguiling, such as the laments sung at various points in the five years of mourning which follow a death. The laments are especially intriguing because they also do service at certain moments (of sepa- ration and parting) in weddings. Exotic but probably less beguiling, however, is the rite that marks the end of the five-year mourning period—the exhuma- tion of the bones of the dead and their consignment to the village ossuary, where the deceased individual becomes one of the general dead, remembered henceforward only collectively.

Between death and exhumation the rites of mourning seek to maintain, sug- gests Danforth, the social relationship between the living and the dead. 'The manner in which the living interact with the dead is in effect', he claims, 'an extension of the manner in which the living interact with each other.'[85] Thus women typically care for their men by housekeeping at their graves, which will be tended, washed, scrubbed, and cleaned, perhaps on a daily basis. But the essence of the relationship he pictures as carrying on a 'conversation'. So the widows will also sit by the grave to keep the dead company. And the living address the dead directly, in the formal and sometimes dialogic laments which punctuate the passage of the five-year period of mourning. As Danforth sees it, 'These moving attempts to converse with the dead are an expression of the

---

[85] Danforth, *The Death Rituals of Rural Greece*, 130.

strong desire on the part of the living to continue to communicate with those who have recently died'.[86] Death after all, comes 'as a premature interruption of a conversation, a conversation that is the essence of social life itself'.[87] Thus during the five years that separate the death and the exhumation, that conversation is sustained; only with the exhumation is it abruptly and painfully brought to a close.

Danforth's is a stunning tale, beautifully photographed and elegantly narrated, but marred by one distinctly false note—the attribution to the participants in the burial rites and exhumation of what I am terming 'superstition'. Specifically he argues that the participants in these rites are governed by two contrasting and competing outlooks—a 'religious perspective' and a 'commonsense perspective', the former being the supposed vehicle of superstition.

As he sees it, the religious perspective involves 'the belief that the dead continue to exist as sentient beings who are somehow aware of the activities performed by the living on their behalf'. 'Many women', he says, 'claim that, by the grace of God...the souls of the dead are able to perceive the care and attention that women in mourning lavish upon them.'[88] On the other hand, the commonsense perspective denies this claim, on which, however, he suggests the rites of mourning are predicated. There is a 'contradiction'[89] between the common sense and religious perspectives, he tells us, though 'paradoxically' the perspectives 'seem to be held jointly by the women of rural Greece'.[90] He thus construes the period of mourning as a battle between these perspectives.

> During the early portions of the long liminal period that lasts from the time of death until the exhumation, the attitudes of those in mourning tend to be dominated by the religious perspective...in spite of the occasional expression of an awareness of the contradictions between this religious perspective and the reality of death. As long as the religious perspective is subjectively maintained, a woman in mourning can continue to inhabit the socially constructed reality that existed prior to the death of the relevant significant other. She can continue to interact with the deceased; she can carry on a reality-sustaining conversation with him through the performance of death rituals in his memory.

With the passage of time, however, the religious perspective becomes increasingly difficult to maintain.[91] The 'religious perspective' is finally worn down, so

---

[86] Danforth, *The Death Rituals of Rural Greece*, 128.

[87] Danforth, *The Death Rituals of Rural Greece*, 130.

[88] Danforth, *The Death Rituals of Rural Greece*, 177. Danforth seems to cite no Orthodox or other authority as teaching the possibility of such perception on the part of the dead. He presents the belief in this perception as a popular—and chiefly female—belief: 'Men are much more likely to express skepticism concerning the continued existence of the soul after death and its ability to perceive or benefit from the services performed for it by women in mourning' (136).

[89] Danforth, *The Death Rituals of Rural Greece*, 139.

[90] Danforth, *The Death Rituals of Rural Greece*, 140.

[91] Danforth, *The Death Rituals of Rural Greece*, 140–41.

it seems, by 'commonsense'. And it is the exhumation which is the final nail in the coffin, so to speak, for the religious outlook. A caption to one of the photographs makes the point:

> When the women who have gathered around the grave confront a pile of bones instead of the person they buried five years earlier, their hopes are crushed. The joy they anticipated is transformed into grief and pain. They are forced to realize that although the exhumation can return the remains of the deceased to the upper world, it cannot reverse the process of decomposition, which has reduced a person to bones. It cannot bring the dead back to life.[92]

It is a nice story, but it surely will not do. A rather large clue to the utterly unsatisfactory nature of this explanation comes a couple of photographs back from the one with the caption just quoted. In this photograph two small groups of quite small children (mostly girls) stand on a wall and peer down at the exhumation going on just below them in the graveyard. Given that children have a habit of growing up—or, to put the point conversely, given that grown-ups have an even more reliable habit of having been children—we may safely assume that the women who gather for the exhumation will be familiar with the usual outcome of exhumations, namely a pile of bones. The village ossuary is, after all, one supposes, far from empty. Thus to interpret the exhumation as the painful crushing of the fictions and false expectations supposedly involved in the 'religious perspective' seems hopelessly implausible as a serviceable explanation of what is going on. (Positing 'denial' from time to time, as Danforth does, doesn't do anything to shore up the proposed explanation, since though it lends the account an air of authority, the posit presupposes what is in question.[93]) In any case, the pain of the exhumation has a perfectly good explanation in the fact that, as Danforth notes, the grave is personified—thus, the women go to visit x, not x's grave. This personification at once facilitates the social relationship during the liminal stage, but also means that the destruction of a grave by the exhumation is especially powerful and disturbing (and hardly stands in need of further explanation).

It is also not only unsatisfactory, but manifestly unnecessary to posit the thought that the dead are not really dead to explain anything else which is observed over the course of the five years of rites—and again, Danforth has the material to hand which might have encouraged him in that thought, though, as it turns out, he doesn't seem minded to attend to it.

To take an example: part of the care which the living provide for the dead is expressed through the 'preparation and serving of food', which is, as Danforth

---

[92] Danforth, *The Death Rituals of Rural Greece*, text accompanying plate 29.

[93] 'By caring for the dead as they care for the living the women of rural Greece are able to deny, symbolically and temporarily at least, the reality of death' (133)—though not very well, one would have thought.

notes, 'an essential feature of social life in rural Greece and is the epitome of the expression of love and solidarity within the family.'[94] That 'the distribution of food is an important event at all rites associated with death' is thus a striking exemplification of the claim that care for the dead is typically constructed as a continuation of care for the living. Danforth does not stop here but makes the further claim that 'This food, which is actually consumed by the living, is believed to make its way into the other world where it benefits the dead directly.'[95]

Now it is not generally, you might say, for the stay-at-home reader, from his or her armchair, to correct the intrepid anthropologist, who has after all braved the field, on the matter of what the anthropologist's informants do or do not believe—indeed this would normally be a 'cannot' not a 'should not'. But if the anthropologist, as here, claims that 'the belief [which is posited about food reaching the dead] is illustrated . . . by the following account', when the 'following account' illustrates no such thing, the stay-at-home reader may surely feel emboldened. The account goes as follows:

> Paraskevi had eight children. When one of her daughters married and left home, Paraskevi was distraught. She was so upset that when she cooked meals for her children, she could not bring herself to prepare only seven plates of food. She continued to prepare eight plates of food, even though her daughter was no longer there. She would give her daughter's serving to a young girl, an orphan, who lived nearby. She felt comforted because she knew that her daughter's serving was being eaten. It was as if her own daughter were eating it herself.[96]

This, very plainly, however, does not illustrate the 'belief' which Danforth posits, that food consumed by the living 'makes its way' to the dead and 'benefits them directly'. In the first place, Paraskevi's daughter is not dead. In the second place, the food is certainly not supposed to benefit even the still-living daughter directly—in the claim that 'it was as if her own daughter were eating it', the words 'it was as if' can safely be assumed, I think, to be doing some work. In fact Paraskevi's 'feeding' of her absent daughter makes perfect human sense without positing that a benefit reached her—and is a telling example of a capacity to find consolation for loss by caring for someone who can represent that other who precisely cannot receive care. (Thus a father whose son who had died from AIDS expresses his continuing—and possibly previously poorly expressed—love for his son in volunteering for a charity which prepares meals for housebound and dying victims of AIDS.[97]) Paraskevi's practice makes human sense whether her daughter is alive or dead—but in neither case

[94] Danforth, *The Death Rituals of Rural Greece*, 131.
[95] Danforth, *The Death Rituals of Rural Greece*, 131.
[96] Danforth, *The Death Rituals of Rural Greece*, 131.
[97] An instance from Bender, *Heaven's Kitchen: Living Religion at God's Love We Deliver* (Chicago, 2003).

need it depend upon the sort of belief which the practice is said to presuppose in Danforth's account.

There is much that is good in Danforth's treatment of the death rituals of rural Greece, and suggestive for any explication of practices of keeping the dead close—and we will need to return to that in due course. But the readiness of Danforth to find superstition in mourning is a fault that is strikingly replicated in another highly suggestive ethnography. *The Secret Cemetery* by Francis, Kellaher, and Neophytou is a study of 'the emotional and symbolic meaning attached' to bodies, as evidenced in the various rituals of burial, mourning, and commemoration observed in certain London cemeteries.[98] And while it will serve us well, I think, in seeking to make sense of the parental wishes expressed at Alder Hey, its readiness to point a finger at imagined superstitions indicates something of the degree of opacity of mourning even to reflective contemporary analysis and observation.

We can approach this study in three steps. First, we will notice something of the elaborate practices of mourning which are displayed in the cemeteries studied. But then, and in the second place, we will notice that the authors of this study themselves show some ambivalence towards some of the practices they describe, and are tempted to construe (or possibly construct) them as superstitious—in a way which is analogous, perhaps, to the habits of interpretation which were evident in response to Alder Hey. We shall conclude in the third place, however, that the subtlety and depth of the mourning practices revealed by the study generally need no such construal or construction, and that the significance of *The Secret Cemetery* is in its revealing the depth of articulate, coherent, and morally serious practices of mourning in late twentieth- and early twenty-first-century Britain of a kind which were neither anticipated nor understood by many of those connected with the controversies associated with Alder Hey.

As the authors see it, 'The bereaved, as members of an increasingly secularized and individualistic English society, are "on their own" to cope with loss'.[99] Death, as is commonly observed, has been more and more kept at a distance in Britain over the last hundred years in a number of different ways—it typically now occurs in a hospital; the body of the deceased is only rarely returned to or kept at home; and that body is normally handed over to professionals who may take responsibility not only for its preparation for burial or cremation and its storage the meanwhile, but may also arrange any service or rite which

---

[98] D. Francis, L. Kellaher, and G. Neophytou, *The Secret Cemetery* (Oxford, 2005). If time and space permitted, it would also be useful to locate the wishes of the Alder Hey parents in the wider context of the creative and flexible use of material culture to keep the dead more than just in mind, so to speak, even without the body. See e.g. E. Hallam, J. Hockey, G. Howarth, *Beyond the Body: Death and Social Identity*, (New York, 1999) and E. Hallam and J. Hockey, *Death, Memory and Material Culture* (Oxford, 2001).

[99] Francis et al., *The Secret Cemetery*, 58.

accompanies the final parting. Cremation may signal a further distancing, with the disposal of the body being more effectively concealed from view in a tidy fashion.[100] However that may be, an aspect of the distancing, or at least accompanying it, has been what the authors refer to as the 'privatizing of mourning', noting that 'In contemporary, secular English culture, bereavement is often described as personal and private, without formal guidelines and customs'.[101]

Of course, like many such descriptions, this one also serves as a prescription—and anything other than rather formal and contained expressions of loss and grief are unwelcome in normal social contexts and effectively prohibited. (Even the widely accepted and seemingly permissive notion of there being stages in grief itself serves to encourage or require adjustment and moving on, thus giving notice of a social expectation of an ending to even those moderate displays of public grief which are permitted.) It follows from this distancing and privatizing of death and mourning, that the cemetery has become a place apart, 'where grieving behaviour, often marginalized by society, is both evoked and managed by cemetery procedures and peer practices'.[102] Visited and cared for, the plots become an embodiment of the deceased and thus allow 'the creation of an ongoing relationship with the physically located and grounded identity of the departed'. Thus 'for the bereaved who visit cemeteries, these burial grounds are special, sacred spaces of personal, emotional and spiritual reclamation where the shattered self can be "put back in place" '[103] through a newly constituted relationship with the deceased. Through the 'creation of memory and the construction and reconstruction of the identity of both the deceased and the mourner, the dead are remembered and the living and dead remain linked'.[104]

What is observed then, where grieving is not merely permitted but fostered and modelled, is a rich range of practices, mediated by 'the enduring presence of the body buried in soil', which serve to 'express loss and perpetuate memory'[105]—and which will seem to those of us who are used to these observances perfectly regular and obvious, even if remarkable when you stop and think about them. The most basic activity is visiting, but this may take many different forms. Most commonly there will be a pattern of visiting on particular days or anniversaries, and of placing flowers on a grave. (The choice of flowers may itself often be significant, as the deceased's favourites, and care may be expressed not only in the choice but even in obtaining the flowers: ' "The roses and carnations on the grave I have grown especially for her from seedlings" '.[106]) The incidence of visits may decline markedly after a short time, but in other

---

[100] And it would be interesting to compare practices of memory and mourning which occur after cremation (where ashes are interred in a cemetery or alternatively scattered in a cemetery or elsewhere) with the practices revealed in this study of burial.

[101] Francis et al., *The Secret Cemetery*, 6.   [102] Francis et al., *The Secret Cemetery*, 6.

[103] Francis et al., *The Secret Cemetery*, 3.   [104] Francis et al., *The Secret Cemetery*, 80.

[105] Francis et al., *The Secret Cemetery*, 26.

[106] Francis et al., *The Secret Cemetery*, 85.

cases regular visiting takes place over a long period and at considerable effort of time and trouble. An 87-year-old unmarried man, who had visited a grave twice a month for very many years, explained—' "I lived with my parents and they lived with me. They're the only ones I've got to remember; I don't want to give up my memories of them".'[107] Other common practices include bringing cards on Mother's Day or at Christmas, often with long messages for the deceased, which are not meant to be read by other mourners or visitors.[108] And in the same vein, and perhaps most significant in continuing and even developing relationships, is the conversing with the dead which was commonly observed and reported, mediated by the presence of the body.

It is these conversations which are the most striking and remarkable part of the ethnography. They differ in character, it seems, depending on whether the occupant of the grave is a child, sibling, spouse, or parent to the visitor, and, as one might expect, by the nature or quality of the relationship between the mourner and the deceased.[109] Thus the conversations could serve quite different purposes and express quite diverse emotions. For example, the authors found that 'Many of the adult children from each cemetery site said they continued to talk to their deceased parents at home as well as in the cemetery, seeking their approval and their reassurances, soliciting their consent, asking their assistance, or thinking through problems with them.'[110] Others, however, conversed not to maintain a parental relationship on which they had relied, but to resolve or heal it: ' "Coming here, I am spending time—sort of making up" ',[111] reported one visitor. One Jewish mother reported going to the cemetery ' "To say things you did not say or could not say, because they were too difficult or too painful." '[112] Thus, as the authors say, '[F]or some individuals, cemetery visits seemed to share some of the processes and tasks of psychotherapy and to offer the possibility of self-healing over time'.[113] For others, neither guidance nor healing seemed at the forefront of the visiting and conversing. ' "There is someone here to come to" ' said one. ' "It's a comfort to come here to talk" ' said another; ' "we were married fifty-three years" '. ' "I look forward to coming on a Thursday; it's visiting the wife, visiting the memory" '.[114] According to the authors: 'Such comments suggest that the cemetery is a place where a continuing relationship with the deceased can be maintained, despite death, through conversation and by being "near" the other. Couples still grow old together'.[115] And what is said specifically of a conversation with parents, applied across the various relationships: 'For many, this "dialogue", spoken in

---

[107] Francis et al., *The Secret Cemetery*, 157.   [108] Francis et al., *The Secret Cemetery*, 121.

[109] Again, the grave can be a medium for the 'reconstruction of domestic relationships' (21) and 'can express a range of familial connections—from those of positive meaning, affection and belonging to those suggesting disappointment, conflict or negative memories' (21–22).

[110] Francis et al., *The Secret Cemetery*, 90.   [111] Francis et al., *The Secret Cemetery*, 159.

[112] Francis et al., *The Secret Cemetery*, 152.   [113] Francis et al., *The Secret Cemetery*, 159.

[114] Francis et al., *The Secret Cemetery*, 162.   [115] Francis et al., *The Secret Cemetery*, 162.

a "low conversational tone" was a significant component of keeping the dead parent "alive".[116] For some, talking discontinued after a relatively brief period even though they continued to visit; for others the conversations continued with the visiting. Perhaps the most striking of all the conversations occurs when widows and widowers discuss remarriage with former partners, and even introduce the new partner at the graveside.

The authors' conclusion is that their 'research suggests that the cemetery must be appreciated as an important site for the creation of culture and memory'. Grave visiting here in north London may be practised, if not quite as intensively and as extensively as in Greece, at least in a highly developed and committed way. And through this visiting of the dead, 'the notions and practices of kinship—of ongoing ties between the living and dead—are articulated, reinforced, contested, renegotiated and reconstructed through memorial behaviour and personal conversation'.[117] This is an important appreciation, then, of the morally sophisticated work of mourning. It seems, however, that the authors find something in the maintenance of the ties somewhat dubious—even that they are tempted to think that some sort of mistake may be involved in the practices they reveal.

The use of scare quotes in the following passage ought to alert us to the issue:

> The basic funerary practices of those who are the focus of this book, such as cleaning the memorial stone and refreshing the flowers, draw on and elaborate connections between body, home and garden to negate or resolve the paradox of death as a part of life. Our research suggests that these transformative ritual acts resurrect and symbolically 'reconstruct' the body, control nature and, by implication, 'control' death, and so keep the departed 'present' and 'alive'.[118]

The scare quotes, here and elsewhere in the book, function, it seems, to alert us to the fact that the bodies are not *really* reconstructed, death is not *really* controlled, and the departed are not *really* present and alive. But why, I wonder, do we need to be scared away from such literalism? It is surely only if there is danger that we might think that by means of these memorial practices the departed are, for example, imagined as quite simply present and alive, that we need the scare quotes to save us from the error. I don't, for example, write that the time 'flew' by, since I don't think you are in danger of imagining that time passed us by with its wings flapping. Nor do I tell you that we confront a 'thorny' problem here, for the same reason. So why are we warned that the departed were 'present' and 'alive', not simply present and alive?

---

[116] Francis et al., *The Secret Cemetery*, 157.
[117] Francis et al., *The Secret Cemetery*, 177.
[118] Francis et al., *The Secret Cemetery*, 25.

The root of the anxiety seems to be revealed in the observation that 'Commemorative visits to the graves of parents...had different meanings over the life course, and the nature of such visits appeared to be related to a number of factors' including 'whether or not the mourner believed that connection between the world of the living and the world of the dead was possible'.[119] Now, of course, it would be hard to deny a connection between the world of the living and the world of the dead—the cemetery is itself proof of this very connection. But the authors are getting at belief in a different sort of connection than this, which they characterize as follows:

> Whereas the 'soul' or 'spirit' exists in the eternal time of heaven, the cemetery-based 'spirit'—the corpse—and the identity and memory of the deceased are maintained in linear time. Cemetery-based commemorative practices rely on the premise that the identity of the individual is closely allied with the physical body and that in death the cemetery-based 'spirit' retains a connection to the interred body—the physical self—and is sentiently aware of events among the living.[120]

What is unclear to me, however, is just how much of the behaviour described (i.e. the 'cemetery-based commemorative practices') relies on any sort of premise at all, let alone upon the specific premise that the dead are 'sentiently aware of events among the living'—which seems here to be regarded as a presupposition of 'cemetery-based commemorative practices'.

There is no need to repeat the critique of Danforth. Indeed, even in place of that critique, it might have been better simply to cite the trenchant remarks of Wittgenstein directed at a fellow Fellow of Trinity College, Cambridge, Sir James Frazer, whose *Golden Bough: A Study in Magic and Religion*, construed religion and magic as resting on various (false) hypotheses.[121] But, says Wittgenstein, this 'is not how it is in connexion with the religious practices of a people; and what we have here is not an error'.[122] Amongst his withering remarks aimed at Frazer's general approach Wittgenstein notes that 'towards morning, when the sun is about to rise, people celebrate rites of the coming day, but not at night, for then they simply burn lamps'.[123] Or, to take an example which is apposite to our case, and which Frazer might have pondered for himself: 'Kissing the picture of a loved one. This is obviously *not* based on a belief that it will have a definite effect on the object the picture represents. It aims

---

[119] Francis et al., *The Secret Cemetery*, 199.

[120] Francis et al., *The Secret Cemetery*, 123.

[121] According to Rush Rhees, the editor of Wittgenstein's *Remarks on Frazer's* Golden Bough (Retford, 1979), Wittgenstein wrote the major portion of these remarks in 1930–31, and the remainder 'not earlier than 1936 and probably after 1948' (vi). Wittgenstein read the abridged version of Frazer's *Golden Bough*, published in 1922.

[122] Wittgenstein, *Remarks on Frazer's* Golden Bough, 2.

[123] Wittgenstein, *Remarks on Frazer's* Golden Bough, 12.

at some satisfaction and it achieves it. Or rather, it does not *aim* at anything; we act in this way and then feel satisfied'.[124] Laying flowers on a grave would surely fall into the same category. Only a modern-day Frazer would search for the premise on which this practice or the cemetery practices observed in north London rest.

Of course, there is no reason to maintain that there are no superstitions, either in the cemeteries of north London or in the villages of rural Greece. Francis and her collaborators do indeed have an informant who claims of a relative that '"I know he's here, I speak to him; he really hasn't left us. We keep him informed of all the news, we do not just come and put flowers on the grave and move away. He's listening".'[125] But others do not: '"I know she's not there, really, the body deteriorates—but it's nice to have somewhere to come to appreciate the life we had together".'[126] The point is thus and simply that the dead can be present and alive, without any scare quotes, in a normal and regular way, and conversations with them may make perfect human sense without any beliefs and hypotheses concerning post-mortem communication of a quasi-telephonic kind.

If one were forced to offer an analogy to make sense of something which in fact makes sense to the participants without the need for such intermediary terms, one might simply say that the dead here have become like characters in a novel or a play or film, about whom and with whom we think dialogically in perfectly familiar ways. We do not trouble about the ontological status of such characters, and we certainly don't worry whether they are 'really' alive. A person, textual or subterranean, can interrogate, disclose, unfold, reveal, challenge, question, and forgive our emotions, concerns, dispositions, and perspectives. The engagement can help us understand the self, the other, and the narrative of our lives and relationships. And it can be conducted honestly or truthfully or not, as can other dialogues. But it need not necessarily be conducted superstitiously.

To complete the point, one might note further that there is nothing here— and not much elsewhere in this study—to justify a lazy reliance on the notion of denial, which crops up from time to time. Does one really need to say that 'At a deeper level of sacred meaning, to keep the stone and garden is possibly to forestall the effects of time, disorder and forgetting and to deny the inevitable decomposition of the body—to keep the person "alive"....'?[127] And what of the even more extravagant claim that cemeteries 'exist to obscure the terrifying fact of death through ritual practice. This is the central secret of the cemetery, circumvented and generally unspoken by most of our study participants',[128] a

---

[124] Wittgenstein, *Remarks on Frazer's* Golden Bough, 4.
[125] Francis et al., *The Secret Cemetery*, 157.
[126] Francis et al., *The Secret Cemetery*, 164 and 167.
[127] Francis et al., *The Secret Cemetery*, 124.
[128] Francis et al., *The Secret Cemetery*, 214.

secret unspoken and yet intuited by the authors? 'Cemetery users, standing at the gravesite, sometimes came close to revealing their inner and existential thoughts about the death of the other and the future loss of the self, but it was evident that much could not be put into words if a degree of reincorporation were to be achieved.' How lucky the anthropologists were there to overhear what was only on the verge of being said.

V MOURNING WITHOUT SUPERSTITION

The catalogue of a recent exhibition which explored the medieval cult of relics ends with an essay on 'The Afterlife of the Reliquary', pointing us to the life of relics beyond what it is easy to regard as the weird and wonderful early medieval practices of collecting arm bones, skulls, foreskins, and the like, disinterring bodies and breaking them up, and sending them round the world, even as far as Hippo. It contains an illustration of a lock of Dürer's hair, allegedly taken by his pupil Baldung and now found in a museum in Vienna. It might just as well have used a picture of a lock of Newton's hair found in the Wren Library of Trinity College, alongside his solemnly preserved walking stick. As the writer of the essay says of another more modern instance: 'the protocols of relic worship are restaged'.[129]

Our willingness to restage the protocols of relic worship in relation to the favoured dead has not inured us against a readiness to find superstition in any regard for the remains of the less worthy dead. It is striking, I suggest, that Augustine, having overcome the thought that belongs to an earlier tradition that mourning is a sign of lack of faith, and yet maintaining his highly tuned sensitivity to the wiles of paganism, is able and willing to vindicate and script modest burial, measured mourning, and a decent or devout care for the dead. He finds human and Christian meaning in popular practices, while acquitting them of suspicions of superstition. (Even his early protests in 388 against feasting at the tombs of the dead are directed at the drunkenness, not at the feasting per se, it seems, which does the dead no good, but us no harm.)[130]

I mentioned at the outset that the pictorial or iconographic tradition of the high Middle Ages represents Christ's death as but the beginning of a protracted path of highly affective mourning leading solemnly towards a much

---

[129] A. Nagel, 'The Afterlife of the Reliquary', in M. Bagnoli, H. A. Klein, C. G. Mann, and J. Robinson, eds., *Treasures of Heaven: Saints, Relics and Devotion in Medieval Europe* (London, 2011), 215.

[130] See *Letters* 22 in *The Work of Saint Augustine: A Translation for the 21st Century*, pt. 2, 4 vols, trans. R. J. Teske (Hyde Park, NY, 2001–5), Exposition 1 of Psalm 48, 15, and *On the Morals of the Catholic Church*, ch. xxxiv.

lamented burial. This tradition felt compelled to give Christ, thereby, the burial he deserved, whether or not he received it. We, it seems, have been set on a different path, intent not on magnifying the mourning of the dead, but on minimizing it—to the point that we have begun to notice our own ineptitude in knowing what to do with the dead. But only partially do we notice it—for we have been so successful in a certain manner of speaking in accomplishing this minimization, that we have rendered mourning almost wholly opaque, such that we very readily convict grieving parents of emotionalism, irrationality, and superstition. And we can even discover anthropologists to second the bioethicists (from whom nothing better could have been expected) in finding no sense in such goings on. (The shallow mockery of mourning practised with great comic effect by Evelyn Waugh and Nancy Mitford had at least the excuse that for the sake of a joke, a writer may be obliged or at least tempted to make the worst of what is observed. It is not clear what plea in mitigation others can make.)

How can we begin to make proper and better sense of the attachment to the body evinced by very many of the Alder Hey parents? For what is the body needed? What is expressed by the desire for restoring bodily integrity to the deceased, even when what is missing may amount to no more than fragments or scraps of tissue? How do these body parts and the body in general figure in mourning and what does that mourning signify or accomplish? What work is done by grieving and how is the work of grieving frustrated by the absence of the body or of body parts?[131]

Augustine's modest apology for mourning, in conversation with the more constructive findings of ethnography, ought to allow an everyday ethics to begin to develop a proper account of the deep and subtle moral labour which is accomplished at the grave. And for all that I have been critical of aspects of the two ethnographies I have discussed, their significance, especially that of the second, is in uncovering a deep, articulate, coherent, and morally serious practice of mourning in the late twentieth century of a kind which was neither anticipated nor allowed for by many of those connected with the controversies associated with Alder Hey.

In his study of the cult of relics, Peter Brown tells us that if we listen with sufficient care, we can find behind what may seem odd or disturbing, 'the strains of an alien music'.[132] The same listening with care might allow us to rehabilitate practices that are in danger of occlusion. And since, as I suggest in the next chapter, learning to mourn well is a cognate practice to learning to remember well, these practices may stand not at the fringes of our religions and moral lives, but at their very centres.

---

[131] On which question see especially A. C. Robben, 'State Terror in the Netherworld: Disappearance and Reburial in Argentina', reprinted in *Death, Mourning, and Burial: A Cross Cultural Reader*, ed. A. C. Robben (Oxford, 2004).

[132] P. Brown, *The Cult of the Saints*, 108.

7

Remembering Christ and Making Time Count: On the Practice and Politics of Memory

I INTRODUCTION: ON NOT FORGETTING TO REMEMBER

The Creeds, from which this book has taken its starting point, have their current prominent place in the liturgy as a result of some rather curious historical and political contingencies.

The creeds developed out of spare baptismal confessions—a simple formula, such as 'Jesus is Lord', in due course became a widely used threefold affirmation of Father, Son, and Spirit, serving as a mark of the acceptance of the belief of the Church on one's reception in to it.[1] The Nicene Creed, however, took matters 'a stage further...[and] was no longer...a test of belief for those entering the church from outside'.[2] Nor was it devised for liturgical use. It was devised as a solemn affirmation of belief for those within the Church and with the intention of ruling out Arians (with the clause naming Christ as 'God of God'). The Nicene Creed gained liturgical use locally and only in AD 473, when the Monophysites took it up in the liturgy to display deference to the Council of Nicea, as opposed to the Council of Chalcedon, to whose formulae they objected. And 'when by the vicissitudes of political fortune the orthodox once more secured control of the See of Constantinople, they dared not incur the odium of seeming to attack the memory of Nicea by discontinuing this use of the creed: and so this originally heretical practice became a permanent feature of the Byzantine liturgy'.[3] By these and other curious contingencies, the creeds made their way into liturgical use more generally, though Rome held out against the novelties until 1014.

---

[1] For references, see A. Richardson, 'Creed, Creeds', in *A New Dictionary of Liturgy and Worship*, ed. J. G. Davies (London, 1986).

[2] G. Dix, *The Shape of the Liturgy* (London, 1945), 485.

[3] Dix, *The Shape of the Liturgy*, 486.

This liturgical happenstance with its origins in the rough and tumble of early Byzantine ecclesiastical politics is, however, fortuitous, for placed as they are, the creeds are emphatic about something of great importance. In the Eucharist, for example, they provide us with a remembrance within a remembrance of a remembrance which itself referenced another remembrance—and thereby make something of a point.

Let me explain. The creeds remember, as we have noted, Christ's life: that he was conceived, born, suffered, died, and buried. And this remembrance itself occurs in the middle of a remembrance (the Eucharist) of the supper Christ had with his disciples on the night before he was betrayed. But the Eucharist is a remembrance of Christ's own remembering—since in his actions on the evening to which the Eucharist refers, he, with bread and wine, recalled and remembered his own life. For the bread and wine, which was, like his life, taken, blessed, broken, and given, thereby remembered that life. The Eucharist remembers this remembering, which itself remembered the Passover.[4] With this Russian doll of remembering, Christianity, so we might say with certain warrant and some understatement, is a practice of remembering.

Christianity remembers. But how? And what is the quality of this remembrance? And in what way does this remembrance underscore other Christian practices, supposing it does? And, to take another question, how does this manner of remembrance stand in relation to our contemporary culture with its own distinctive patterns and styles of remembrance?

In Section II, I will start with the how question, reflecting on the depth and thoroughness of the practice of remembering in the Christian life, relying on du Boulay's ethnography of a Greek mountain village to draw attention to one particularly articulate manifestation of a practice which is common to the central Christian tradition in different forms, and which construes calendar time as a memorial to Christ.

In Section III, I will turn from the fact of remembering to its quality. What is the character of the practice of remembering? After all, just as we can imagine a religion that isn't primarily a religion of remembering, so we can imagine a religion which remembers but in quite different tones, registers, or keys, one from another. 'Remember, remember the Fifth of November, Gunpowder, Treason, and Plot', is remembrance in one key, but there are certainly other possible keys. The adverbs which might qualify remembering are numerous to the point of being countless; one might remember resolutely, severely, uncompromisingly, charitably, fondly, negligently, self-servingly, critically, and so on and so on. We shall need to ask whether there is an especially Christian adverb for remembering, and again I take up du Boulay's ethnography to find the specific quality of the practice of remembering Christ in the Christian life as

---

[4] On the role of memory within Judaism, see Y. H. Yerushalmi's important and influential study *Zakhor: Jewish History and Jewish Memory* (Seattle, 1982).

it is expressed in a day-to-day remembrance. I suggest that in the practice of mourning in the Greek village du Boulay describes, remembering is performed forgivingly—and that it is this tone of remembrance, taken from the larger context of Christian remembrance into the practice of everyday life, that might be deemed the authentic form of Christian remembrance.

In Section IV I turn to Augustine's conception of how criminals are to be held in remembrance as expressed in his customary practice and defence of seeking clemency for those liable to the death penalty. (His defence of clemency is repeated in a sermon which condemns the Christians of Hippo for their tacit acceptance of the lynching of a deeply unpopular and wicked government official.) I ask about the grounds for requesting judicial forgiveness and suggest that Augustine imagines the forgiving remembrance of sins as the Christian response to the forgiving remembrance of God himself. I briefly contrast this practice with the recriminatory relationship to offenders which is arguably institutionalized in their treatment within our society.

In Section V I consider attempts by two thinkers to vindicate a practice of remembrance that is not one of revenge or recrimination. Both are concerned with the question whether our resentment and grievances can be so governed as to preclude retaliation, revenge, and counter-violence. I contrast the tones of the two cases (while noting that they seem to share much in common), and draw attention to the shaping and freighting of modern memory in ways inimical to the hopes of a practice of remembering forgivingly. I take the practice of Holocaust remembrance as especially important and especially problematic in the modern history of remembering. It is not, I stress, Holocaust remembrance itself that is problematic; what is problematic is that a pattern of remembrance appropriate to events of a specific and horrifying kind should come to provide a paradigm for the everyday remembrance of other and quite different crimes and wrongs. Holocaust remembrance is ill-suited to provide a pattern for an everyday ethics, even if that is what it has done (thereby overwhelming, it seems, the sort of reasoned cases for non-recriminatory remembrance advanced by our two thinkers).

In conclusion (in section VI), I take note of a particular proposal for moderating the unmitigated retributivism of current penal practices—a proposal that draws attention only too clearly to the challenge involved in the non-recriminatory, forgiving recollection which for Christianity amounts to remembering well.

II ON REMEMBERING THOROUGHLY

When such and such a religious group gathers they...Well—what can we say? There is plainly no good *a priori* answer to such a question and experience provides a range of answers. But of Christians, as we have already noted, we might be tempted to say that they gather to remember. Whom they remember, we answer very quickly. They remember Christ; and in particular, in the Eucharistic rites which are central forms of worship for many traditions, they remember the supper he had with his disciples on the night before he was betrayed. But as we have previously remarked, this remembrance is of Christ's own remembering, since in his actions that evening with bread and wine, he recalled his own life. The bread and wine, like his life, were taken, blessed, broken, and given, and were taken, blessed, broken, and given for a remembrance of that life. So Christians remember this remembering in this one central rite. But it is not only this rite that is a practice of remembrance, for this remembrance is itself set within a wider and complex framework of remembrance, which we refer to as the Christian year. Time itself is thus construed and constructed as a remembrance in this most thorough-going and resolute practice of remembering.

There is a moment in liturgical history that seems to be of some consequence in the development of this intense and extensive framework of remembering—but unlike the proliferation of the liturgical use of the Nicene Creed, we can find behind this innovation not happenstance, but a deep and implicit logic.

The liturgical innovation, whenever precisely it occurred, is reported with some enthusiasm by a pilgrim to Jerusalem, the deeply pious Egeria, probably a nun, who writes home (probably to Galicia) to tell of a novelty with which she was obviously very taken (and which is reasonably supposed to have been an introduction of Cyril, Bishop of Jerusalem c.350 to 387). This novelty was simply that at the time of the pious pilgrim's visit:

> there is a whole daily round of offices at Jerusalem, from the Night Office an hour or two after midnight lasting till Lauds at cock-crow, on through Sext and None daily (public Terce is still specially reserved for Lent) and ending with Vespers, which lasted until after sunset.[5]

But what are we to make of this innovation (besides its adding to the enjoyment of pilgrims)? As Dix sees it:

> It is nothing less than the reception for the first time into the public worship of a secular church of the monastic ideal of sanctifying human life as a whole, and the passage of time, by corporate worship. It marks the end of the pre-Nicene tradition that corporate worship should express only the separateness of the 'holy church' from the world out of which it had been redeemed.[6]

---

[5] Dix, *The Shape of the Liturgy*, 329. For Egeria's writings, see J. Wilkinson, ed. and trans., *Egeria's Travels*, 3rd ed. (Warminster, 1999).

[6] Dix, *The Shape of the Liturgy*, 329.

And the introduction of the offices goes along with the development of the Eucharist, which in Dix's account shifts from being a vigil of eschatological expectation in which the liturgy withdrew the Christian from the world which was passing away, into a service that sought to touch the world and time. Thus as 'the monk and his imitators gave the church the divine office', so the Eucharist was itself developing to express a notion of worship as consummating the '*whole* life of man' and not as 'the contradiction of daily life'.[7] Out of these developments, suggests Dix, comes the Christian calendar—the mark of the acceptance of the unfolding of time.

Well, Dix may be wrong here, so it seems, in at least two respects.[8] First, a pattern of daily offices may have 'had origins…in popular parochial practice'[9] and not in the monastery alone. And second, the supposed shift (from eschatological preparedness and social reserve, to an acceptance of the world and unfolding time after Constantine), was perhaps not quite as dramatic as he suggests. 'Eschatology and history go hand in hand even in the first three centuries.'[10]

But about the logic implicit in the forms of worship which become standard in the late fourth century, however and whenever they developed, Dix surely makes an important point. Modernity has been told—through a rather simplistic misreading of the evidence—to think of the early Christians as highly ambivalent about the body. Well that is for another occasion, but plainly in the early period, the one thing about which there may have been some ambivalence was time. This ambivalence could be expressed in a question. Should the liturgy take us out of time or take it over? Should it seek to remove us from time or to shape it? But, whether monastic in origin or not, and whether or not expressive of strands of quite early attitudes, what is clear is that the provision and spread of daily prayer amounted to a determined claiming of time, which in the invention of the liturgical year is even more explicitly declared. The intensive bid for time made by the daily offices becomes extensive with this further elaboration (which is a development with its own twists, turns, and contingencies). Between them, however, these two practices colonized and owned time through and through, as the weekly remembrance of the Eucharist was framed by a daily and a yearly patterning of Christian time which was, to use a pejorative term, hegemonic to a degree.[11]

Juliet du Boulay's *Cosmos, Life and Liturgy in a Greek Orthodox Village* describes the compelling and thorough-going form this colonization takes in

---

[7] Dix, *The Shape of the Liturgy*, 332.

[8] See, e.g. Baldovin, 'The Empire Baptised', referencing P. F. Bradfield, *The Search for the Origins of Christian Worship* (Oxford, 2002), R. F Taft, *Beyond East and West: Problems in Liturgical Understanding* (Rome, 1997), and T. J. Talley *The Origins of the Liturgical Year*, 2nd ed. (Collegeville, MN, 1991).

[9] Baldovin, 'The Empire Baptised', 112.   [10] Baldovin, 'The Empire Baptised', 112.

[11] On the importance within Christianity of the shaping of time as sacred time, making reference back to the Christ's life and death, see Paul Connerton's important and properly influential

Orthodoxy, which constructs the year as the Christian year by saturating time with references to Christ's life and death, thus locating other time in relation to his in a complex pattern. (Though there are particularities in the Orthodox calendar, its general form is common to most of Christianity. Easter is a central and moveable feast, which itself determines two seasons, Lent and Pentecost, occuring on either side of it. Other feasts, related to the life of Christ and the Virgin Mary, and to the life and death of saints, occur at fixed points through the year according to different logics or simply according to historical happenstance.) The result is the creation of 'liturgical time', which is, says du Boulay, 'many-layered, creating a complex harmony of several cycles of differing length, which tell again and again variants of the same story using the materials provided by the natural world'.[12]

There is much in the detail deserving of comment, but it serves here simply to notice that the broad mapping out of the liturgical year not only necessarily relates Christian time to simple calendar time, but furthermore comments on and colours the natural seasonality of the year, constructs the week in a particular fashion, and even styles the natural rhythms of the day after its own concerns. Thus, to take a few examples provided by du Boulay, the birth of Christ is associated with the solstice as the overcoming of darkness, for example (as for Augustine, when Christmas day and the solstice fell at the same time), the transfiguration with the height of summer (and thus with the intensity of light), and the nativity of John the Baptist with the summer solstice, and thus with the fading and giving way of the sun (as John must diminish as Christ increases). The week, in turn, has its own patterning as a weekly recollection of both the whole of cosmic history (since Sunday is both the first day of the week signifying creation, and also the eighth day, pointing beyond time), and of the drama of salvation history (since Wednesday is the day when Christ was taken, Friday when he died, and both therefore fast days). Thus, 'Every week throughout the year is in this way an image of Holy Week, constantly commemorating in miniature the events of the Passion, and every Sunday is an image both of the beginning of the world, and the triumph of Christ over

study, *How Societies Remember* (Cambridge, 1989), especially ch. 2: 'Christianity stands or falls with the tie that binds it to its unique historical origin. It originates at a definite historical moment and at all subsequent points in its history it explicitly and elaborately refers back to that moment. . . [T]he vocation of the Christian is to remember and commemorate the history of that intervention' (46).

[12] du Boulay, *Cosmos, Life and Liturgy*, 105. The complexity here, which I note but pass over, is that Easter is the centre of one cycle, but that there is another and 'second cycle'. For circling through the whole year from autumn to autumn, and including the three chief movable feasts as part of their round, is the sequence formed by the Twelve Great Feasts'. These twelve themselves form two sets, one for Christ and one for Mary, and the time span of the latter contains the former, which itself contains Christmas (with associated feasts) and transfiguration. The nesting of these cycles within cycles creates its own further associations, connections, and inflections of meaning.

death and inauguration of a new creation.'[13] Even the day partakes of a liturgical temporality which parallels that of the year, since both are governed by
the sun, but like the liturgical year, the 'principal characteristic' of the day is
that it 'runs not from sunrise to sunrise, but from sunset to sunset', so that
it moves from darkness to light, and not other way round. The effect is 'that
the twenty-four hours of any holy period are inaugurated not on the morning
of the day concerned but on its "eve", and any ritual custom or prohibition
associated with a holy day—and there are many—becomes relevant from the
time the church bell rings at 6 p.m.'[14] Darkness is the herald of coming of light
(and thus of night's negation), just as the winter solstice heralds the coming
of Christ.

Since the year has this thorough patterning, since every Sunday is a feast
and every Wednesday and Friday fasts, and since each day is itself construed
Christianly, 'it is easy to see how this liturgical rhythm becomes grafted on to
the rhythm of work and rest, and forms an inseparable part of the village understanding of time'.[15] Of course, as du Boulay says of the complex pattern she
describes, this 'intellectual architecture' is not expressed or explicit, but 'present
as an undefined set of assumptions which has brought into being a time world
which is accepted without reflection'; but that 'the villagers live imaginatively
in this view of time' is manifested time and again, 'when they grieve anew over
the recently crucified Christ lying before them and refrain from eating because
"Christ died today", or rejoice anew in his resurrection in words which bring
his defeat of death into the present moment: "Christ is risen!"'.[16] And 'while it
is clear that those engaging in subsistence living cannot afford to be anything
other than relentlessly practical in the way they organise their daily activities,
the sacred world is echoed in these activities at every point'.[17]

Nothing suggests the success of the complex interweaving of the 'seasonal
and liturgical cycles [which] govern village time' as clearly as the joining of
saintly with agricultural names to identify particular periods and occupations.
Thus at the feast of his birth just after summer solstice, John the Baptist is
referred to as St John the Oregano-Gatherer. And the feast of the Entry of the
Mother of God into the Temple on 21 November (based on a story from the
non-canonical *Infancy Gospels of James*, when Mary was taken to the temple
by Joachim and Anna), gives its name to the season which is thus referred to as
'the Mother of God Half-Way-Through-The-Sowing'.[18] '[T]he name of a sacred
person is set as a transcendent sign over the appropriate season.'[19]

---

[13] du Boulay, *Cosmos, Life and Liturgy*, 124.
[14] du Boulay, *Cosmos, Life and Liturgy*, 125.
[15] du Boulay, *Cosmos, Life and Liturgy*, 125.
[16] du Boulay, *Cosmos, Life and Liturgy*, 132–33.
[17] du Boulay, *Cosmos, Life and Liturgy*, 113.
[18] du Boulay, *Cosmos, Life and Liturgy*, 106.
[19] du Boulay, *Cosmos, Life and Liturgy*, 133.

In summary, then, in the liturgy 'the timeless reality of the sacred world enters into the cycles of time', gives 'its inner pattern to the whole of life', and does so while harmonizing with the seasons.[20] Liturgy and seasons together 're-enact variants of the same story; and through this continual return to the same story with the experience of time that it involves, there occur in the villagers' lives moments, however fleeting, when they are caught up into a dimension which is "both now and ever"—a world beyond time'.[21]

But what does all this remembering, minutely and thoroughly choreographed in the Christian year, subserve, since it is no end in itself? If Christians remember thoroughly, why do they do so? Well, to put it awkwardly perhaps, Christians remember Christ (and Christ's remembering), for the sake of being re-membered by him, even in their remembering. So what is the character or quality of the remembering that this thorough-going and central practice of remembering intends?

III ON REMEMBERING WELL

That Christians remember and remember thoroughly is one thing. But what is the quality or value of this remembering? After all, just as we can imagine a religion without remembering, so we can imagine a religion that remembers a great deal, but remembers in quite different tones or keys. As we have said, any number of adverbs could, in principle, qualify remembering: 'resolutely', 'severely', 'uncompromisingly', and many others, all fit. So what is the adverb for the Christian practice of remembering? Again, I go to du Boulay to hear an echo of the meaning and significance of the overall practice of remembering in the tone or quality of a day-to-day instance of remembering—to find, in other words, the contribution of the cult of remembering Christ to the practices of the wider moral economy.

Besides the thoroughly scripted remembrance of Christ, the other most importance practice of remembrance in the life of the village du Boulay depicts

---

[20] du Boulay, *Cosmos, Life and Liturgy*, 133.

[21] du Boulay, *Cosmos, Life and Liturgy*, 133. The reference here and elsewhere to a 'world beyond time' hints at an issue that can only be mentioned, but not discussed here, concerning the relationship between what one might term the sacred or the transcendent, and history itself. du Boulay notes that the Orthodox imagination of time is 'cyclical' and that 'Christianity in the Orthodox world has in general been less concerned with mapping time as a linear movement from creation to apocalypse, and less troubled by millennial anxieties' (102). This contrast is linked too, of course, to what to much Western Christianity would seem a problematic (and Platonic) understanding of *anamnesis*, or recollection (see 131ff). A contrast would need to be explored between the liturgy as relating human history to eternity, as against bringing sacred history to bear on the present. If the former is characteristic of Orthodoxy, the latter may be characteristic of Western thought, and plainly the issues between them deserve elaboration and discussion.

is that of recalling the dead, and this possesses a tonality imparted to it by the remembrance of the Christian year. du Boulay notices one very striking element in the mourning of the dead:

> it emerges in the talk about the person who has died, for the conversation about this person is natural and straightforward, but is radically altered from the previous everyday attitudes. The customary reference to the dead, both at the wake and for a period after it, is to couple the name with the adjective 'forgiven'—as in 'Maria, the forgiven one'—and although the life which is now ended is called to mind with clarity and sharpness, the comparisons and judgements which operated in life are, at the wake, entirely absent.[22]

The 'clarity and sharpness' of the recollections means, as she says, that the life will be recalled in all its colour (so-and-so was a wastrel, a drunk, or whatever), 'yet the tones of contempt or mockery so often used about him in his lifetime have disappeared', for accompanying the clarity of recollection, there will be heard:

> like a litany, repeating itself at intervals, the comment of extraordinary acceptance and mercy: 'That's how God has made us, to every person his own character.' The entire wake is in its way a rehearsing of the life of the dead person as people recall this and that characteristic, but the competitive relations of daily life are entirely absent, and the forgiveness evoked is no abstraction but a concrete reality expressed by all who come.[23]

A modern reader will be quick, perhaps, to suspect hypocrisy here, thinking that the mourners are pretending to a compassion, with this 'so and so the forgiven', which they don't necessarily feel. And if we place this practice in the wider context of the harsh and contentious life of the village, described vividly in du Boulay's earlier *Portrait of a Greek Mountain Village*,[24] we will have even more cause to wonder about the quite remarkable gap between the compassionate tone of post-mortem remembrance and the severe, critical, competitive, and suspicious comments that make up the exchanges and gossip of everyday life. But this gap can be acknowledged, along with the radical transformation (i.e. we needn't suppose that indifference and hostility is the genuine and underlying truth here), just if we reckon with the power of a 'common awareness of the common need for mercy and forgiveness'[25] to overcome very real animosities. That it does just this is evidenced, however, not only by the change it induces in references to and thus relations with the deceased, but also by its affecting relations between the living. Thus, just as those who have been at odds with the deceased will take part in the rites of

---

[22] du Boulay, *Cosmos, Life and Liturgy*, 245.
[23] du Boulay, *Cosmos, Life and Liturgy*, 246.
[24] J. du Boulay, *Portrait of a Greek Mountain Village* (Oxford, 1974).
[25] du Boulay, *Cosmos, Life and Liturgy*, 251.

mourning (except in the very rarest circumstances), so too those who have been at odds with each other will overcome any such differences to share in the communal tasks of mourning and burial. The wake is a community event and is 'undertaken with a kind of healing familiarity and pragmatism'[26]—and the healing is evidenced not only in the character or quality of allusions to the deceased, but also in the reordering of relations among the living. 'The community's response to death is forgiveness, and at the wake it is not just the dead who need, and who receive, forgiveness, but the living also.'[27]

The thought that is expressed in the appellation, 'the forgiven', takes its origins from the central remembrance of the Christian life—the remembrance of Christ's prescribed remembrance of his death. For this prescribed remembrance, as we will have cause to note presently, frames that recollection forgivingly, since his death is remembered not as a charge against us, so to speak, but as a gift for many. But, so we must ask, can this quality of remembering take form amongst us not only at the wake, but elsewhere? Can this modality of remembering shape not only the recollection of the dead, as we have discussed here and in the last chapter, but also our remembrance of the living? (Or must we accept Beowulf's instruction, given in a social world like ours, which knows something of the Christian conception of human life but feels the strong pull of another: 'Wise sir, do not grieve. It is always better to avenge dear ones than to indulge in mourning.'[28]) What contribution can the practice of remembering Christ make then, to a wider moral economy?

IV ON REMEMBERING SIN—FORGIVINGLY

Societies remember the dead with grief; but they remember and grieve not just the dead, but other grievances—wrongs done, crimes committed, violence suffered. And how?

Take the following case: members of a small terrorist faction have confessed to committing vicious acts of violence against two officials. One official has been ambushed and murdered. Another was taken from his home, beaten, and mutilated: one of his eyes was gouged out and a finger cut off. The death penalty is available to the magistrate who is set to pass sentence. How is this crime to be remembered?

A colleague of the murdered and the maimed officials writes first to one and then to another senior magistrate, to ask that those guilty of the crime be treated leniently. He has a 'very great worry' that the criminals will be punished

---

[26] du Boulay, *Cosmos, Life and Liturgy*, 246.
[27] du Boulay, *Cosmos, Life and Liturgy*, 256.
[28] *Beowulf*, trans. S. Heaney (London, 1999), 46.

with 'the great severity' which the law allows; he wishes, however, that they should be left alive and in no way mutilated themselves, even though they have killed and mutilated others. In passing judgement, he advises the first magistrate, remember 'to be humane', eschewing any 'desire for revenge'. To the second, he insists that even were there no way of curbing the violent criminals except by putting them to death, he would still prefer that they go free than the death penalty be used, but, since imprisonment will serve, a gentler sentence is certainly in order. In a third letter, to that first magistrate again, he repeats his plea that any punishment should 'not involve the death penalty', and for good measure mentions that if the two magistrates to whom he has written don't accept his recommendation he will appeal (or maybe has appealed, the translation is uncertain) to their superior.

This instruction to magistrates on how they are to remember crime comes in letters of Augustine, appealing for clemency for Circumcellions and Donatists who had confessed to the violence I have described, committed against two Catholic clergy.[29] In making the appeals Augustine seems to find it hard to hit exactly the right note—on the one hand he has no standing in the proceedings and no authority over the magistrates (Marcellinus and Apringius), but on the other hand, he speaks as a bishop to members of the church. He hovers, therefore, somewhat awkwardly between requesting and demanding: 'I as a Christian beg the judge and as a bishop warn a Christian.'[30] But if there is a hint of awkwardness in finding the right tone for making an appeal for clemency, there is no sense of hesitancy whatsoever as regards his obligation, as a Christian, to make just that appeal.

What is striking, however, is not just the seemingly 'it goes without saying' assumption that a bishop will appeal for clemency for those condemned to death, but equally the 'it goes without saying' character of the appeal itself. Augustine does not so much make a case for clemency, as take it for granted that the case for clemency a bishop is bound to advance will be understood without any elaboration. The letters to which I have referred admittedly mention points in favour of clemency: the sufferings of the Catholic servants of God would be 'marred by the blood of their enemies', for then it would seem as though those who suffered 'have returned evil for evil';[31] the judges should 'use goodness to contend with the evil', and '[o]n account of Christ hold back from' spilling the blood of the convicted criminals;[32] Christian judges, should 'be angry at wickedness', but only 'in such a way that [they] remember to be humane, and do not turn the desire for revenge upon the atrocities of sinners,

[29] Augustine, *Letters* 133, 134, and 139, in *The Works of Saint Augustine: A Translation for the 21st Century*, pt. 2, 4 vols., trans. R. J. Teske (Hyde Park, NY, 2001-5). Subsequent references will be to the number of a Letter, followed by section (if the Letter is in sections) and page number.

[30] Augustine, *Letters*, 134, 2 (206).

[31] Augustine, *Letters*, 134, 3 and 4 (206).   [32] Augustine, *Letters*, 134, 4 (207).

but apply the will to heal to the wounds of sinners'.[33] But these points do not so much make a case as refer to it; Augustine doesn't argue, but assumes. 'When their convicted enemies are treated rather gently, men usually appeal against a milder sentence, but we love our enemies so that, if we do not presume too much upon your Christian obedience, we appeal against your severe sentence.'[34] But that love of enemies really requires what Augustine requests and that it obliges judges in the way Augustine suggests—this is more taken for granted than it is established by sustained argument.

Ironically, the two recipients of these letters would themselves be executed very shortly after receiving these appeals, caught up in an intrigue hatched by allies of the Donatists, implicating them in a rebellion against Emperor Honorius. But shortly after their deaths, Augustine had occasion to make a fuller case. Whether genuinely or simply for the sake of encouraging a fuller statement from Augustine on the issue of clemency, Macedonius (a senior legal administrator for Africa), having granted a petition from Augustine on behalf of a condemned man, writes to ask whether it really belongs to 'our religion' that the clergy should 'intervene on behalf of the guilty'.[35] He puts the sceptical case by asking about its consistency with the contemporary practice of penance within the Church: 'if the Lord forbids sins so that after the first penance he does not give a chance for a second penance, how can we claim in the name of religion that we should forgive a crime, not matter of what sort it is?' But behind that question of consistency with Church practice, there is another and seemingly more general doubt about the case for forgiveness, expressed in the thought that 'when we want [a crime] to go unpunished, we of course approve of it' and that makes us 'accomplices in guilt', since we thus allow the guilty to go free.[36] Letter 153 (of 413 or 414) is a detailed response to these queries, providing Augustine with occasion to make an articulate case for clemency (fitting with the argument of the probably earlier Sermon 302).

Augustine admits that it 'is easy and natural to hate evil persons because they are evil, but it is rare and holy to love those same persons because they are human beings'. This, however, is our duty—and one 'which comes from our religion', since God, who knows what each and every person is and will be, 'makes...his sun to rise over the good and the evil and sends rain upon the just and the unjust'.[37] Christ exhorts us to follow this 'marvellous goodness': 'Love your enemies; do good to those who hate you, and pray for those who persecute you in order that you may be children of your Father'. If we do not, as Paul warns us in Romans, we misuse God's leniency 'to our own destruction', judging harshly those who do only what we ourselves do.

---

[33] Augustine, *Letters*, 133, 2 (203).   [34] Augustine, *Letters*, 134, 4 (207).
[35] Honorius's letter appears as Letter 152 in Augustine's *Letters*.
[36] Augustine, *Letters*, 152.
[37] Augustine, *Letters*, 153 (392).

We are, then, bound to love the wicked. This is commanded. To love the wicked is not, however, to love wickedness, but rather to allow occasion for repentance.

If this, in essence, is the case for clemency, Augustine nonetheless returns, and most persistently, to the need for the judge to recollect his very own need for mercy (implicit in that reference to the words of Paul). God, who stands in need of mercy from no one, extends mercy to human beings. How then 'should we human beings behave toward other human beings? For, no matter how much praise we have accumulated for this life of ours, we do not say that it is free of sin'. And this, he says, is the very force of Jesus's words when the woman taken in adultery was brought before him: 'let whoever of you who is without sin be the first to throw a stone at her'. The words 'frightened' them— and 'called back to mercy' those who would have put her to death. Even her husband, so Augustine speculates, supposing he were present, 'once he heard these words of the Lord...was filled with fear and turned his mind away from the desire for vengeance to the will of pardon'.[38] In the case of all those present, 'their anger collapsed as their conscience trembled',[39] for 'a consideration of our common weakness breaks down' our indignation.[40] Thus he says to the judge Macedonius: 'I think that you understand that we said truthfully rather than insultingly that we intercede before sinners'[41]—not just for, but as sinners before sinners.

The text of a textually confused sermon (302) employs the story of the woman taken in adultery to the same effect in a less discursive context. One sermon (on the feast day of the great Roman martyr St Lawrence) lacked an end, and another (against some outrage, most likely, it seems, the lynching of a deeply unpopular and corrupt government official) lacked a beginning. According to the editor, someone must have had the bright idea of solving the problem by simply putting them together. However that may be, the argument of the second part of the sermon involves Augustine appealing yet again for the right remembrance of sin, though not this time to magistrates, but to his very own congregation.

The atmosphere in which Augustine preaches is tense. The sermon is at once direct, imploring, sometimes indignant, and admonitory; at other times, it is despairing and almost tetchy. There is no question that the dead soldier was corrupt—'it was a bad man that died!' he imagines the congregation as saying, and he does not dispute the point. 'I am not defending bad men, or saying that bad men aren't bad.' Nor is he complaining chiefly that the task of judging belongs not to the crowd, but to others, though that is true. His central point is rather that all judgement should be practised by consciences pricked by Christ's words to the crowd surrounding the adulterous woman;

---

[38] Augustine, *Letters*, 153 (394).   [39] Augustine, *Letters*, 153 (396).
[40] Augustine, *Letters*, 153 (395).   [41] Augustine, *Letters*, 153 (398).

and 'When those who were thirsting for blood withdrew, they left behind them a miserable woman and mercy'. Thus, 'It is only bad people who vent their rage on bad people'. The congregation should distance itself 'from these bloody deeds'—'Your only concern, when you see or hear such things, should be to feel pity...So let it be your business, my brothers and sisters, to grieve, let it be your concern to grieve, not to vent your rage.'[42] 'Bad people are to be mourned much more, because after this life they are caught in the clutches of eternal pains.'[43]

In attending to Augustine's pleas for remembering crimes forgivingly we find ourselves not at the margins of his theological concerns but at its very centre. To appeal to human solidarity in sin is the very heart of his anti-Pelagianism. Pelagianism, as he liked to say, heaps 'cruel praise' on human nature. When Hamlet asks that the players be well bestowed and Polonius proposes to use them according to their 'desert', Hamlet exclaims, 'Use every man after his desert and who should scape whipping?' The Pelagian praise of human nature and its capacity to know and will the good is cruel then, since the heightening of the praise heightens the just deserts which is that praised nature's due—if the Pelagian account of freedom of the will and our knowledge of good and evil is right, we shall scarcely 'scape whipping'.

The immediate cruelty of Pelagianism in the specific context of our discussion, would be in favouring a judicial practice which would take up the concept of desert unforgivingly and untempered by Augustine's reminder that intercession is made not only on behalf of sinners, but is addressed by sinners to sinners. Or, as Shakespeare puts it in *The Merchant of Venice*: 'Though justice be thy plea, consider this, that in the course of justice none of us should see salvation. We do pray for mercy; and that same prayer doth teach us to render the deeds of mercy.'

In principle, it might be said, our penal systems can be construed as incorporating some notions of forgiveness, or if not that exactly, a notion of measured retributivism such that certain punishments expiate certain crimes, so that criminals are not criminals for life, but become ex-criminals. But in practice, even after prison, many prisoners, to use a resonant phrase, 'continue to wear "invisible stripes"'; which is to say that stigmatization continues, effectively

---

[42] Augustine, *Sermons*, 302, 18 (309).

[43] Augustine, *Sermons*, 302, 18 (309). It is moreover, not enough that the congregation may claim not to have had any part in the lynching, nor that they now lament 'these bloody deeds'. They should, he says, have done what was 'in [their] power to prevent' them. There is not a single household in the city where there isn't a Christian. There isn't a single house in which there aren't more Christians than pagans. 'These bad events wouldn't have occurred, if Christians hadn't wanted them to. You haven't got an answer to that.' They could, he insists, have restrained their slaves or sons—'by warning, persuading, teaching, correcting', indeed 'by any kind of threats' *Sermons*, 302, 19 (310).

excluding prisoners 'from employment, educational, and social opportunities' ever afterwards.[44]

'May she rot in hell'—so said the *Sun's* headline on the death of Myra Hindley. 'I felt like opening a bottle of champagne' said a Home Secretary on the death by suicide of a prisoner (Harold Shipman), for whose welfare the Home Secretary was responsible. These are perhaps unpromising subjects for lengthy meditation. But they raise for us, alongside the more general stig-matization of prisoners, the question as to whether our culture can and does remember forgivingly (as Augustine commends) or otherwise.

V ON REMEMBERING THEN AND NOW

Augustine's concern was that the judicial recollection of crime should be a rec-ollection with mercy. The authors of two modern discussions of the virtues and vices of remembrance of wrongs are likewise concerned to temper the tendency for such remembrance to beget recrimination and retaliation. They share sur-names (Butler) and an initial (J). But besides this superficial and coincidental resemblance between them, and even besides other more significant resem-blances in the cases they make, I want to notice a significant difference in tone in the cases they advance—since it is a sign, I suggest, of a cultural shift in the history and practice of remembering which poses a problem for any contempo-rary venture of merciful recollection. Thus we will find ourselves sympathetic to the intention and ambitions of both writers to construct a reasoned case for restraining resentment, even while we notice the existence of a cultural climate that has become increasingly inimical to remembering forgivingly.

In two of his famously careful and lucid sermons, Joseph Butler sets out to provide what amounts to a grammar of resentment and an account of the virtues and vices of remembering faults. In Sermon VIII ('Upon Resentment'), Butler proposes to vindicate the 'passion' of resentment, even while distin-guishing 'abuses' of it.[45] The abuse occurs, so he argues, when resentment of wrongs done to ourselves and others (which is natural and serves a useful pur-pose) turns to pure retaliation and revenge—for 'hatred, malice and revenge, are directly contrary to the religion we profess, and to the nature and reason of the thing itself'.[46]

---

[44] S. Maruna, 'Re-entry as a Rite of Passage', *Punishment and Society*, 13.1 (2011), 12 and 5. The phrase 'invisible stripes', Maruna takes from T. P. LeBel, 'Invisible Stripes? Formerly Incarcerated Persons' Perception of and Responses to Stigma', an unpublished doctoral dissertation at the University of Albany (New York, 2006).

[45] *The Works of Joseph Butler*, ed. W. E. Gladstone, vol. II, *Sermons* (Oxford, 1897), Sermon VIII, 4 (117).

[46] Butler, Sermon VIII, 4 (116).

Although Butler refers to the religious proscription of hatred, his ambition in this sermon and in Sermon IX, 'Upon Forgiveness of Injuries', is to establish the case against hating our enemies not by religious proscription, but on grounds of reason alone. And so his argument against what he takes to be a principle of demotic Greek ethics, that 'Thou shalt love thy neighbour, and hate thine enemy',[47] proceeds in his cool and rational fashion.

He distinguishes two kinds of resentment: 'hasty and sudden' (called anger) and 'settled and deliberate'. Both are justified—'resentment against vice and wickedness...is one of the common bonds, by which society is held together; a fellow-feeling, which each individual has in behalf of the whole species, as well as of himself'[48]—but both have their abuses. The abuse of natural anger is tetchiness and ill temper. The abuses of settled anger are twofold. In the first place it may blind us to the nature of the injury done, leading us to magnify the malice from which it arose or the harm we have suffered. In the second place (and this is the main object of his critique), it may lead to 'the dreadful vices of malice and revenge',[49] 'when pain or harm of any kind is inflicted merely in consequence of, and to gratify, that resentment, though naturally raised'.[50] But on what grounds is revenge or retaliation objectionable, or unlawful as Butler puts it? The key thought is that if resentment is 'indulged or gratified for itself', then it is 'doing harm for harm's sake', and thus is contrary both to what our 'nature and condition require' and to our 'obligation to universal benevolence':[51]

[L]ove to our enemies, and those who have been injurious to us, is so far from being a *rant*, as it has been profanely called, that it is in truth the law of our nature, and what everyone must see and own, who is not quite blinded with self-love.[52]

Our second Butler—not Joseph but Judith—speaks to a quite different context, though her starting point, like his, is a concern with the vices of remembrance (and in particular with those evidenced in response to 9/11 and the rush to the 'war on terror'). Just as the other Butler finds a place for resentment, so Judith Butler means to find a place for grief and mourning of the violence

---

[47] Butler claims to find this principle referred to in Aristotle's *Nichomachean Ethics* (Sermon VIII, 3 [116]); it is certainly taken to be a nostrum of popular ethical thought in Book 1 of Plato's *Republic*.

[48] Butler, Sermon VIII, 8 (119).   [49] Butler, Sermon VIII, 19 (126).

[50] Butler, Sermon VIII, 14 (123).   [51] Butler, Preface, 28 (17).

[52] Butler, Sermon IX, 12 (135). Butler admits, however, that 'to be convinced that any temper of mind, and course of behaviour, is our duty, and the contrary vicious, hath but a distant influence upon our temper and actions'; thus he adds 'some few reflections, which may have a more direct tendency to subdue those vices in the heart, to beget in us this right temper, and lead us to a right behaviour towards those who have offended us: which reflections however shall be such as will further show the obligations we are under to it.' The main reflection is that 'though injury, injustice, oppression, [and]. . . ingratitude, are the natural objects of indignation. . . yet they are likewise the objects of compassion, as they are their own punishment. . . No one ever designed injury to another, but at the same time he did a much greater to himself' (139). Second, since we know that we would not want to face implacable judgement, we should not be implacable judges ourselves (140).

suffered by the US; the question is, however, whether grief and mourning must lead to retribution: 'If we are interested in arresting cycles of violence to produce less violent outcomes, it is no doubt important to ask what, politically, might be made of grief besides a cry for war.'[53] Her suggestion is that loss 'has made a tenuous "we" of us all' and that on the 'basis of vulnerability and loss' we can reimagine 'the possibility of community'.[54] 'Loss and vulnerability', claims Butler, 'seem to follow from our being socially constituted bodies, attached to others, at a risk of losing those attachments, exposed to others, at risk of violence by virtue of that exposure.'[55] It is on the basis of this condition of our humanity that we can and should re-imagine international politics.

Judith Butler's argument depends on the thought that in grief and mourning, 'something about who we are is revealed, something that delineates the ties we have to others, that shows us that these ties constitute what we are, ties or bonds that compose us'.

> It is not as if an 'I' exists independently over here and then simply loses a 'you' over there, especially if the attachment to 'you' is part of what composes who 'I' am. If I lose you, under these conditions, then I not only mourn the loss, but I become inscrutable to myself. Who 'am' I, without you? When we lose some of these ties by which we are constituted, we do not know who we are or what we do. On one level, I think I have lost 'you' only to discover that 'I' have gone missing as well. At another level, perhaps what I have lost 'in' you, that for which I have no ready vocabulary, is a relationality that is composed neither exclusively of myself nor you, but is to be conceived as *the tie* by which those terms are differentiated and related.[56]

So, contrary to the thought of grief as privatizing and depoliticizing, Butler contends that it, in fact, 'furnishes a sense of political community of a complex order', 'bringing to the fore the relational ties that have implications for theorizing fundamental dependency and ethical responsibility. If my fate is not originally or finally separable from yours, then the "we" is traversed by a relationality that we cannot easily argue against; or, rather, we can argue against it, but we would be denying something fundamental about the social conditions of our very formation.'[57] To put it another way, though we often talk about the relationships we 'have', this way of speaking attempts to 'minimise the relationality'. But in grief, this misleading 'narrative falters'—for 'what grief displays...is the thrall in which our relations with others hold us.'[58] Desire may reveal the same condition of our being. It is not that we have relationships, but that we are relationships.

> This way of imagining community affirms relationality not only as a descriptive or historical fact of our formation, but also as an ongoing normative dimension

[53] J. Butler, *Precarious Life: The Powers of Mourning and Violence* (London, 2004), xii.
[54] Butler, *Precarious Life*, 20.   [55] Butler, *Precarious Life*, 20.
[56] Butler, *Precarious Life*, 22.   [57] Butler, *Precarious Life*, 22–23.
[58] Butler, *Precarious Life*, 23.

of our social and political lives, one in which we are compelled to take stock of our interdependence.[59]

Thus 'Grief contains the possibility of apprehending a mode of dispossession that is fundamental to who I am'.[60] It reveals a vulnerability we cannot will away; instead we must 'attend to it, even abide by it, as we begin to think about what politics might be implied' by it.[61]

The question grief poses then becomes a question for politics: does it return us to our 'sense of human vulnerability' and also to a sense of 'our collective responsibility for the physical lives of one another?'[62] Can this grief be a resource for an international politics in which all lives are recognized as 'grievable', and not just our own? 'From where', asks Butler, 'might a principle emerge by which we vow to protect others from the kinds of violence we have suffered, if not from an apprehension of a common human vulnerability?'[63]

We could mark various differences and similarities between the two arguments, but I note first one similarity and then one difference. The similarity is that both arguments are exercises in moral reasoning, appealing to a variety of considerations, prudential and principled, but also asking us essentially to reflect on our nature as human beings (constituted in one case by certain passions or sentiments, in the other by certain needs and vulnerabilities). The difference is in the tone of the arguments and the context to which this tone bears witness.

Joseph Butler's case has the high confidence of the early Enlightenment, where reason is expected to make its way quite successfully in restraining and disciplining the mild disorders of human nature. His argument has the air of the drawing room, as if the only task is to deal with the mildly unreflective incivilities to which even gentlemen may be prone, but which can, quite easily, be corrected. Judith Butler's argument, notwithstanding its similarity in nature, is a less than fully optimistic intervention into a context where argument is not expected to make such headway. Joseph Butler confidently seeks to correct some relatively minor failings of reasoning and reflection that mar the practice of social civility; Judith Butler is conscious of struggling to find grounds that will, in practice, check the rather grosser incivilities of international relations. Both Butlers want to reason us towards the proper limits of resentment of and grieving over wrongs. But the confidence implicit in the first case has altogether dissipated in the second, which is far more acutely aware of the limits of reason.

Of course, an important part of the change in intellectual context between the eighteenth century and now, is in the abandonment of the Enlightenment's

---

[59] Butler, *Precarious Life*, 27.
[60] Butler, *Precarious Life*, 28.
[61] Butler, *Precarious Life*, 29.
[62] Butler, *Precarious Life*, 30.
[63] Butler, *Precarious Life*, 30.

intellectual optimism (and its own Pelagian faith in humankind's ability to know and propensity to will the good). The second Butler has less confidence than the first that getting an argument straight will straighten out our practice and politics. But the context is made more difficult still by a profound shift in the practice of remembering.

The history of more than 250 years of remembering is not to be written in the space of a few pages, but we must at least note something of the social dynamics that have shaped the nature and character of modern remembering and thus created the difficult conditions in which the second of the two Butlers seeks to intervene.

There has, according to many commentators, been a memory boom which began in the late 1970s. The story, say certain commentators on these commentators, goes something like this:

> Following the decline of postwar modernist narratives of progressive improve-
> ment through an ever-expanding welfare state, nation-states turned to the past as
> a basis for shoring up their legitimacy. The decline in utopian visions supposedly
> redirected our gaze to collective pasts, which served as a repository of inspira-
> tion for repressed identities and unfulfilled claims. Without unifying collective
> aspirations, identity politics proliferated. And most often, these identities nursed
> a wound or harboured a grudge. The memory boom thus unleashed a culture of
> trauma and regret. . .[64]

As will be plain, the writers of that comment indicate a wish to maintain a critical distance on the story they repeat, allowing them to challenge, nuance, and correct it in various ways. But about the rise of memory and its growing importance in our politics, they are not dissenters, and like others, they would locate somewhere near the centre of this modern history of memory, the influ-ence of the Holocaust.

'Whoever says memory, says Shoah' is Pierre Nora's celebrated assertion of this point.[65] Nora's assertion could be accepted while doubts remain whether it is the Holocaust itself which has made memory and remembering vital cul-tural forms. As Olick et al. suggest, the causal significance of the Holocaust (as a supposed 'civilizational rupture') should not simply be assumed. The matter is quite complex. Our perception of the Holocaust has, as they point out, changed very significantly in the years since 1945, and it is only since the 1960s that the term has had any very general currency. The various and different mobilizations of the memories of the Holocaust are not then them-selves explained immediately and simply by the Holocaust itself, but by refer-ence to other, diverse social forces and interests. What is clear, however, these

---

[64] Introduction, *The Collective Memory Reader*, eds. J. K. Olick, V. Vinitzhy-Seroussi, and D. Levy (Oxford, 2011), 3.
[65] Cited in Olick et al., Introduction, *The Collective Memory Reader*, 29.

subtleties apart, is that the Holocaust has a central place in the contemporary imagination and thus now in shaping the practice of memory. Or to put it another way: 'the iconographic status of Holocaust memories is reflected in and contributes to the formation and practice of a global memory imperative'.[66]

Some believe that this current cultural imperative is the source of many woes.[67] Maier, in particular, has claimed that we suffer from a 'pathology of post-Holocaust' memory expressed in 'a culture of complaint and competition among victims'.[68] As Maier sees it, 'Modern American politics...has become a competition for enshrining grievances. Every group claims its share of public honor and public funds by pressing disabilities and injustices. National public life becomes the settlement of a collective malpractice suit in which all citizens are patients and physicians simultaneously'.[69] Whatever is to be made of these larger claims, it is easy enough to entertain the more modest thought that 'Increasingly, memory worth talking about—worth remembering—is memory of trauma'.[70]

Maier's dramatic pathology of post-Holocaust memory concerns the creation of victims. I am concerned, however, with what we might think of as the other side of the coin: not with the aspect of the remembrance of the Holocaust which may or may not have something to do with the supposed current prestige of victimhood, but rather with how the practice of Holocaust remembrance may relate to our recollection not of those who have suffered wrong, but of those who have done it.

The issue can be stated quite simply for all that it bears careful and further analysis. The great imperative which emerged from the Holocaust is, of course, to remember. This imperative was both backward- and forward-looking. The attempted erasure of the Jewish people should, at one and the same time, be defeated and prevented from ever happening again by determined remembrance. And the battle for this remembrance of the Holocaust, against indifference and purported scepticism, has been hard fought. Against the risk of forgetting, the imperative to remember has preserved the memory not only

---

[66] Olick et al., Introduction, *The Collective Memory Reader*, 31.

[67] 'For many critics. . . the sum total of these developments has been what Maier. . . called a "surfeit of memory", which is intended as an understatement, for the diagnosis is substantially more grim than a "surfeit". According to Dominick LaCapra. . . "Recently the concern with the problem of memory has become so widespread and intense that one is tempted to take a suspicious view and refer to fixation." The literary critic Geoffrey Hartman. . . refers to a Proustian *Schwärmerei* or unwholesome swarming. Maier. . . argues that "we have in a sense become addicted to memory" and asks "whether an addiction to memory can become neurasthenic and disabling"'. Olick et al., Introduction, *The Collective Memory Reader*, 32–33.

[68] Olick et al., Introduction, *The Collective Memory Reader*, 33.

[69] Cited by Olick et al., Introduction, *The Collective Memory Reader*, 33.

[70] 'Introduction: Forecasting Memory', in *Tense Past*, eds. P. Antze and M. Lambek (London, 1996), xii. For the wider cultural history of trauma and its place in the contemporary moral economy, see D. Fassin and R. Rechtman, *The Empire of Trauma: An Inquiry into the Condition of Victimhood* (Princeton, 2009).

of identifiable individuals (as in Primo Levi's recollections of 'a gallery of people who remained irreducibly individual in the lowest circles of hell', in Clendinnen's words[71]), but also of countless faceless victims, by means of the systematic, detailed, and patient cataloguing of the era's countless crimes. And as it has conserved the sites of the crimes as the most pertinent scene for the evocation of memory, so also has it created new sites for memorialization, most prominently in Berlin, Jerusalem, and Washington, to name just a few.

Those sites, particularly the one in Berlin, have provided, as might be expected, a focus for controversy over precisely how the Holocaust should be remembered. But one central and common characteristic of the practice of Holocaust remembrance seems to be that it is static. It is not a remembrance that anticipates some sort of resolution or closure, and for sure, not a resolution by way of forgiveness.[72]

The point here is not to argue that Holocaust remembrance should have such a concern. What gives the Holocaust its particular character as an event at or beyond the bounds of human comprehension, is that we are more than hard put to begin to think about it in terms of redemption or forgiveness. Nor is the difficulty merely contingent, as if it were only to do with who would now forgive whom; the difficulty is rather to do with what it might be to forgive wrongs of this kind or character. But this is by the way. The point here is that the very reasons which encourage us to think there may be something *sui generis* about the Holocaust, at the same time explain why it is highly unsuitable as a paradigm for everyday memory. Insofar as Holocaust memorialization is adamantine (without an 'horizon' or 'eschatology' to use Ricoeur's terms[73]), it serves as a poor paradigm for the practice of the remembrance of other wrongs. Remembrance, *a fortiori*, can never be about forgetting *tout court*, but remembering with mercy is plainly teleological in a way that Holocaust memorialization is not.

The two Butlers are divided by more than the Holocaust—but if 'to say memory is to say Shoah' as Nora suggests, one of the things that stands between them is a new, dominant, and iconographic practice of remembrance that surely serves to discourage a move beyond resentment and grievance. The first Butler speaks in tones of gentle but confident reasonableness. The second Butler speaks with none of that confidence. And one of the reasons for that change in tone may be the particular and important work to which memory has been put in the recent past, which is chiefly that of resolutely testifying and witnessing to an egregious wrong. A practice of memory so formed may

---

[71] I. Clendinnen, *Reading the Holocaust* (Cambridge, 2002), 183.

[72] A fuller discussion would need to acknowledge ('confess' might be a better word) that the roots of the Holocaust emerge from Christianity's harbouring and nursing a notion of racial guilt which itself admitted of no resolution.

[73] P. Ricoeur, *Memory, History, Forgetting*, trans. K. Blamey and D. Pellauer (Chicago, 2004), 457.

not be readily overcome by other possible forms of practice. What is apparent, however, is that if we are seeking a policy for the treatment of sex offenders, let us say, which goes beyond permanent stigmatization, we will indeed need to imagine or better still practise some different forms of remembering.

VI CONCLUSION: RIGHT RITES FOR REMEMBERING RIGHTLY

In a sermon to the newly baptised explaining the structure of the Eucharist, Augustine notes that after the remembering Christ's forgiving remembrance in the prayer of consecration, and after the saying of the Lord's Prayer (with its 'forgive us our sins'), 'comes the greeting, Peace be with you, and Christians kiss one another with a holy kiss. It's a sign of peace; what is indicated by the lips should happen in the conscience; that is, just as your lips approach the lips of your brothers and sisters, so your heart should not be withdrawn from theirs'.[74]

The order of things here is significant. The Christian imagination is turned first of all to a remembrance of Christ's forgiving remembrance. The lips follow (with words and gestures of peace), and after the lips the heart—what is thought is then said, and after what is said or mouthed, the will (or heart) should follow. We might say that the right remembering of remembering, invoked and expressed in ritual practice, is to serve as the basis for a wider practice which flows from the heart.

If the Christian imagination is nourished by stories of Christ's forgiving life, the contemporary imagination is shaped, it can seem, by quite different tales— the most favoured stories of modern life seem to be stories of retribution and vengeance. They are often stories of good and evil, in which good will and must triumph, but in which its triumph does not resolve the conflict inclusively, but closes it by exclusion, or by damnation, to use another notion. In our present context then, we do not lack stories in which wrongs are remembered, blame assigned, and punishment inflicted, but we may reflect that we need stories also of remembrance, but which end in harmonious peace.

Twelve years ago, the Home Office's then Director of Prisons spoke of 'the immorality of our treatment of some prisoners and the degradation of some establishments'.[75] In early April 2013, Her Majesty's Inspectorate of Prisons reported on the case of two disabled prisoners at Winchester confined in their cells for twenty-three and half hours a day, with no easy access to showers.[76]

---

[74] Augustine, *Sermons*, 227, 255.
[75] Cited by A. Liebling, *Prisons and Their Moral Performance: A Study of Values, Quality, and Prison Life* (Oxford, 2004), vii.
[76] See <www.bbc.co.uk/news/uk-england-hampshire-21845935>.

This needs no comment. But an aspect of the treatment of prisoners that does deserves further comment is not the nature of the conditions they endure while in prison, but their treatment ever after—the fact, to which I referred earlier, that even after prison, many prisoners 'continue to wear "invisible stripes"'.[77]

It is the distinct and significant merit of an article by Shadd Maruna, 'Re-entry as a Rite of Passage', that it draws attention to this aspect of the unmitigated retributivism (if that is not a contradiction in terms) of our penal practices. Prisoners, Maruna notes, are unsuccessfully reintegrated into society. The figures for reoffending are terrible. So too are the life chances of those who leave prison, and rates of suicide amongst ex-offenders are, unsurprisingly, high.[78]

Maruna asks whether part of the failure of this reintegration can be understood as a result of the premature or unsatisfactory curtailment of what can be seen as the ritual process of imprisonment. The convicted prisoner is, like other ritual subjects (according to van Gennep's classic account of rites of passage), first separated from the community—here with solemn and symbolic degradations, such as loss of everyday clothes, name, possessions, and so on. The central act of the rite is imprisonment itself, whereby, or so we hope, the prisoner is transformed and emerges as a new subject. But it is at the third stage, the stage of re-entry, that the rites definitely fail us. We have, says Maruna, no effective or well-established rites for marking the new status of the prisoner as they are brought back into the moral and civil order from which they are been removed. This re-entry is typically 'stealthy and private', with prisoners, for example, merely slipping out of prison at dawn. For the sake of the prisoners and for the sake of society, we need, says Maruna, rites of reintegration to declare and enact the restored status of the former prisoner and thus the end of his or her stigmatization.

The friend of Oscar Wilde who stood amidst a hostile crowd for many hours waiting for the convicted man to appear in his prison garb on his way to a further and humiliating appearance in a dock (this time in the bankruptcy court), and who solemnly and silently raised his hat to him as he passed by, understood something of the power of ritual (without the benefit it seems, of having read van Gennep). And Maruna is surely right to try to imagine a rite that would do something to address the parlous state of prisoners who, without a clear and unequivocal marking of a new status, are left to wear invisible stripes long after their sentences have officially ended.

The problems of inventing and institutionalizing such a rite are considerable—but towards those who attempt it, what should the Christian ethicist do but wish them well? Happily, there are examples of Christian work in receiving and supporting prisoners on the other side of the prison gates—such as in the Community Chaplaincy project, which has its origins in Canada and operates

---

[77] Maruna, 'Re-entry as a Rite of Passage', 12.
[78] Maruna, 'Re-entry as a Rite of Passage', 4, for references.

throughout the UK—that attempt to provide models of what it might be for us to take seriously our fellowship in humanity and sin with fellows sinners.[79] But such practice, of course, as Maruna's wish for new rites itself intuits, itself emerges from rites of the kind Augustine explicated for the sake of the newly baptized. Christian remembrance, whether in grieving death or other grievances, must be done, if it is to be done, Christianly, after the practice of Christ, which is to say forgivingly.[80] So if this practice is to take form amongst us, it is not a matter of Christians inventing new rites, but of living in accordance with the rites of remembrance that we already have and that seek to colonize our life and times and re-member Christ's.

---

[79] See *International Journal of Community Chaplaincy*, 2013 (1), for references to Community Chaplaincy. Of course, this work, like the work of L'Arche, deserves ethnographic study, explication, and critique.

[80] For an extremely helpful elucidation of the wider theological issues that would need to be addressed in a fuller treatment of the topic, see N. Biggar, 'Forgiveness in the Twentieth Century: A Review of the Literature, 1901–2001', in *Forgiveness and Truth*, eds. A. McFadyen and M. Sarot (Edinburgh, 2001). Such a treatment would also need to attend to the work of South Africa's Truth and Reconciliation Commission and its wider influence. On South Africa, see, for example, R. A. Wilson, *The Politics of Truth and Reconciliation in South Africa* (Cambridge, 2001) and T. Goodman, *Staging Solidarity: Truth and Reconciliation in a New South Africa* (Boulder, CO, 2009). For South Africa and elsewhere, see N. Biggar, ed., *Burying the Past: Making Peace and Doing Justice after Civil Conflict*, new ed. (Washington, DC, 2003).

8

In Conclusion: Some Final (but Not Last) Words

I FROM ALDER HEY TO MORAL THEOLOGY (VIA SOCIAL ANTHROPOLOGY)

The origins of what I have tried to achieve in this book—which is to reconceive the practice of moral theology, to do so especially through a closer engagement with social anthropology, and to begin (but only to begin) the practice so reconceived—lies in a very particular problem or concern which I have mentioned on a number of occasions. This problem came into focus in certain events connected with Alder Hey Children's Hospital in Liverpool. These perplexing events were revelatory, so I came to believe, of some quite general deficiencies in the appreciation and understanding of the nature of ethics and the moral life that afflict general moral discourse especially as it is shaped by certain strands of moral philosophy, bioethics, and moral theology. Since social anthropology, however, works with a better account of everyday ethics, I came to see that it offers tools and resources for a moral theology concerned to take up its proper tasks.

The story of what happened at Alder Hey, told as a story of the various motivations, concerns, objectives, and actions of the main players, unfolding over twenty years or more, would be very complex. But as I have briefly touched on previously, one small moment in the story particularly caught my notice. This moment does not concern any specific action of the particular pathologist at the centre of what would become the scandal; the pathologist, it will be recalled, retained a vast, unsystematic collection of body parts and tissues after post-mortem on children, neither seeking parental consent in advance of the retention, nor notifying the parents afterwards. After all, his actions might be said, whether rightly or wrongly, to be those of a rogue individual—which is what presidents of Royal Colleges or other leaders of professional bodies are very naturally ready to say of such occurrences. And, of course, if what is said is accepted as true, the actions are thereby rendered of little general significance. But there was an event in the middle of this story which is uncontroversially of general significance. It occurred after the scandal came under the spotlight of a parliamentary inquiry when the hospital officials began to return body parts but while *still* retaining parts of the parts without seeking parental consent.

What this utterly extraordinary episode suggests is that the parents' requests for the return of their children's body parts were deeply opaque to official understanding in the hospital. But not only in the hospital. For what became clear as the whole scandal unfolded was that the requests were opaque to the medical profession and to health administrators more generally, and even to bioethics, the discipline that might have served, so one would have thought, to explicate those parental requests. But to very many of these actors and commentators, the parental wishes were evidence of mere confusion, error, sentimentality, or emotionalism; they had to be reckoned with or managed, to be sure, but they couldn't be understood and didn't need to be genuinely respected.

Reflecting on these events led me to pose a host of questions. How should one understand this social incomprehension, on the one side of which were parents who plainly regarded what they did as natural and right, and on the other side an establishment that found no sense in what the parents wanted? Why did bioethics not only fail to provide any means of comprehension, but actually very often took on the task of justifying the professional disdain? And would moral theology have done any better in trying to give an account of the parental requests?

With these questions in mind, I chanced upon a review by Ian Hacking in the *London Review of Books*. Hacking is an immensely distinguished philosopher and his name caught my eye in the first instance, not the book under review, which was Lesley Sharp's *Strange Harvest: Organ Transplants, Denatured Bodies and the Transformed Self*.[1] But encouraged by the review, I read Sharp's book and in it found the key to making some sense of and moving beyond the social incomprehension revealed by Alder Hey.

Lesley Sharp is a social anthropologist at Columbia University and her book is an ethnography of aspects of organ transplantation in the United States. One element of the practice that interests her in particular is the difference in the understanding and framing of heart transplantation between medics on the one side, and organ recipients and the kin of deceased donors on the other. A single striking example of such a difference will suffice for our purposes.

In the US, the recipients of organs sometimes develop relationships with a deceased donor's family—and this despite the discouragement, which often amounts to an attempted prohibition, on the part of medical practitioners and administrators. According to Sharp, medical professionals commonly consider 'attempts to communicate as evidence of pathology—that is, [as evidence] that the recipient was unable to come to terms with his or her altered

---

[1] Hacking's review was published on 14 December 2007.

life course'.[2] The suspicion is that the recipient is troubled by receiving an organ from a dead donor. And on the basis that the wish to communicate is pathological, attempts at communication between recipients and donor families have generally been discouraged or forbidden.

What, however, emerges from these contacts, when such meetings do nonetheless occur, despite lack of official sanction or even despite official proscription? In Sharp's observation, what sometimes occurs is that out of these meetings the recipient and the donor kin 'develop...long-standing bonds of intimacy'.[3] These 'bonds of intimacy' are configured in various ways, but one recurring feature of their construction or shaping is the resort to what Sharp refers to as 'fictive kinship'—that is, to use Sharp's account, the deployment of 'the strategy of rendering those unrelated to us either by blood or marriage as close kin'.[4] Thus, in one case, the donor's mother refers to the recipient as 'Son' and the recipient calls her 'Mom', and her children 'Bro' and 'Sis'.[5] In another, a donor's mother refers to a family including a child who has received her son's heart as 'distant cousins'.[6] Again, in a third case, a donor mother writes to the recipient of her daughter's kidney that 'Meeting you is like finding a long-lost child'.[7] On the basis of these new bonds of kinship, a recipient may send a card to the dead donor's mother on Mothering Sunday, for example, just as a mother may send a recipient a card on her dead son's birthday. In the same vein, she may well mourn this new son and the old one again if that new son dies with the failure of the new organ.

What are we to make of these bonds, which develop even in the face of what Sharp refers to as 'bureaucratic constraints on social desire'?[8] We could, of course, describe the participants as making a mistake, as sentimental, emotional, superstitious, and so on—this would fit with the 'still dominant [medical] assumption that a recipient's identification with the donor is pathological'[9] and would conform to the official construction put on the 'social desire' of the Alder Hey parents. Sharp, however, draws a different conclusion. As she sees it, in emotionally fraught and unfamiliar territory, the donor families and recipients deploy 'terms of fictive kinship' in 'creative configurations' that help to 'define and legitimate these deeply peculiar new forms of association'.[10] As Sharp puts it: 'donor kin–recipient communication is about building community in highly unconventional ways... [T]he beauty of fictive kinship lies in the

---

[2] Sharp, *Strange Harvest*, 166.

[3] Sharp, *Strange Harvest*, 40. It is worth adding that just because the likely source of donor hearts are poor young males who have died violently and the likely recipients well-off and middle aged, apart from any other difficulties, these meetings often involve crossing some quite strong boundaries of wealth, status, and even in some cases, race.

[4] Sharp, *Strange Harvest*, 171.   [5] Sharp, *Strange Harvest*, 188.

[6] Sharp, *Strange Harvest*, 184.   [7] Sharp, *Strange Harvest*, 173.

[8] Sharp, *Strange Harvest*, 161.   [9] Sharp, *Strange Harvest*, 181.

[10] Sharp, *Strange Harvest*, 40.

astonishingly flexible ways that such practices create bonds between radically disparate parties, thus undermining the strangeness of the hybrid recipient rejuvenated by parts derived from the dead'.[11] To put it in other words: the participants do subtle and serious moral work in negotiating and constructing relationships that acknowledge and meditate on facts of loss, unmerited gift, new beginnings, and unresolved endings.

According to Lesley Sharp, attributing the claim to Gregory Bateson, 'careful anthropological investigation can illuminate the hidden complexity and grace of a cultural ethos—that is, an unconscious moral code that guides human actions, thoughts, and language within a particular social group'.[12] And this is precisely what she achieves, it seems to me, in her account of that aspect of organ donation which I have mentioned: she identifies and maps a largely unspoken moral world and its logic and grace, and does so in just the sort of territory where the deficient assumptions deployed at Alder Hey expected and consequently found mere confusion, mistake, or pathology.

But if this is *what* anthropology can do, what *enables* it to do it? Put bluntly and briefly I would say this: social anthropology knows implicitly that morality exists as a practice of such a kind that if the meaning, logic, sense, or significance of morality is to be fathomed, it will be fathomed by the sort of approach and manner of investigation characteristic of anthropology's ethnographic method or probably not at all. Why should this be so? Well, because, as the title of a recent collection on the anthropology of ethics suggests (*Ordinary Ethics* edited by Michael Lambek[13]), ethics is not something we do only with huge fanfare, in great debates about deep dilemmas or overriding principles, but can be and usually is really rather quiet and regular: ' "ordinary" [says Lambek] implies an ethics that is relatively tacit, grounded in agreement rather than rule, in practice rather than knowledge or belief, and happening without calling undue attention to itself'.[14] It is this aspect of ethics which explains the sense its practitioners have that ethics is rather obvious and given—and explains also, therefore, their inability to give an immediate, ready, reasoned, and articulate account of their ethics when challenged. It is a similar inability, of course, to that of the speakers of a language who are typically less than forthcoming when asked to give an account of its grammar. For ethics—like grammar—often goes with saying.

I suggested in Chapter 1 that philosophy has rather forgotten about the ordinariness of ethics—or at least moral philosophy in its dominant Kantian and consequentialist strains, the strains chiefly responsible for the woeful character of much bioethics. Moral philosophy demands rules, principles, and rationales which are enunciated out loud and if it doesn't find them straight

---

[11] Sharp, *Strange Harvest*, 204.   [12] Sharp, *Strange Harvest*, 4.
[13] Lambek, *Ordinary Ethics*, 'Introduction'.
[14] Lambek, *Ordinary Ethics*, 'Introduction', 2.

off, it finds no ethics at all. (Some anthropologists, it is sometimes said, too wedded to certain philosophical constructions of morality, have ended up finding that their natives speak pure Heidegger; bioethicists would likely commit an equal and opposite fault, concluding that their natives don't have ethics because they don't speak pure Mill or Kant.) But ethics often goes without saying—and because it goes without saying, it will only be noticed and understood by the patient ethnographic enquirer.

So, with the discovery that anthropology offers a way of understanding the morality which was misunderstood and misconstrued at Alder Hey, I was left to wonder why moral theology's engagement with social anthropology has been relatively limited—and I have proposed in this book that moral theology can and should be reconceived through an engagement with social anthropology, and in the light of a need for what I have been terming an everyday ethics.

Such an everyday ethics is one potentially open to noticing that the moments of Christ's human life mentioned in the creeds—his conception, birth, suffering, death, and burial—figure in and configure most human lives. These moments are paradigmatically human. And it would notice, too, that these events would feature in any outline syllabus for a course in social anthropology, and in such a course would be noticed as structuring, but also sometimes perplexing or troubling, our imagination of the human. It is here, in living out the course of life, that the practice of what it is to be human is worked out. Thus, were moral theology to address itself to the stuff of everyday life, and so to set out its imagination of the human, it would find itself immediately in dialogue with other, perhaps contrary imaginations of human being, as these are narrated especially in social anthropology.

This dialogue, so I proposed, would have a number of gains for moral theology. In the first place, social anthropology serves to provide Christianity with models and methods by which it can better understand and explicate its own framing of our moral lives and world. In the second place, just as social anthropology provides accounts of alternative moral visions of the human, so it allows Christian moral theology to engage therapeutically or evangelically with these counter visions or conceptions (but also, as I have allowed, to learn from them). Thus, so I submitted, a moral theology reconceiving its nature as concerned with everyday ethics and resourced by its engagement with social anthropology, would escape from two characteristic failings: its tendency to be an ethics of hard cases and not of the life course; and its complacent acceptance of a simple naming of the good and bad as sufficient fulfilment of its obligations.

The first failing I have mentioned on a number of occasions (and perhaps especially in discussing IVF and related technologies). As it is presented and received, it is too often the case that the centre and heart of the subject can seem to lie in solving difficult cases. Thus, to take one example, the discussion of so-called end of life issues (euthanasia, advance directives, assisted suicide, and the like), can leave the impression that the scope of the subject is a matter of the licitness (or otherwise) of certain ways of avoiding or ceasing to be old and dependent—but not about why and how one might conceive of living well in this state.

The second failing with a Christian ethics of hard cases is its lack of interest in fully narrating the good or the bad. Too often, I think, moral theology has been content to imagine how and why we act—this in contrast to social anthropology (or at least, to good social anthropology), which to repeat that phrase from Joel Robbins, seeks to render human action 'psychologically and socio-culturally realistic'. Anthropology endeavours to understand the springs of human action. But moral theology must itself come to such an understanding of the moral worlds from which actions arise and in virtue of which they seem compelling, if it is to be therapeutic—or in theological terms, evangelical. Only thus can it present the deep logic of the living of the life course which it commends, and counterwise, discover the logics that shape other lives quite differently. Without this perspicuous presentation, its judgments are unable, I suspect, to move or touch moral lives.

I hope that my discussion of conception and childbearing in Chapters 2 and 3, for example, has illustrated both why and how these failings can be addressed, and that that is best done with the assistance of social anthropology. It can seem from Christian ethics as standardly conceived, that the central matter of the subject belongs to asking and answering the question as to what means are licit or illicit in becoming, avoiding, or ceasing to be pregnant. So it was that the would-be mothers in Klassen's study searched in vain (even in religious traditions known to them) for something other than a merely medical framing of what it is to have a child. In the same way, those who have failed to achieve a birth after a long course of IVF are in turn failed by moral theology's lack of understanding of the specific cultural logics which render having a child of one's own an object of overwhelming and consuming desire, and by its further failure to narrate a counter logic which, in virtue of the creation of spiritual kinship, denies the desperateness of childlessness just as it denies the possibility of having a child of one's own. And so too the Alder Hey parents—most felt that receiving their children's body parts for burial or cremation belonged to their responsibilities as parents and was a proper expression of their grief; it was not an expression of a mere preference. And yet I think the parents would have been hard put to find within contemporary Christian discourse an articulation of the practice and meaning of mourning as part of human being and life (which I began in Chapter 6).

On these topics and others, I have tried to display something of the promise of an ethnographically informed and sensitive moral theology, which consists in its potential to be something other and better than an ethics of hard cases in narrating the life course and in doing so therapeutically. Such a moral theology will attempt to do prescriptively what is done descriptively in Juliet du Boulay's book, to which I have returned on many occasions— that is, to provide a theological ethnography that displays life shaped through and through by a theological imagination of the human. It will aim to display something of the socio-cultural and psychological possibility of living in accordance with a Christian imagination of the human. But if it is to do this, moral theology must learn from the skills of the anthropologist so as better to describe and articulate and render explicit what goes without saying in relation to burying, conceiving, suffering, mourning, remembering, and so on. But as moral theologians begin to practice in the light of an anthropological understanding of morality, they will find that they have much to say about those everyday things about which an ethics of hard cases says nothing. That is, as moral theology goes back to the Christian imagination of the human in ritual, art, literature, prayer, hymns, sermons, and so on (being highly eclectic in its openness to diverse sources), a script will be discovered for everyday ethical life. And it is this script which must be the concern of moral theology to elaborate and exhibit, with something of the richness and subtlety of the best social anthropology.

Scripts can be more or less full. This book has roughed out some main lines, drawing widely and freely on some of the vast resources of the Christian tradition. But a more fully detailed script, which would seek to describe and narrate the good in something approaching ethnographic specificity, would only result from a far more demanding and extensive programme of study. I have had to content myself, in making this proposal for a new direction for moral theology, with sketching some elements in the Christian imagination of the human. Without becoming social anthropology, moral theology could and should seek to locate its prescriptive imagination of the human in a more fully realized account of the form of life in which this imagination might flourish and pass from prescription to description.

Moral theology can only be therapeutic or evangelical as it renders good and bad comprehensible—it cannot liberate us from one form of life for the sake of another unless it enters into the imagination of both. An ethics of hard cases is an ethics which passes judgement, but does not necessarily comprehend the desires of contemporary life. Social anthropology may allow us to begin to fathom and chart choices for the good and the bad, which may otherwise remain opaque and puzzling and thus beyond engagement. Moral theology, in its dominant and received forms, deals with the wrong problems and it deals with them inadequately. How can moral theology be better? How can it learn to practise and provide an everyday ethics that would sustain and support the Christian imagination of the human, and yet address pastorally and therapeutically other ethical imaginaries and forms of life? According to that great anthropologist of what we call rites of passage, van Gennep: 'If I did not somewhat fear the reproach of exaggeration, I would say that in the twentieth century ethnography will be the foundation on which a new philosophical conception of humanity will be built.'[15] He was, I fear, badly wrong about the contribution that ethnography would make to philosophy—at least in the Anglophone world. My hope is that a moral theology which is open to an encounter with social anthropology may itself provide a fuller and better account of the human.

II SEEING CHRIST IN THE WORLD: SPENCER'S *TRAVOYS ARRIVING WITH WOUNDED AT A DRESSING-STATION, SMOL, MACEDONIA, SEPTEMBER 1916*

I began with a painting and now at the end I conclude with a painting—two brackets enclosing the text, the first asking whether we can see the world in Christ, this second answering the question by finding Christ in the world.

The picture with which I began—the *Mérode Altarpiece*—was the opening bracket, and is a solemn annunciation that makes us, the viewers, present at Christ's conception, inviting us to conceive our conceivings in the light of the conception of Christ. What is it, that picture asks, for the conception of Christ to be not an historical event which is over and done with, not an occurrence in one human life, but an event that might govern, inflect, and modulate later conceptions, whether in Flanders in 1425 when the picture was painted, or here and now. My closing picture and bracket (Stanley Spencer's *Travoys Arriving with Wounded at a Dressing-Station, Smol, Macedonia, September 1916*[16]) looks at things from the other side, so to speak, and tells of that very governing, inflection, and modulation (see Plate 6).

We, the viewers, look down from an elevated position over the rough thistles or holly which stand at the front edge of the picture, and towards a brightly illuminated dressing station. There, in the background on a rough table, lies a shrouded patient attended by two medics, one holding a mask and ready to administer choloroform, another concerned with the patient's wound. Around this dressing station are gathered the mules pulling the travoys of the title—travoys being a sort of horse-drawn sledge, traditionally used for moving logs over ground so rough that it will not bear wheels, and thus especially suited to the mountainous terrain of Macedonia. But here the cargo is not logs, but wounded men.

---

[15] Given as an epigram on the page opposite the new 'Introduction' by Deborah Ross, to V. and E. Turner, *Image and Pilgrimage in Christian Culture*, first published 1978 (New York, 2011).
[16] In the Imperial War Museum, London.

The mules, with heads raised and ears pricked, are all attention. Their cargos on the travoys are, in contrast, seemingly oblivious to what is going on—the bodies are covered in blankets and the faces in gauze to prevent mosquito bites. The wounded are quiescent, presumably under the influence of morphine, awaiting their turn to be treated. And they are attended by the orderlies and soldiers of the medical corps, who seem to steady the mules, the travoys, and the wounded all at the same time—their calming and gentle hands mirroring the actions of the healing hands in the makeshift surgery. And these soldiers and orderlies, like the mules or horses, are drawn to the spectacle at the back of the scene. So too, the orderly in the right foreground, with the awkward cast on his arm, and the equally awkward pose, looks back over his shoulder towards that brightly lit improvized operating theatre. And we, the viewers of this picture, join him and the others and become spectators ourselves, adding to the avid throng around the single patient and the two who attend him.

The painting was begun and finished in 1919—the first work done by Stanley Spencer after the war. Spencer was just twenty-three years old when the war broke out. He enlisted in 1915 in the Royal Army Medical Corps and worked in a hospital, and was then sent to Macedonia. In 1917 he volunteered for the infantry and spent time at the front line. In September of 1918 one of his brothers was killed on the Western Front, and in December he was invalided out of the army and returned to Cookham.

The picture recalls an incident which occurred while Spencer was still with the Field Ambulance Unit: 'About the middle of September 1916', Spencer later wrote 'the [22nd] Division made an attack on Machine Gun Hill on the Doiran Vardar Sector and held it for a few nights. During these nights the wounded passed through the dressing stations in a never-ending stream'. 'I was standing a little way from the old Greek church' (now become the dressing station), 'and coming there were rows of travoys... crammed full of wounded men.'[17]

When Spencer came to paint this scene some three years after he had witnessed it, he had 'buried so many people' and seen 'so many dead bodies', as he said, that his recollections must have been chiefly painful or even horrific. And yet even as he witnessed the scene at the time, so he claimed, he had an inkling of how it should be read or interpreted or understood in terms other than those simply of loss or suffering or pain: 'One would have thought that the scene was a sordid one, a terrible scene... but I felt there was grandeur.'[18]

'Grandeur' may seem an odd thing to perceive in a stream of wounded and dying men being dragged on makeshift stretchers to a rough-and-ready clinic. Other wartime artists might well—and quite reasonably—have seen only horror, and had Spencer chosen to conjure up the pain and the suffering and anguish of that night in Macedonia, when the scale of losses compared with

[17] T. Hyman and P. Wright, *Stanley Spencer* (London, 2001), §20.
[18] T. Hyman and P. Wright, *Stanley Spencer* (London, 2001), §20.

the killing fields of the Somme and Verdun, his painting might have resembled others that hang near it in the Imperial War Museum in London—such as Paul Nash's nightmarish visions of desolate landscapes illuminated by the lightning of the relentless shells of trench warfare. But Spencer saw something else besides the horror—'I felt there was grandeur', and he has given us a scene of monumental calm and stillness.

Of course, as Spencer himself said, the picture 'is not in any material... sense a truthful representation of the scene it is supposed to depict'.[19] It is not a depiction of what was there, but a representation—a re-presentation. And what he has done, I think, it to re-present or transfigure the stream of dead, dying, and wounded arriving at the dressing station as if present at the nativity.

Spencer has disposed the figures around the ruined church which has become a dressing station just as figures are disposed, spatially, in any number of representations of the birth of Christ. The ruined church stands in place of the stable. The wounded and those who accompany them, replace the shepherds, the bystanders, or the kings. The horses stand in for ox and ass. Instead of a manger we have an operating table, itself possibly the simple altar from the church. Instead of the holy family—the attentive Mary and the usually brooding Joseph and the fragile baby—we have the doctors or orderlies and the fragile patient.

Of course this nativity, just as indeed many of the medieval ones, contains references to the crucifixion, here rather explicit, as if nativity and crucifixion are joined. We have the red crosses on the sleeves of the soldiers; there are the outstretched arms of the figures in the centre as if they are about to be nailed to crosses; there are those huddled bodies on the stretchers, treated, as Spencer says, 'with the same veneration and awe as so many crucified... Christs'.[20] And we have a different sort of cross, a disciple's cross, supporting that basin of water in the makeshift operating theatre—the basin itself suggestive of a baptismal font.

The form into which Spencer has transfigured the original scene is the form of a nativity, with hints of the crucifixion; as in a nativity, we have humans and animals gathered as avid spectators of a mysteriously illuminated scene. But if this is the form Spencer has chosen, why has he chosen it? What is the substance which makes this the right form? What is it that captured Spencer's imagination on that night in 1916 so that he read and re-presented the original scene in this way? What is it, we might ask alternatively, that causes that soldier with his arm in the sling, even while leaving, to turn back to behold the spectacle? What is it that draws the orderlies, and even the mules, as spectators of all this—and invites our fascinated attention too? What is there to see as we join this band of spectators gathered as at a nativity?

---

[19] T. Hyman and P. Wright, *Stanley Spencer* (London, 2001), §20.
[20] T. Hyman and P. Wright, *Stanley Spencer* (London, 2001), §20.

If one were to try to explain what it is that makes the original nativity a spectacle to behold, there would be many things to say—but one thing would be this: that something of its grandeur consists in its being a moment of peace framed by force and violence. At the original nativity that great and grand colonial power, Rome, asserts its will and determination to tax its subject people, requiring them to go to their tribal homes. No sooner is the baby born than a petty tyrant (Herod), a client of the greater tyrant, jealous of his power and position, has the infants of Bethlehem massacred on the basis of a rumour of a prophecy delivered by wandering magicians. The framing of the original nativity is force and conflict and violence born of base human motives and fears, fuelled by wild superstitions and dodgy divinations. The central moment, the moment when the child is displayed to human view, the moment that draws the spectators, is the all-too-brief moment when peaceful tender care becomes a fragile interlude between the violent before and the violent after.

Spencer depicts a similar moment. It was plainly conflict and violence which led to the dressing station, Smol, Macedonia, 1916, and plainly there will be violence and death on the other side of this event. But Spencer has not illustrated the dreadful and tragic events that frame this moment, although he alludes to them, but the moment in which is born peace, comfort, and care, when there is redemption and healing—no matter what there is outside the frame. Here a few men are snatching something back from the chaos. 'Inserting peace in the face of war'—this was Spencer's phrase. 'It was possible even in war', he asserted, 'to establish to a greater or lesser degree a peaceful atmosphere, ... [so] hope and some sort of constructive life was sustained'.[21] And the grandeur Spencer discerns here in the midst of conflict is just the insertion of peace in the midst of violence; it is this intervention that allows and encourages Spencer to transfigure the stream of wounded and dying into a nativity.

In 1934, some fifteen years after this picture was completed, some artists got together to publish a book of sermons.[22] They seem to have done it in response (possibly retaliation) to a group of clergy who themselves had got together to exhibit their paintings in London. And in the collection of sermons there is one by Spencer. But however well Spencer's sermon may compare with the clergymen's paintings, Spencer had no need to write sermons when his paintings preach as powerfully as does this one, bidding us too, in his phrase, to 'Insert peace!'

The painting with which I began, the *Mérode Annunciation*, depicts the conception of Christ, and asks us whether we can conceive our conceivings in the light of that conception. This picture, with which I end, answers that question by finding and depicting the nativity of Christ in the humble efforts at care in an improvized dressing station in a ruined church on the outer edge

---

[21] Cited in F. MacCarthy, ed., *Stanley Spencer: An English Vision* (New Haven, 1997), §7.
[22] S. Spencer, *Sermons by Artists* (London, 1934).

of a world in the throes of a conflict of almost unprecedented horror. Even here, the painting tells us, we can depict and envision and imagine our world through that great and original story.

This painting is not usually counted among Spencer's later visionary works—it is not classed with the famous *Resurrection at Cookham*, with bodies rising from the tombs of an English village churchyard on a gentle summer's afternoon. There is in this painting none of the 'weird ebullience' (as one critic puts it),[23] which is expressed by the wild fancy and distortion of some of his other great pictures. But this is indeed a great visionary work—for it holds up a renewed nativity and calls us to pray and hope and act for the sake of other and similar nativities, where, amidst the conflicts and violence of our everyday social worlds, peace is inserted, and there come to birth forms of tenderness and care and love and solidarity in a world given to conflict and war and alienation.

The imagination of Christ's life provides a rich and vibrant imaginary of a new social topography, which even now seeks to take form amongst us, perhaps in the work of L'Arche communities where the handicapped are accompanied in their lives, in the work of Community Chaplaincy where criminals are remembered forgivingly, and in hospices where the dying are accompanied in their deaths. The task of an everyday Christian ethics is, in its own lesser part, to imagine, recount, and thereby hopefully sustain the practice and enactment of human being after the measure of Christ's human being.

---

[23] F. MacCarthy, 'Spencer, Sir Stanley (1891–1959)', *Oxford Dictionary of National Biography* (Oxford, 2004).

Bibliography

Aelius Aristides, *Apology*.

Alfani, G. and Gourdon, V., eds., *Spiritual Kinship in Europe, 1500–1900* (London, 2012).

Almeling, R., *Sex Cells: The Medical Market for Eggs and Sperm* (Berkeley, 2011).

Ambrose, *De Obitu Valentiniani Consolatio, Consolation on the Death of Emperor Valentinian*, trans. R. J. Deferrari, in *Funeral Orations of St Gregory Nazianzen and St Ambrose*, in R. J. Deferrari, ed., *The Fathers of the Church*, vol. 22 (Washington, DC, 1953).

Ambrose, *First Oration On the Death of his Brother Satyrus*, trans. R. J. Deferrari, in *Funeral Orations of St Gregory Nazianzen and St Ambrose*, in R. J. Deferrari, ed., *The Fathers of the Church*, vol. 22 (Washington, DC, 1953).

Anon., *Beowulf*, trans. S. Heaney (London, 1999).

Antze P. and Lambek, M., 'Introduction: Forecasting Memory', in P. Antze and M. Lambek, eds., *Tense Past* (London, 1996).

Appiah, K. A., 'Anthropology' in *Encyclopedia of Ethics*, eds. Becker and Becker.

Arendt, H., *The Human Condition*, 2nd ed. (Chicago, 1998).

Ariès, P., *Centuries of Childhood: A Social History of Family Life* (London, 1979).

Ariès, P., *The Hour of Our Death* (London, 1981).

Aristotle, *Nichomachean Ethics*.

Ashley B. M. and O'Rourke, K. D., *Ethics of Health Care*, 3rd ed. (Washington, DC, 2002).

Atkinson, D. W., *The English Ars Moriendi* (New York, 1992), vol. 5 of E. Bernstein, ed. *Renaissance and Baroque Studies and Texts*.

Augustine, *City of God*, trans. H. Bettenson (Harmondsworth, 1984).

Augustine, *Confessions*, trans. H. Chadwick (Oxford, 1991).

Augustine, *Expositions of the Psalms*, trans. M. Boulding, in *The Works of Saint Augustine: A Translation for the 21st Century*, pt. 3, 6 vols. (Hyde Park, NY, 2000–2004).

Augustine, *Letters*, trans. R. J. Teske, in *The Works of Saint Augustine: A Translation for the 21st Century*, pt. 2, 4 vols. (Hyde Park, NY, 2001–2005).

Augustine, *On the Gospel of John*, trans. J. Gibb, in P. Schaff, ed., *Nicene and Post-Nicene Fathers*, 1st series, vol. 7 (Edinburgh, 1991).

Augustine, *On the Morals of the Catholic Church*, in *Writings against the Manichœans and Donatists*, trans. R. Stothert, in P. Schaff, ed., *Nicene and Post-Nicene Fathers*, 1st series, vol. 4 (Edinburgh, 1989).

Augustine, *Sermons*, trans. E. Hill, in *The Works of Saint Augustine: A Translation for the 21st Century*, pt. 3, 11 vols. (Brooklyn, NY, 1990–7).

Augustine, *The Care to be Taken for the Dead*, trans. J. A. Lacey, in *Treatises on Marriage and Other Subjects*, R. J. Deferrari, ed., *The Fathers of the Church*, vol. 27 (Washington, DC, 1955).

Bailey, S., *Sponsors at Baptism and Confirmation: An Historical Introduction to Anglican Practice* (London, 1952).

Bakke, O. M., *When Children Became People: The Birth of Childhood in Early Christianity* (Minneapolis, 2005).

Baldovin, J. F., 'The Empire Baptised', in G. Wainwright and K. B. Westerfield Tucker, eds., *The Oxford History of Christian Worship* (Oxford, 2006), 77–130.

Banner, M. C., 'Catholics and Anglicans and Contemporary Bioethics: Divided or United?', in L. Gormally, ed., *Issues for a Catholic Bioethics* (London, 1999), 34–57.

Banner, M. C., 'Moral Philosophy: The Philosophy of What?', *Studies in Christian Ethics*, 24 (2011), 232–41.

Barclay, J. M. G., 'The Family as Bearer of Religion', in H. Moxnes, ed., *Constructing Early Christian Families* (London, 1997), 66–80.

Barnard, A. and Spencer, J., eds., *The Encyclopedia of Social and Cultural Anthropology* (London, 2002).

Barnes, J., *Levels of Life* (London, 2013).

Barth, K., *Church Dogmatics*, III/4, trans. A. T. Mackay et al. (Edinburgh, 1961).

Becker, G., *The Elusive Embryo: How Women and Men Approach New Reproductive Technologies* (Berkeley, 2000).

Becker, L. C. and C. B., eds., *Encyclopedia of Ethics*, 2nd ed. (London, 2001).

Bellarmine, R., *De Arte Bene Moriendi* (Rome, 1619), in *Spiritual Writings*, eds. and trans. J. P. Donelly and R. J. Teske (New York, 1989).

Bender, C., *Heaven's Kitchen: Living Religion at God's Love We Deliver* (Chicago, 2003).

Benedict, *The Rule of St Benedict*, trans. J. McCann (London, 1976).

Bennett, J. M., *Water is Thicker Than Blood: An Augustinian Theology of Marriage and Singleness* (New York, 2008).

Bialecki, J., Haynes N., and Robbins, J. 'The Anthropology of Christianity', *Religion Compass* (2008), 1139–58.

Biehl, J., *Vita: Life in a Zone of Social Abandonment* (Berkeley, 2005).

Biggar, N., ed., *Burying the Past: Making Peace and Doing Justice after Civil Conflict*, new ed. (Washington, DC, 2003).

Biggar, N., 'Forgiveness in the Twentieth Century: A Review of the Literature, 1901–2001', in A. McFadyen and M. Sarot, eds., *Forgiveness and Truth* (Edinburgh, 2001), 181–217.

Bonaccorso, M., *Conceiving Kinship: Assisted Conception, Procreation and Family in South Europe* (New York, 2008).

Bonaccorso, M., 'Making Connections: Family and Relatedness in Clinics of Assisted Conception in Italy', *Modern Italy*, 9 (2004), 59–68.

Bossy, J., *Christianity in the West* (Oxford, 1985).

Bossy, J., 'Blood and Baptism: Kinship, Community and Christianity in Western Europe from the Fourteenth to the Seventeenth Centuries', in D. Baker, ed. *Sanctity and Secularity: The Church and the World* (Oxford, 1973), 129–43.

Bradfield, P. F., *The Search for the Origins of Christian Worship* (Oxford, 2002).

Brock, B., 'Supererogation and the Riskiness of Human Vulnerability', in H. S. Reinders, ed., *The Paradox of Disability* (Grand Rapids, MI, 2010), 127–39.

Brown, P., *Poverty and Leadership in the Later Roman Empire* (Hanover, NH, 2002).

Brown, P., *The Body and Society: Men, Women and Sexual Renunciation in Early Christianity* (London, 1988).

Brown, P., *The Cult of the Saints* (Chicago, 1981).

Brown, P., *Through the Eye of a Needle: Wealth, the Fall of Rome, and the Making of Christianity in the West, 350–550 AD* (Princeton, 2012).

Brown R., *The Death of the Messiah*, 2 vols. (New York, 1994).

Butler, J., *The Works of Joseph Butler*, W. E. Gladstone, ed., vol. 2, *Sermons* (Oxford, 1897).

Butler, J., *Precarious Life: The Powers of Mourning and Violence* (London, 2004).

Bynum, C. W., *The Resurrection of the Body in Western Christendom, 200–1336* (New York, 1995).

Cadell, D. P. and Newton, R. R., 'Euthanasia: American Attitudes towards the Physician's Role', *Social Science and Medicine*, 40 (1995), 1671–81.

Campbell, A. V. and Willis, M., 'They Stole My Baby's Soul: Narratives of Embodiment and Loss', *Medical Humanities*, 31 (2005), 101–104.

Carruthers, M., *The Craft of Thought: Meditation, Rhetoric, and the Making of Images* (Cambridge, 1998).

Carruthers, M., *The Experience of Beauty in the Middle Ages* (Oxford, 2013).

Carsten, J., *After Kinship* (Cambridge, 2004).

Cátedra, M., *This World, Other Worlds: Sickness, Suicide, Death, and the Afterlife among the Vaqueiros de Alzada of Spain*, trans. W. A. Christian (Chicago, 1992).

Chadwick, H., *The Church in Ancient Society* (Oxford, 2001).

Chouliaraki, L., *The Spectatorship of Suffering* (London, 2006).

Clendinnen, I., *Aztecs: An Interpretation* (Cambridge, 1991).

Clendinnen, I., *Reading the Holocaust* (Cambridge, 2002).

Cohen, D. and Eisdorfer, C., *Loss of Self* (London, 1986).

Cohen, E., *The Modulated Scream: Pain in Late Medieval Culture* (Chicago, 2010).

Cohen, L., *No Aging in India: Alzheimer's, the Bad Family, and Other Modern Things* (Berkeley, 1998).

Congregation for the Doctrine of the Faith, *Donum Vitae* (*Instruction on Respect for Human Life in its Origin and on the Dignity of Procreation*) (London, 1987).

Connerton, P., *How Societies Remember* (Cambridge, 1989).

Corbier, M., 'Child Exposure and Abandonment', in S. Dixon, ed., *Childhood, Class and Kin in the Roman World* (London, 2001), 52–73.

Coster, W., 'Purity, Profanity and Puritanism: The Churching of Women, 1500–1700', *Studies in Church History*, 27 (1990), 377–87.

Craig, E., ed., *The Encyclopedia of Philosophy* (London, 1998).

Cressy, D., *Birth, Marriage and Death: Ritual, Religion and the Life-Cycle in Tudor and Stuart England*, new ed. (Oxford, 1999).

Cressy, D., 'Purification, Thanksgiving and the Churching of Women in Post-Reformation England', *Past and Present*, 141 (1993), 106–146.

Cross, G., *The Cute and the Cool: Wondrous Innocence and Modern American Children's Culture* (New York, 2004).

Cummings, B., *The Book of Common Prayer* (Oxford, 2011).

Cunningham, H., 'Histories of Childhood', *The American Historical Review*, 103 (1998), 1197–99.

Danforth, L. M., *The Death Rituals of Rural Greece* (Princeton, 1982).

Davidson, A. I. 'Ethics as Ascetics: Foucault, the History of Ethics, and Ancient Thought', in G. Gutting, *The Cambridge Companion to Foucault* (Cambridge, 1994), 115–40.

Davis-Floyd, R. E. and Sargent, C. F., eds., *Childbirth and Authoritative Knowledge* (Berkeley, 1997).

Davis-Floyd, R. E., *Birth as an American Rite of Passage* (Berkeley, 1992).

de Vos, D., *The Flemish Primitives* (Princeton, 2002).

Dix, G., *The Shape of the Liturgy* (London, 1945).

Dixon, S., *The Roman Family* (Baltimore, 1992).

Driver, M. W., 'Mirrors of a Collective Past: Re-considering Images of Medieval Women' in J. Taylor and L. Smith, eds., *Women and the Book* (British Library, 1997), 75–93.

du Boulay, J., *Cosmos, Life, and Liturgy in a Greek Orthodox Village* (Limni, 2009).

du Boulay, J., *Portrait of a Greek Mountain Village* (Oxford, 1974).

Duclow, D. F., 'Dying Well: The *Ars moriendi* and the Dormition of the Virgin', in E. E. DuBruck and B. I. Gusick, eds., *Death and Dying in the Middle Ages* (New York, 1999).

Duffy, E., *Marking the Hours* (New Haven, 2006).

Edel, M. and A., eds., *Anthropology and Ethics: The Quest for Moral Understanding* (Cleveland, 1959).

Edwards, J., Franklin, S., Hirsch, E., Price F., and Strathern, M., eds., *Technologies of Procreation: Kinship in the Age of Assisted Conception* (Manchester, 1993).

Elliott, C., *Better than Well: American Medicine Meets the American Dream* (New York, 2003).

Eusebius, *The History of the Church from Christ to Constantine*, trans. G. A. Williams, rev. and ed. A. Louth (London, 1989).

Faubion, J., *An Anthropology of Ethics* (Cambridge, 2011).

Faubion, J., ed., *The Ethics of Kinship: Ethnographic Enquiries* (Oxford, 2001).

Faubion, J., 'Toward an Anthropology of Ethics: Foucault and the Pedagogics of Autopoiesis', *Representations*, 74 (2001), 83–104.

Fassin, D., 'Beyond Good and Evil? Questioning the Anthropological Discomfort with Morals', *Anthropological Theory*, 8.4 (2008), 333–44.

Fassin, D., *Humanitarian Reason: A Moral History of the Present* (Berkeley, 2012).

Fassin, D., '*Noli Me Tangere*: The Moral Untouchability of Humanitarianism', in E. Bornstein and P. Redfield, eds., *Forces of Compassion: Humanitarianism between Ethics and Politics* (Santa Fe, NM, 2011), 32–52.

Fassin, D. and Rechtman, R., *The Empire of Trauma: An Inquiry into the Condition of Victimhood* (Princeton, 2009).

Fassin, D., ed., *A Companion to Moral Anthropology* (Oxford, 2012).

Feeney, D., *Caesar's Calendar: Ancient Time and the Beginnings of History* (Berkeley, 2007).

Finaldi, G., ed., *The Image of Christ* (London, 2000).

Fisher, A., *Catholic Bioethics for a New Millennium* (Cambridge, 2012).

Florence, M., 'Foucault, Michel, 1926– ', in *The Cambridge Companion to Foucault*, ed. G. Gutting (Cambridge, 1994), 314–19.

Ford, D., *Christian Wisdom* (Cambridge, 2007).

Fontana, A. and Smith R., 'Alzheimer's Disease Victims: The "Unbecoming" of Self and the Normalization of Competence', *Sociological Perspectives*, 32.1 (1989), 35–46.

Foucault, M., *The History of Sexuality*, in three vols, trans. R. Hurley (Harmondsworth, 1979–1986).

Foucault, M., 'Subjectivity and Truth', in M. Foucault, *The Essential Works*, vol. 1., *Ethics*, ed. P. Rabinow, trans. R. Hurley (Harmondsworth, 1997), 87–92.

Francis, D., Kellaher L., and Neophytou, G., *The Secret Cemetery* (Oxford, 2005).

Franklin, S., *Biological Relatives: IVF, Stem Cells and the Future of Kinship* (Durham, NC, 2013).

Franklin, S., *Embodied Progress: A Cultural Account of Assisted Conception* (London, 1997).

Franklin, S., 'Deconstructing "Desperateness": The Social Construction of Infertility in Popular Representations of New Reproductive Technologies', in M. McNeil, I. Varcoe, and S. Yearley, eds., *The New Reproductive Technologies* (London, 1990), 200–229.

Franklin, S., 'From Blood to Genes? Rethinking Consanguinity in the Context of Geneticization', in C. H. Johnson, B. Jassen, D. W. Sabean, and S. Teuscher, eds., *Blood and Kinship: Matter and Metaphor from Ancient Rome to the Present Day* (New York, 2013), 285–306.

Franklin, S., 'Life', in *Encyclopedia of Bioethics*, ed. Reich, 456–62.

Frier, B. W., 'Demography', in A. Bowman, P. Garnsey, and D. Rathbone, eds., *The High Empire, A.D. 70–192, The Cambridge Ancient History*, 2nd ed., vol. 11 (Cambridge, 2000), 787–816.

Freud, S., *Introductory Lectures on Psychoanalysis*, trans. J. Strachey (London, 1973).

Fulton, R., *From Judgment to Passion: Devotion to Christ and the Virgin Mary, 800–1200* (New York, 2005).

Giardina, A., 'The Family in the Late Roman World' in A. Bowman, A. Cameron, and P. Garnsey, eds., *The Crisis of Empire, A.D. 193–337, The Cambridge Ancient History*, 2nd ed., vol. 12 (Cambridge, 2005), 392–415.

Glaser, B. G. and Strauss, A. L., *Time for Dying* (Chicago, 1968).

Goodman, T., *Staging Solidarity: Truth and Reconciliation in a New South Africa* (Boulder, CO, 2009).

Goody, J., *The Development of the Family and Marriage in Europe* (Cambridge, 1983).

Green, J. W., *Beyond the Good Death* (Philadelphia, 2008).

Guilhot, N., 'The Anthropologist as Witness: Humanitarianism between Ethnography and Critique', *Humanity*, 3.1 (2013), 81–101.

Hacking, I., 'Whose body is it?' Review of L. Sharp, *Strange Harvest: Organ Transplants, Denatured Bodies, and the Transformed Self*, in *London Review of Books* (14 Dec. 2007).

Hall, A. L., *Conceiving Parenthood: American Protestantism and the Spirit of Reproduction* (Grand Rapids, MI, 2008).

Hallam E. and Hockey, J., *Death, Memory and Material Culture* (Oxford, 2001).

Hallam, E., Hockey, J., and Howarth, G., *Beyond the Body: Death and Social Identity* (New York, 1999).

Hamilton, B. E., Martin, J. A., and Ventura, S., 'Births: Preliminary Data for 2011', *National Vital Statistics Report*, 61.5 (2012), 1–20.

Hauerwas, S., *The Peaceable Kingdom* (London, 1984).

Heintz, M., ed., *The Anthropology of Moralities* (New York, 2009).

Hendrick, H., *Children, Childhood and English Society, 1880–1990* (Cambridge, 1997).

Herskovits, E., 'Struggling over Subjectivity: Debates about the "Self" and Alzheimer's Disease', *Medical Anthropology Quarterly* 9 (1995), 146–64.

Hockey, J., *Experiences of Death: An Anthropological Account* (Edinburgh, 1990).

Hogan M. C., et al., 'Maternal Mortality for 181 Countries, 1980–2008: a Systematic Analysis of Progress Towards Millenium Development Goal 5', *The Lancet*, 375 (2010), 1609–23.

Howell, S., ed., *The Ethnography of Moralities* (London, 1997).

Howes, G., *The Art of the Sacred* (London, 2007).

Humphrey, C., 'Exemplars and Rules: Aspects of the Discourse of Moralities in Mongolia', in S. Howell, ed., *The Ethnography of Moralities* (London, 1997).

Humphrey, C., 'Reassembling Individual Subjects: Events and Decisions in Troubled Times', *Anthropological Theory*, 8 (2008), 357–80.

Hyman, T. and Wright, P., *Stanley Spencer* (London, 2001).

Ingold, T., ed., *The Companion Encyclopedia of Anthropology* (London, 1994).

Inhorn, M. C., *Reproductive Disruptions: Gender, Technology, and Biopolitics in the New Millennium* (New York, 2007).

Inhorn, M. C. and Birenbaum-Carmeli, D., 'Assisted Reproductive Technologies and Culture Change', *Annual Review of Anthropology* (2008), 37, 177–96.

Jalland, P., *Death in War and Peace: A History of Grief and Loss in England, 1914–1970* (Oxford, 2010).

John Paul II, *Evangelium Vitae*, English trans. (London, 1995).

Kahn, S. M., *Reproducing Jews: A Cultural Account of Assisted Conception in Israel* (Durham, NC, 2000).

Kant, I., *Groundwork of the Metaphysic of Morals*, trans. H. J. Paton as *The Moral Law* (London, 1948).

Kaufman, S., 'Dementia-Near-Death and Life Itself', in A. Leibing and L. Cohen, eds., *Thinking about Dementia: Culture, Loss and the Anthropology of Senility* (New Brunswick, NJ, 2006).

Kastenbaum, R., *On Our Way: The Final Passage Through Life and Death* (Berkeley, 2004).

Kenna, M. E., 'Review of J. du Boulay, *Cosmos, Life, and Liturgy in a Greek Orthodox Village*', in *Journal of the Royal Anthropological Institute*, N.S., 17 (2011), 205.

Klassen, P. E., *Blessed Events: Religion and Home Birth in America* (Princeton, 2001).

Kleinman, A., 'Medicine, Anthropology of', in *Encyclopedia of Bioethics*, ed. Reich.

Kleinman, A. and J., 'The Appeal of Experience; The Dismay of Images: Cultural Appropriations of Suffering in our Times', in A. Kleinman, V. Das, and M. Lock, eds., *Social Suffering* (Berkeley, 1997).

Kontos, P., 'Embodied Selfhood: An Ethnographic Exploration of Alzheimer's Disease', in A. Leibing and L. Cohen, eds., *Thinking about Dementia: Culture, Loss and the Anthropology of Senility* (New Brunswick, NJ, 2006).

Kozhimannil, K. B., Law, M. R., and Virnig, B.A., 'Cesarean Delivery Rates Vary Tenfold Among US Hospitals', *Health Affairs*, 32.3 (2013), 527–35.

Kusserow, A., *American Individualisms: Child Rearing and Social Class in Three Neighbourhoods* (New York, 2004).

LaFollette, H., ed., *The Oxford Handbook of Practical Ethics* (Oxford, 2003).

Laidlaw, J., 'For an Anthropology of Ethics and Freedom', *Journal of the Royal Anthropological Institute*, 8 (2002), 311–32.

Laidlaw, J., 'Review: Jarrett Zigon, *Morality: An Anthropological Perspective*', in *Ethnos*, 74 (2009), 436.

Laidlaw, J., 'Social Anthropology' in J. Skorupski, ed., *The Routledge Companion to Ethics* (London, 2010), 369–83.

Laidlaw, J., *The Subject of Virtue: An Anthropology of Ethics and Freedom* (Cambridge, 2014).

Lambek, M., ed., *Ordinary Ethics: Anthropology, Language, and Action* (New York, 2010).

Lambek, M., 'The Anthropology of Religion and the Quarrel Between Poetry and Philosophy', *Current Anthropology*, 41 (2000), 309–20.

Lambek, M., 'Value and Virtue', *Anthropological Theory*, 8 (2008), 133–57.

Lancy, D., *The Anthropology of Childhood: Cherubs, Chattel, Changelings* (Cambridge, 2008).

Lavi, S. J., *The Modern Art of Dying* (Princeton, 2005).

LeBel, T. P., *Invisible Stripes? Formerly Incarcerated Persons' Perception of and Responses to Stigma*, unpublished dissertation, University of Albany (New York, 2006).

Levinson D. and Ember, M., eds., *Encyclopedia of Cultural Anthropology* (New York, 1996).

Liebling, A., *Prisons and Their Moral Performance: A Study of Values, Quality, and Prison Life* (Oxford, 2004).

Luther, M., *Disputation Against Scholastic Theology*, trans. H. J. Grimm, in *Luther's Works*, vol. 31 (Philadelphia, 1957).

Luther, M., *Ninety-Five Theses*, trans. H. J. Grimm, in *Luther's Works*, vol. 31 (Philadelphia, 1957).

Lynch, J. H., *Godparents and Kinship in Early Medieval Europe* (Princeton, 1986).

MacCarthy, F., ed., *Stanley Spencer: An English Vision* (New Haven, 1997).

MacCarthy, F., 'Spencer, Sir Stanley (1891–1959)', *Oxford Dictionary of National Biography* (Oxford, 2004).

MacGregor, N., *Seeing Salvation: Images of Christ in Art* (London, 2000).

MacIntyre, A., *After Virtue* (London, 1981).

Mahoney, J., *The Making of Moral Theology* (Oxford, 1987).

Maruna, S., 'Re-entry as a Rite of Passage', *Punishment and Society*, 13.1 (2011), 3–28.

Mathewes, C. 'The Scandalous Present (and Future Promise) of Christian Ethics', an unpublished paper given in Cambridge in 2012.

May, E. T., *Barren in the Promised Land: Childless Americans and the Pursuit of Happiness* (Cambridge, MA, 1995).

Meeks, W., *The Origins of Christian Morality* (New Haven, 1993).

McLean, A., *The Person in Dementia: A Study of Nursing Home Care in the US* (Peterborough, ON, 2007).

McManners, J., *Death and the Enlightenment* (Oxford, 1981).

McNeill, J. T., *A History of the Cure of Souls* (Chicago, 1951).

Merbeck. M. B., *The Thief, the Cross and the Wheel: Pain and the Spectacle of Punishment in Medieval and Renaissance Europe*, 2nd ed. (Chicago, 1999).

Michaelson, K. L., ed., *Childbirth in America: Anthropological Perspectives* (South Hadley, MA, 1988).

Milbank, J., *Theology and Social Theory: Beyond Secular Reason* (Oxford, 1990).

Mill, J. S., *Utilitarianism*, ed. R. Crisp (Oxford, 1998).

Mills, R., *Suspended Animation: Pain, Pleasure and Punishment in Medieval Culture* (London, 2006).

Modell, J., *A Sealed and Secret Kinship: The Culture of Policies and Practices in American Adoption* (New York, 2002).

Modell, J., *Kinship with Strangers: Adoption and Interpretations of Kinship in American Culture* (Berkeley, 1994).

Moltmann, J., *The Crucified God*, trans. R. A. Wilson and J. Bowden (London, 1974).

Montgomery, H., *An Introduction to Childhood: Anthropological Perspectives on Children's Lives* (Chichester, 2010).

Morrison, K. F., *'I am You': Hermeneutics of Empathy in Western Literature, Theology and Art* (Princeton, 1988).

Morrison K. F. and Bell, R. M., eds., *Studies on Medieval Empathies* (Turnout, Belgium, 2013).

Moxnes, H., 'What is Family? Problems in Constructing Early Christian Families', in H. Moxnes, ed., *Constructing Early Christian Families* (London, 1997), 13–41.

Murray, A., *The Curse on Self-Murder*, vol. 2 of A. Murray, *Suicide in the Middle Ages* (Oxford, 2000).

Nagel, A., 'The Afterlife of the Reliquary', in M. Bagnoli, H. A. Klein, C. G. Mann, J. Robinson, eds., *Treasures of Heaven: Saints, Relics, and Devotion in Medieval Europe* (London, 2011), 211–22.

Nelson, J., 'Parents, Children, and the Church in the Earlier Middle Ages', in D. Wood, ed., *The Church and Childhood* (Oxford, 1994), 82–83.

O'Connor, M. C., *The Art of Dying Well: The Development of the* Ars Moriendi (New York, 1941).

O'Donnell, J. J., *Augustine's Confessions*, 3 vols. (Oxford, 1992).

O'Donovan, O. M. T., *Resurrection and Moral Order: An Outline for Evangelical Ethics*, 2nd ed. (Leicester, 1994).

Olick, J. K., Vinitzhy-Seroussi, V., and Levy, D., eds., *The Collective Memory Reader* (Oxford, 2011).

O'Malley, J., *Trent: What Happened at the Council* (Cambridge, MA, 2013).

Origen, *Contra Celsum*, trans. H. Chadwick (Cambridge, 1980).

Pächt, O., *Van Eyck and the Founders of Early Netherlandish Painting*, trans. D. Britt (London, 1994).

Paxton, F. S., *Christianizing Death: The Creation of a Ritual Process in Early Medieval Europe* (Ithaca, NY, 1990).

Péguy, C., *Œuvres complètes en prose* (Paris, 1992).

Pelikan, J., *The Shape of Death: Life, Death and Immortality in the Early Fathers* (London, 1962).

Perkins, W., *A Salve for a Sicke Man* (Cambridge, 1595).

Pius XII, 'Encyclical Letter', *Divino Affiante Spiritu* (Rome, 1943).

Plato, *The Republic*.

Plotinus, *Eneads*.

Ragoné, H., 'Chasing the Blood Tie: Surrogate Mothers, Adoptive Mothers and Fathers', *American Ethnologist*, 23.2 (1996), 352–65.

Rapp, R., *Testing Women, Testing the Fetus: The Social Impact of Amniocentesis in America* (New York, 1999).

Rawls, J., *A Theory of Justice* (London, 1972).

Rebillard, E., *The Care of the Dead in Late Antiquity*, trans. E. Trapnell Rawlings and J. Routier-Pucci (Ithaca, NY, 2009).

Reich, W. T., ed., *Encyclopedia of Bioethics*, rev. ed. (New York, 1995).

Reimer, K. S., *Living L'Arche: Stories of Compassion, Love and Disability* (London, 2009).

Reinders, H. S. 'Being with the Disabled: Jean Vanier's Theological Realism' in B. Brock and J. Swinton, eds., *Disability in the Christian Tradition: A Reader* (Grand Rapids, MI, 2012), 467–511.

Reinis, A., *Reforming the Art of Dying: The* Ars moriendi *in the German Reformation (1519–1528)* (Farnham, Surrey, 2007).

Report of the Committee of Inquiry into Human Fertilisation and Embryology (commonly known as the *Warnock Report*) (London, 1984).

Report of the Royal Liverpool Children's Inquiry (London, 2001).

Richards, M., Pennings, G., and Appleby, J. B., eds., *Reproductive Donation: Practice, Policy and Bioethics* (Cambridge, 2012).

Richardson, A., 'Creed, Creeds', in J. G. Davies, ed., *A New Dictionary of Liturgy and Worship* (London, 1986).

Ricoeur, P., *Memory, History, Forgetting*, trans. K. Blamey and D. Pellauer (Chicago, 2004).

Robben, A. C., 'State Terror in the Netherworld: Disappearance and Reburial in Argentina', reprinted in A. C. Robben, ed., *Death, Mourning, and Burial: A Cross Cultural Reader* (Oxford, 2004), 134–48.

Robbins, J., *An Anthropology of the Good* (forthcoming).

Robbins, J., *Becoming Sinners: Christianity and Moral Torment in a Papua New Guinea Society* (Berkeley, 2004).

Robbins, J., 'Beyond the Suffering Subject: Toward An Anthropology of the Good', *Journal of the Royal Anthropological Institute* (N.S.) 19 (2013), 447–62.

Robbins, J., 'Where in the World are Values? Exemplarity, Morality and Social Process', forthcoming in collection of essays in honour of C. Humphrey.

Robinson, J. A. T., *The Priority of John* (London, 1985).

Roman Catholic Church, *Catechism of the Catholic Church* (London, 1994).

Rousseau, J.-J., *Émile*.

Rouselle, A., *Porneia: On Desire and the Body in Antiquity* (Oxford, 1988).

Sabat, S. R., *The Experience of Alzheimer's Disease* (Oxford, 2001).

Sahlins, M., *What Kinship Is—And Is Not* (Chicago, 2013).

Salmon, M. H., 'Anthropology, Philosophy of', in *The Encyclopedia of Philosophy*, ed. Craig.

Scharen, M. and Vigen, A. M., eds., *Ethnography as Christian Theology and Ethics* (London, 2011).

Schiefflin, E. L., *The Sorrow of the Lonely and the Burning of the Dancers* (New York, 1976).

Schneider, D. M., *American Kinship: A Cultural Account*, 2nd ed., (Chicago, 1980; first published in 1968).

Schopenhauer, A., *On the Basis of Morality*, trans. E. F. J. Payne (Indianapolis, 1995).

Seale, C., *Constructing Death: The Sociology of Dying and Bereavement* (Cambridge, 1998).

Sharp, L., *Strange Harvest: Organ Transplants, Denatured Bodies, and the Transformed Self* (Berkeley, 2006).

Shaw, B. D., 'The Family in Late Antiquity: The Experience of Augustine', *Past and Present*, 115 (1987), 3–51.

Skorupski, J., ed., *The Routledge Companion to Ethics* (London, 2010).

Smith, J. Z., *Imagining Religion: From Babylon to Jonestown* (Chicago, 1982).

Sontag, S., *Regarding the Pain of Others* (London, 2005).

Spencer, S., *Sermons by Artists* (London, 1934).

Steinbeck, D., ed., *The Oxford Handbook of Bioethics* (Oxford, 2007).

Stolcke, V., 'New Reproductive Technologies—Same Old Fatherhood', *Critique of Anthropology*, 6.3 (1986), 5–31.

Stolcke, V., 'New Reproductive Technologies: The Old Quest for Fatherhood', *Reproductive and Genetic Engineering: Journal of International Feminist Analysis*, 1.1 (1988), 5–19.

Strathern, M., *After Nature: English Kinship in the Late Twentieth Century* (Cambridge, 1992).

Strathern, M., *Reproducing the Future: Anthropology, Kinship and the New Reproductive Technologies* (Manchester, 1992).

Swanson, R., *Religion and Devotion in Europe 1215–1515* (Cambridge, 1993).

Sweet, V., *God's Hotel: A Doctor, A Hospital and A Pilgrimage to the Heart of Medicine* (New York, 2012).

Taft, R. F., *Beyond East and West: Problems in Liturgical Understanding* (Rome, 1997).

Talley T. J., *The Origins of the Liturgical Year*, 2nd ed. (Collegeville, MN, 1991).

Taylor, J., *The Rule and Exercises of Holy Dying* (1651).

The President's Council on Bioethics, *Controversies in the Determination of Death* (Washington, DC, 2008).

The President's Council on Bioethics, *Taking Care: Ethical Caregiving in our Aging Society* (Washington, DC, 2005).

Thomas, K., *Religion and the Decline of Magic* (London, 1971).

Thompson, C., *Making Parents: The Ontological Choreography of Reproductive Technologies* (Cambridge, MA, 2005).

Thompson, C., '"Quit Snivelling Cryo-Baby, We'll Work Out Which One's Your Mama"—Kinship in an Infertility Clinic', in R. Davis-Floyd and J. Dumit, eds., *Cyborg Babies: From Techno-Sex to Techno-Tots* (London, 1998), 4–66.

Tocqueville, A. de., *Democracy in America*, trans. G. Lawrence, ed. J. P. Mayer (New York, 1969).

Turner, V. and E., *Image and Pilgrimage in Christian Culture*, first published 1978, with a new introduction by D. Ross (New York, 2011).

Van der Meer, F., *Augustine the Bishop: Church and Society at the Dawn of the Middle Ages* (New York, 1961).

Vatican II Council, *Optatam Totius* (Decree on the Training of Priests) (1962–1965).

Verhey, A., *The Christian Art of Dying* (Grand Rapids, MI, 2011).

Viladesau, R., *The Beauty of the Cross: The Passion of Christ in Theology and the Arts—From the Catacombs to the Eve of the Renaissance* (Oxford, 2006).

Viladesau, R., *The Triumph of the Cross: The Passion of Christ in Theology and the Arts from the Renaissance to the Counter-Reformation* (Oxford, 2008).

Walter, T., *The Revival of Death* (London, 1994).

Ward, P., ed., *Perspectives on Ecclesiology and Ethnography* (Grand Rapids, MI, 2012).

Welles-Nyström, B., 'Parenthood and Infancy in Sweden', *New Directions for Child and Adolescent Development*, 40 (1988), 75–96.

Wilkinson, I., *Suffering: A Sociological Introduction* (Cambridge, 2005).

Wilkinson, J., ed. and trans., *Egeria's Travels*, 3rd ed. (Warminster, 1999).

Wilson, R. A., *The Politics of Truth and Reconcilation in South Africa* (Cambridge, 2001).

Wittgenstein, L., *Remarks on Frazer's Golden Bough*, trans. R. Rhees and A. C. Miles (Retford, 1979).

Wrigley E. A. and Schofield, R. S., *The Population History of England 1541–1871* (London, 1981).

Yerushalmi, Y. H., *Zakhor: Jewish History and Jewish Memory* (Seattle, 1982).

Young M. and Wilmot, P., *Family and Kinship in East London* (London, 1957).

Zelizer, V., *Pricing the Priceless Child: The Changing Social Value of Children* (New York, 1985).

Zigon, J., *Morality: An Anthropological Perspective* (Oxford, 2008).

Index

Printed and bound by CPI Group (UK) Ltd, Croydon, CR0 4YY